PRAISE FOR

Major

"Balf revels in the bicycle's bone-shaking evolution and the top-gun fraternity of daredevils who literally risked life and limb to race."

—*Entertainment Weekly*

"The Lance Armstrong of the 19th century . . . in Balf's hands, Taylor becomes an earthbound figure, brooding about civil rights, swooning over his wife . . . Balf gives McFarland [Taylor's bigoted rival] the kind of inspired devilry that makes him seem like the next obvious role for Daniel Day-Lewis." —*New York Times*

"Balf has written the definitive biography . . . and re-creates the [races] in pulse-pounding prose. . . . Why does Hollywood waste time with innocuous sports fiction when real-life dramatic gold of this quality remains unmined?" —*Washington Post*

"Taylor gets his due in a suspenseful narrative that pumps up the drama of big competitions won and lost." —*Boston Sunday Globe*

"[Major Taylor's] rise to fame, and his subsequent fall back into obscurity, is the stuff of Hollywood legend, and Balf tells his story with a cinematic eye, combining strong visual descriptions and sharp characterizations. Like Major Taylor himself, the book is a surefire winner." —*Booklist* (starred)

"Todd Balf has done a masterful job of combining exhaustive historical research with a passion for the sport and a way with words. . . . Highly recommended." —*Toronto Star*

"A fascinating biography . . . as Balf shows, Taylor's racing wasn't the best part of his story." —*Bicycling* magazine

ALSO BY TODD BALF

The Darkest Jungle

The Last River

Major

a black athlete, a white era,

and the fight to be

the world's fastest human being

TODD BALF

THREE RIVERS PRESS

NEW YORK

Frontispiece: Stanley B. Burns, M.D., and The Burns Archive

Library of Congress Cataloging-in-Publication Data

Balf, Todd.
Major : a black athlete, a white era, and the fight to be the world's fastest
human being / Todd Balf. — 1st ed.
Includes index.
1. Taylor, Major, 1878–1932.   2. Cyclists—United States—Biography.   3. African
American cyclists—Biography.   4. Bicycle racing—History.   I. Title.
GV1051.T3B35 2008
796.6092—dc22   2007020747

ISBN 978-0-307-23659-3

Printed in the United States of America

Design by Lenny Henderson

10   9   8   7   6   5   4   3   2   1

First Paperback Edition

To Patty, Celia, and Henry

Contents

In the Age of Progress, Problem

IN THE MID-1920S THE WORLD as many had known it was coming to an end. The Crash was around the corner. In the already slumping western Massachusetts working-class cities of Springfield and Worcester, two older men took an accounting. One white, the other black. One utterly obscure, one only recently forgotten.

Louis "Birdie" Munger was a doer, a thinker, and an extraordinary (if unheralded) inventor. He wasn't a man of reflection, but when he answered the knock at his door in Springfield and signed for the express package something clicked. It wasn't what was inside—a holiday gift from relatives—but the post date on the outside. It had left the Pacific Coast only twenty-six hours earlier, an astonishingly brief span of time. An old, pulse-quickening sensation stirred. His mind raced.

In a subsequent article in the local newspaper, Munger colorfully described a time few remembered. Two photographs accompanying the story seemed to say it all. Both were of him on bicycles. But in one, the earlier one, Munger had short hair, a tidy moustache, and a dark dress suit. He was sitting stiffly upright, formal, gentlemanly. The bicycle was a fashion accessory, like the fluffed silk handkerchief in his lapel pocket. In the companion shot, taken only a few years later, he was wearing a sleeveless T-shirt and tight shorts, and sported a waxed handlebar moustache stretching to the east-west cardinal points. He was hunched over, streamlined, racing. The look on his face was narrow and competitive.

The sport of *that* moment was bicycle racing, and for a decade, from the mid-1890s to the early 1900s, it was all anybody wanted to talk about. Hundreds of professional racers—beautiful, virile gods of sport—competed before millions of spectators at tour stops in San Francisco, Chicago, New York, and dozens of other cities where they were received like heroes, with parades, newly built and record-fast oval tracks, and fan pins and cigarette packs adorned with their handsome images. Scientists were transfixed as the racers hurled themselves against the unknown of terrestrial velocity; they wielded tape measures and calipers to unravel their physiology in the hope of explaining the speeds they attained, but in the end they, too, were stumped and merely hailed the "scorcher" as a new exquisite athletic form, like an evolved species descended from a future world.

Names—hot, fast bicycle names—washed across Munger's mind as if it were yesterday: the Orient, the Yellow Fellow, and his own Birdie Special. He didn't say it, but his bike was the watch charm, the sleekest, most radically designed, most pilot-adored racing bicycle in the world. If you were lucky enough to own a Munger, your intention was plain: you wished to be the fastest thing in existence. He was sought out by the most cyclonic men on the planet to break records, eclipse thoroughbreds, even catch speeding locomotives.

Maybe as much as the time-bending express package, what helped prompt all of this—the interview, the recollections of his time and place in the era, the sifting through scrapbooks for race photographs—was a recent visit (and, as it turned out, the last visit) from his now graying protégé Marshall Taylor. The "colored whirlwind" had begun his own autobiographical project, he told Munger, spending the last several years getting down on paper what he and others could remember before it was too late.

Munger couldn't recall when he initially met Taylor, but he never forgot his first day with him at the track. When he stopped his time-piece after the youngster's mile-long sprint, he shook his head in amazement: 2 minutes and 7/100ths of a second. The world record was just two-hundredths of a second faster. At the time Taylor was sixteen, self-taught, and working as an errand boy at an Indianapolis bicycle shop. The old racer in Munger felt something that tran-scended envy; he felt the goose bumps, the breathless joy of discovery that comes from seeing someone do what you love better than any-one you ever dreamed could do.

At Munger's urging, Taylor had traveled the country, then across the Atlantic, and finally from one end of the earth to the other to compete against the reigning champions of England, Germany, France, Italy, and Australia. Speed was the currency of the moment, and the man, country, and race who could claim to be its master was worth something incalculable. The obstacles abroad were consider-able: rugged overland rail travel, transoceanic steamers, and the vast distances that separated home and away.

At home, it was bleak. In 1899, at the outset of Taylor's assault on the record books, a total of 400 black people were lynched in Geor-gia, Mississippi, and a half dozen other states, the most of any year in U.S. history. It was not a good time to be visible, much less the most prominent and prominently victorious black man in America. On banked outdoor tracks Taylor tucked in behind noisy, steam-belching, rubber-burning, crash-prone motorcycles and raced furi-ously against the clock to see what was possible—a mile a minute? Faster?—but he also raced against flesh-and-blood rivals, wheel to wheel, elbow to elbow, skin to skin. In one of his first professional races, he effortlessly accelerated past a struggling veteran, exhorting as he passed him, "*That* was too easy!"

His victories, and the sensational, crowd-pleasing way in which he won, led to threats, assaults, and the open collusion of his main American race circuit rivals to defeat him. The popular sporting press didn't know what to make of him—he didn't drink alcohol or smoke tobacco, and he stubbornly refused to race on the Sabbath, either for world championship titles or $10,000 race purses. "But I never heard before of an athlete who had conscientious scruples, and no one believes you, Major," a newspaperman protested. Another writer ridiculed him as a Christian Narcissus who "feels the finger of God whirling his pedals round."

In the end there was only one man the competitive equal of Taylor. His name was Floyd McFarland, also an American and of identical age. He came from California—a place where the sheer physical distance to the eastern sporting metropolis had once been insurmountable. He was everything Taylor wasn't—garrulous, school-educated, and white. His father was a well-to-do auctioneer; Taylor's was a poor servant coachman. The McFarland family was storied, a fabled Virginia clan that settled on land where an immense reservoir of oil and natural gas gushed just beneath the tilled surface. Taylor's family was anonymous, neither written about nor recorded as slaves in prewar Kentucky.

They sparred for almost ten years, during which the sport riveted the public's attention the way modern-day NASCAR does. Each became wealthy, made almost daily headlines, and enjoyed unprecedented celebrity as a sportsman, but it was almost as if both feared the lethal consequences of a true championship meeting, of a black striver in the same hot, tight arena with a white master. It was only at the end—of the sport, of the boom, and of the era—that their rivalry finally achieved full form. They took passage for Australia, a seemingly neutral venue halfway around the world and yet a place a local legislator called "the last part of the world in which the higher races can live and increase freely for the benefit of higher civilization."

* * *

"CIRCUMSTANCES HAVE HITHERTO COMBINED to keep these Heroes of the Cycling Path Asunder," announced a promotional poster for the cycling championship of the world on February 27, 1904, in Adelaide, Australia. "They will meet—finally—here." The prize purses in Australia were among the largest ever offered, the promoter the same brilliant rogue who almost a decade later would reprise the black-versus-white stakes with heavyweights Jack Johnson and Tommy Burns. The Taylor and McFarland pairing was his favorite, he said, because it was his first, because it was everybody's first. The World War II generation had their where-were-you moment when the black American Joe Louis stepped into the ring at Yankee Stadium with Nazi Germany's Max Schmeling in the 1938 heavyweight championship of the world; the Vietnam era had trackmen Tommie Smith and John Carlos' black power salute on the 1968 Olympic medal stand in Mexico City. But at the turn of the century, an aging Civil War generation, eager for a battle to decide what had not been decided at Appomattox, also had a defining moment when all thoughts, from north to south, were directed to a faraway track where winter was summer. Royals and American presidents awaited word, as did city gamblers and country church folk, social scientists and old colored troops.

In Australia—not at the broiling racetrack grandstand, because she couldn't bear to watch—Taylor's young, light-skinned wife, Daisy, waited, too, full of love for the man to whom she once addressed a transatlantic letter "The 1 Mile Bicycle King of the World, Paris, France." She had an abiding faith, but it wasn't blind. She had seen too much and been born into hard circumstances few could have imagined. Daisy Victoria Taylor wished she didn't believe that the outcome of a winner-takes-all race between a white man and a black man would fix the prospects of the innocent unborn baby that filled her belly. But she did.

* * *

TWO DECADES LATER TAYLOR PLACED IN FRONT of his old friend Munger an obsessively worked-over manuscript, and they reflected on a story few would believe—especially the ending, when he and Floyd McFarland finally, fatefully met. Tears came. They had been on the move for a long time.

For a moment everything stood quite still.

CHAPTER I

Free

JULY 1865

CITY OF LONDON

ATLANTIC OCEAN

It glides along as though it were alive, and with
a smooth grace . . . everlasting and beautiful to behold.
—*Scientific American*

ARTICLE ON THE EARLY PEDAL-POWERED BICYCLE

THE SOUTH WAS STILL BURNING. Thousands of Confederate POWs remained in Union custody, having refused allegiance to their Yankee victors, and only a partial accounting of the 623,000 war dead had been made. It was a mere eight weeks after Appomattox and the end of the Civil War, but people were already on the move. The promise of America's large northern industrial cities, where work could be had and lives remade, triggered a massive response home and abroad.

The swell of humanity included a twenty-two-year-old French mechanic whose July transatlantic passage was notable because of what he steadfastly towed in a large clanging steamer trunk. Within were the unassembled parts of the first modern-era bicycle to land upon U.S. shores. Pierre Lallement, a baby-faced man with short legs and a penguin's stride, was the first of what would be a very long line of dreamers, schemers, and spectacular failures who would see in the

7

beautiful symmetry of moving bicycle parts a new beginning. His wrought-iron frame didn't look like much, but he won a patent in 1866 and, more incredible still, he rode the thing, nobly taking to the green at New Haven, Connecticut, as a few rubbernecking strollers looked on.

Lallement's bicycle was, in truth, a giant advance that somehow eluded the best and brightest minds for generations, with "two wooden wheels, with iron tires, of nearly equal size, one before the other, surmounted by a wooden perch." The patent description, however, failed to emphasize the genius of the new design—foot pedals that would not just propel it but balance it. For the first time a rider could elevate his feet from terra firma (earlier versions were straddled and powered by hard, scooter-style pushes), drive his wherewithal into foot pedal cranks, and directly propel his earthly volume. One hundred and fifty years later it is the advance that a six-year-old who rides a bicycle for the first time remembers, the moment when the ground gives way, the wind sweetens, and nerve ends spark like dry tinder. It is the moment when doubt and fear release in a simple, fundamental expression of pungent emotion—something that sounds like "Wheeeee!"

Lallement didn't wait around long enough to see his bicycle gain acceptance—after a few years of queer looks and uneventful sales he glumly sailed back to France—but Americans did briefly experience a faddish burst of enthusiasm. It only lasted a year or two before they sharply turned on the contraption, dubbing the hard mechanical horse the "boneshaker." It was uncomfortable, unreliable, and rather awkward (the pedals were attached to the front wheel and not directly beneath the rider). Showcase races at outdoor courses did nothing to help the cause, as even supremely fit men on state-of-the-art velocipedes (the precious-sounding term for the premodern steed) found walking speeds hard to best. It was not a racing bicycle. In a post–Civil War world where urban Americans had lofty expectations of a European-style enlightenment, the bike didn't measure up. By

1870, only five years after Lallement's dodgy transatlantic adventure, the primitive boneshaker was far more dead than alive.

Still, the sense among believers that they were in the proverbial ballpark and that the bicycle might be more than a fling stubbornly prevailed—especially in Europe, where English inventors one-upped their Parisian counterparts with the high-wheeler, the aptly described evolutionary follow-up to the boneshaker. With a lightweight hollow steel frame and cushioning seat spring, the British-made Ordinary was a far better vehicle than the boneshaker—her smooth, fast ride softened the old criticism—but the improvements came at the expense of what appeared to be life and limb. When the first ones were shipped to the United States in the late 1870s (unlike Europeans, it took a while for Americans to shake off the painful memory of its forebear) the new bicycle both enthralled and terrified Victorian America. Of his own experiences the early bicycling advocate Charles E. Pratt wrote, "It runs, it leaps, it rears and writhes; it is in infinite restless motion, like a bundle of sensitive nerves; it is beneath its rider like a thing of life."

The rider was a stratospheric eight feet off the ground, making a first encounter distressingly akin to sitting atop a moving lamppost. Children were particularly endangered. When Major Taylor was first starting to race, the old-timers initiated him by placing him atop the towering Ordinary, then sat back to watch and wait for the expected fall. The pedals were attached to the front wheel, the way they are on a tricycle. Unlike a tricycle, a Sisyphean thrust was required to budge the four-foot-diameter, hard-tired wheel. Brakes were primitive (or nonexistent), and a gentlemanly upright posture made the slightest puff of wind a worthy opponent. Literally and figuratively, a leap of faith was necessary to balance on tiny pedals and grossly dissimilar-sized wheels. The high-wheeler virtually ensured that a stalwart, risk-averse citizen who adored certainty, and for whom dignity was zealously sought in every waking moment, would be monstrously disappointed.

A technical explanation didn't alleviate the concern. Wheels, one small, the other enormous, were aligned so that the oversized rim supported the rider's center of gravity. Once in motion, scientists observed, "the physical forces generated by the rotation of the wheels produced a self steering effect." The technical term was *precession*. Perversely, the stabilizing force that kept one upright increased the faster you went. In other words, you had to risk life in the hope of saving it. The high-wheel bicycle, the popular frame design in America prior to 1890, didn't defy physical law, but it did challenge it.

Despite these immense challenges, a 19th-century person's motivation to learn to ride, once sufficiently teased by seeing others in motion, was unparalleled. Buttoned-up, pickled Victorians had too long stifled the pulsing in their chests. They desperately needed an emotional outlet; they wanted to flush their cheeks with color, expand their lungs with air, and swiftly glide from town to town. As a *Nickell* writer explained, every man was born with some of the "trick instinct." He meant that there was something innate and unseen, like luxurious black oil beneath the earth's still granite mantle, that lay untapped in everyone. Soon America seemed hell-bent on probing the great unknown. Thus, there were a multitude of horrible accidents, but also the kind of magnificence and magic the boneshaker never afforded. Wrote H. G. Wells in his fictional narrative of a neophyte's experience in the English countryside, "[Hoopdriver] wheeled his machine up Putney Hill, and his heart sang within him." Indeed, hearts sang and bicycles led the lovelorn to the bucolic, the exotic, and reputation-making hero climbs such as Ford Hill in Philadelphia. Those who were previously sedentary and waiting tremulously for the inevitable ravages of illness to overtake them flew into delighted, freewheeling motion. Lightness shone through the bleak day-to-day. Underdogs rejoiced.

Unlike in the boneshaker era, being a spectator was nearly as fun.

In the summer of 1878, the same year both Taylor and McFarland were born, a former shoe manufacturer named Albert Pope launched his Columbia brand—the first American-manufactured high-mount— by sponsoring the country's first race on American-made bicycles. It was a precocious moment, bicycles being the hoped-for leader of a burgeoning postwar renaissance in physical sports. There was excited talk of the newly addictive "Athletic Impulse," of the way sports glorified our culture and ennobled the men who gamely partook. A keenness for outdoor sports had emerged, one that made the rising generation "big and lusty and pleasant to look at." Soon records were being broken: all kinds, all places. Neither foot racers nor most fleet thoroughbreds could compare. In a span of only a few years the mile record, the benchmark for true, life-changing speed, was reduced from six minutes to less than three.

Pope's Boston Back Bay velodrome, site of that first American-style bicycle extravaganza, consisted of a planked cycling track inside a mammoth 320-foot-long tent. For several weeks high-wheel racers from Boston and imports from England and France hazarded gale-force winds and bitter Thanksgiving cold, racing distances up to 100 miles on the ten-laps-to-the-mile track. The French champion Charles Terront, an incorrigible ladies' man, wore snug white flannel knee breeches, blue stockings, and a silk ascot. His English rival quoted Shakespeare and went by the racing nom de guerre "Happy Jack." There was an American entry—an ancestral link to future racers Major Taylor, Floyd McFarland, and even Lance Armstrong. Unfortunately, he wasn't deemed important enough to be mentioned by name in the press. Each day they rode with brave, unchecked abandon, their bicycles weighing a thumping thirty pounds.

Fans warmed to the activity in a way that inspired Pope and his rival manufacturers. They saw the potential of the market and began to ramp up. When the American neophyte hit a pole at a top-end speed of 20 mph, an amused London visitor described the bone-snapping collision as "an aerial flight to Mother Earth via the over-the-handles route."

Cycling as an American spectator sport had the necessary toehold.

LOUIS DE FRANKLIN MUNGER, a young hawk-nosed Detroit lad working in a blind-making factory, was one of the thousands of adventure-seeking American men swept into the craze. He had thick, pugnacious features but soft green eyes and almost aboriginal high cheekbones. Heretofore, the factories were the spectacle of his generation. The massive brick establishments, running along America's wide riverbanks, were symbols of progress and power and modernization. The shoppy smell of coal and coke choked the air; the homes nearby were blackened with a sooty film. On the factory floor the cacophony of surfacing machines, water pumps, air compressors, hammers, and pneumatic tools made it impossible to hear—the vibration saturated the body and didn't ever fully dissipate, not even in sleep. Young men such as Munger who had been farmhands, coaxing soft things from a hard earth, were drawn indoors to churn out bales of wire or rivets or some other replicated item in regimented fashion and predictable quantities. They peered into great fires, stamped out molds, and boiled with perspiration from the start of their shift until its conclusion twelve hours later. The hours were fixed, the outcome was known.

But with the certainty of mass employment and production came the sacrifice of an independent life. The factories felt like prisons, and increasingly young men Munger's age fantasized about the outside, daydreaming under the small, shut-tight windows that allowed only dabs of fractured light. Munger found himself particularly ill suited to the regimented factory life.

His father was an Ontario farmer who immigrated to Black

Hawk County, Iowa, in 1859. Theodore wed Mary Jane Pattee, and they began their family in Iowa, with Louis born in 1864, amidst the war. Perhaps because of his Dutch pacifist ancestry, Theodore Munger fled the chaos of wartime America, bringing the family back to his native Canada shortly after Louis's birth.

The Mungers joined a rich and growing collection of exiles in southern Ontario, just across the Detroit River and the U.S. boundary. They included fugitive slaves, former British loyalists, displaced Native Americans, and the most recent exiles, the Civil War runaways and conscientious objectors. For the first ten years of his life, Birdie Munger grew up in a tolerant, diverse, and unusually democratic part of the world. A third of Colchester, one of Ontario's southernmost towns, consisted of black settlers. They'd come from Kentucky and points south, Colchester being the first cross-border stop on the Underground Railroad. In the distinctly egalitarian environs, the black settlers excelled, producing a slew of formidable achievers.

Theodore, a part-time inventor, and Mary brought their five children back to Detroit, where Theodore took work in the state patent office. A young boy such as Louis would have been exposed to one of the most dynamic eras in American ingenuity. In the time after the Civil War the entrepreneurial urge to create was seemingly infinite. There was the telephone, incandescent light, and Coca-Cola. Among the many successful, World's Fair–bound items that passed across Theodore Munger's desk were those of Elijah McCoy, a famous inventor who lived in the area. McCoy was awarded seventy patents, his most famous being a lubricating mechanism that prevented steam engines from overheating. Anywhere but the oddly color-blind border region between Ontario and Michigan, McCoy would've stood out for another reason, too: he was black.

What Birdie Munger kept with him on those long shuttered days in the factory was a sense that anyone, including himself, could do anything. Years later, when he met Taylor, began to coach him, hired him to work for his bicycle-frame-making company in Indianapolis, and then began to brag about him as a prospective world champion, it was as if he was foolishly naive and didn't understand the harsh, racially tinted lens through which all of America seemed to be staring— and he didn't. He was from a much different part of the world, a mere few miles from the border that divided Canada from the United States but an incalculable distance away from the notion that a black man was born inferior to a white one. And he was an inventor's son. Inventors saw what was in front of them, not what was around them. What was in front of inventors, the greatest invention of the moment in a land suddenly teeming with them, was the bicycle. Given his young age, he wasn't ready to build them yet—but he did desperately want to race.

Early American bicycle racers such as Munger were a special breed. They lived and breathed bicycles, a small, ardent community of bachelors who would do anything to go faster and go anywhere to race. They were the spiritual ancestors to dragsters, supersonic pilots, free-falling BASE jumpers. It was like what Tom Wolfe wrote about Chuck Yeager and the first test pilots: "A fighter pilot soon found he wanted to associate only with other fighter pilots. Who else could understand the nature of the little proposition they were all dealing with? And what other subject could compare with it? So the pilot kept it to himself, along with an even more indescribable . . . an even more sinfully inconfessable . . . feeling of superiority, appropriate to him and to his kind, lone bearers of the right stuff."

They were doing what they loved—an indulgence, perhaps, yet irresistible—stepping into a delicious world stripped of everything but the moment-to-moment pursuit of a tingly feeling: how to make wheels spin like marbles on a slick gymnasium floor, or how to master the elemental forces so that riding a bike felt like plunging out of the sky, free-falling with both abandon and control, like an eagle dropping through the middle of a steep thermal. The feeling they craved was a descent, but the direction they had to move *was across the earth,* in touch with the nubby land and all the other elements that conspired to cause slowness. Out of necessity the builders of bikes were racers—who, after all, knew more about speed or wanted more from speed than they did? George Hendee, a rival of Munger's, built a fast bicycle in his Springfield, Massachusetts, shop, then later a faster motorcycle, the fabled Indian. Almost all the pioneers, Munger included, were so consumed with generating speed that the bicycle proved to be only an intermediary step—almost in unison they moved on to motorcycles, then automobiles, and finally airplanes, where they no longer had to deal with the burden of speed-scrubbing Mother Earth.

Munger had ridden a wheel less than two months when he competed in the championship contests at the Detroit Bicycle Club and won every event. The victories literally gave him flight, away from the factory and the crippling family grief that came when his youngest sister, Theodorea, died before her first birthday. As the oldest male sibling, Louis felt an almost parental pang. Racing was an emotional release.

He wasn't a gifted rider, but he seemingly never tired of cranking the pedals. "He had a great habit in his races of taking dangerous headers and then winning the events," marveled a columnist for the *Boston Globe* in November 1885. That same year, after driving rain and a collision with a horse team aborted two earlier attempts in Boston, the twenty-two-year-old rode 259 miles over twenty-four hours, a new American endurance record. (Munger would've bested the 265-mile world record but for his accumulated injuries, which left him banged up and operating at half strength. He said he was afraid to even dismount the bike because he didn't think he'd have the strength to get back on.)

In 1886 Munger shipped himself out to San Francisco and rode his high-wheeler back to New York in an attempt to outdo the

Englishman Thomas Stevens's cross-country record from two years earlier and become the first American transcontinental rider. Like seemingly the rest of America, he had read about Stevens's journey "over the Sierras, through the snow sheds, and across the great desert." Munger wasn't as poetic in describing his ordeal. "It was largely a hike," he confessed years later, though he did gamely try. Following the newly installed Santa Fe line, he removed his rear wheel and rode long stretches on a single wheel. Other times he tried to skirt the margins of canals, sometimes with success, sometimes slip-sliding off the crumbling clay banks into the blue-black water. He reached New York City in 111 days, only seven more than it had taken Stevens, but because he failed to overtake the Englishman his adventure was almost entirely unnoticed. Being the first American to cross the continent didn't seem to matter; he wasn't the fastest.

When he returned he spent the next five years obscurely criss-crossing the country, setting long-distance records in Canada, Boston, Chicago, Indianapolis, and Clarkesville, Missouri. In Columbus, Georgia, he lowered the 50-mile record by seven minutes, finishing in 3:27:34. A year later at the St. Charles Avenue Asphalt Roadway in New Orleans, he slashed five minutes from the 25-mile record. By the turn of the decade he was arguably the best endurance high-wheel racer in the United States—a "rattling good wheelman" whose crashes and daring attacks made him an overwhelming crowd favorite and a man newspapermen fawned over.

Munger loved it all—not to mention the Ordinary itself. To master such an intimidating contraption was an act of machismo that told the world something about who you were—brave, yes; headstrong, certainly; and incorrigibly, irreconcilably eligible. If there had been a popular magazine that attempted to pinpoint the men who were the most desirable to the opposite sex, the men atop the list would've certainly included someone like Munger, someone who rode and raced the brakeless, peril-be-damned high-wheeler.

Louis de Franklin "Birdie" Munger, the old high-wheel racer, master bicycle builder, and Taylor mentor, in an undated portrait. *Source: From the Collection of the Indiana State Museum and Historic Sites*

* * *

THE HIGH-WHEELER, HOWEVER, began to show signs of waning popularity by the end of the 1880s. The fad was losing steam, as
it were. And even the racers began to get frustrated with the performance limits of the heavy-duty frame design. Top-end speeds were
reached, and when they were, both the crowds and the racers grew
increasingly bored.

Moreover, the high-wheeler, so sleek and speedy on the track,
was no match for America's roads. In spring they were quagmires, in
summer dust bowls. Even the congressionally funded National Road,
the main east-west artery, had been abandoned with the advent of the
railroads, thus leaving behind frost heaves, chuckholes, and a long
string of ghost inns. Wagon travelers called the rutted, unpaved rural
roads "gutshakers."

Intrepid cyclists busted forks, folded wheels, and savaged poor
exposed heads. The average rider broke down so often he was required
to bring an anchorlike tool kit almost as heavy as the bike itself. The
same roads that had done in the boneshaker doubly did in the giraffe-
like Ordinary. The English champion F. J. Osmond, the beneficiary of
the world's greatest roads in what he reminded Americans was the
world's greatest civilized nation, returned from a month of racing in
the States riddled with saddle sores and groaning, "I never saw worse
roads anywhere."

Munger might have been the best example of the human damage
America's roads could exact. In 1893, at the dawn of a new age in
racing, he arrived for a week's worth of competition at the World's
Columbian Exposition in Chicago, dreaming of a record-breaking
bonanza. He was still popular among racing fans, a warrior competitor with an easy-to-feel-for tough-luck streak. In a ceremonial cross-
country relay event just prior to the race, he and several other riders
set a new mark for the Boston-to-Chicago section, but Munger was
one of the team's casualties, suffering internal injuries when he col-

lided with a team of horses in Hammond, Indiana. The fact that he
elected to race despite the setback only embossed his ironman reputation. It didn't seem to fully occur to him that he was no longer twenty-
one but rather thirty, possessing the bruised and battered body of a
much older man. As the ten-year veteran of twenty-four-hour road
races, 100-mile time trials, and a cross-country adventure lasting a
Lewis-and-Clark-like 111 days, structurally he mirrored the roads of
Boston, St. Louis, and godforsaken New Mexico—a mess.

At the 1893 Chicago World's Fair, in a championship field "unparalleled in the history of cycling," Munger faced the stern reality that
he was finished. In the 60-mile international championships he didn't
qualify. In the mile tandem at Washington Park his partner, Frank
Waller, called for a final kick in the last lap, but Munger had nothing.
A pair of unheralded cyclists from Buffalo won going away. Perversely,
Munger had saved his most anemic and disheartening performance
for last. As the high-wheel bicycle faded into oblivion it took almost
every one of its pioneer racers with it, most notably Munger. He was
a victim of speed in its purest, most literal form—the jarring pace of
a wheel over rotten road—and, nearly as devastating, of the speed
with which things changed in America. His timing was just a little
off. He had missed the golden age of his sport by the most slender of
margins.

AN ALTOGETHER NEW BICYCLE design hastened the high-mount's
demise. It emerged in Coventry, England, crossed the Atlantic, and
arrived in dozens of cheering American cities like a lifesaving miracle
tonic. Its coming had been whispered over for years, the earliest
looks coming at the big annual bicycle trade shows in Boston, New
York, and Chicago where the latest cycling innovations were introduced to tens of thousands of spectators, then keenly relayed to a
clamoring public in the newspapers and the dozens of national bicycle
journals such as the *Wheel, Wheelmen's Gazette,* and *Wheelmen*

Illustrated (to name but a few). An early report called the design especially welcome for those who "don't want to get their craniums cracked."

The modern "safety" bicycle was nothing like the high-wheeler. It looked, well, rideable. The first unveiling in the mid-1880s drew mixed interest, but by 1890, when the so-called low-mount first appeared at Britain's Stanley trade show with smooth, soft pneumatic tires, the slow-burning love affair was finally consummated. The titillated Indianapolis public was so agog at the prospect of joining the fun that they packed Tomlinson Hall, the city's largest, to get a first glimpse. The scene was duplicated in a half dozen other U.S. cities, including Floyd McFarland's hometown of San Jose, California. Viewed side by side, the two bicycles were the difference between a caravel and a sleek steamship. The "safety" had two wheels about the same size, a chain-based rear-wheel drive, and a linear diamond-shaped frame that felt more like mounting a low stool than a lamppost.

The chain innovation enabled inventors to try a more normal-sized wheel, since speed was determined not by the wheel's diameter but by the gears at the axle of the rear wheel. J. K. Starling, a machinist in Coventry, was looking for a happy medium between the velocipede of old, which was easy to balance and mount, and the high-wheeler, which provided a discernable mechanical advantage but at a difficult-to-swallow risk. His one stumbling point, solid inch-thick rubber tires and stunted spokes that radiated bumps up through the legs and spine, was solved within a few years when the Irishman John Dunlop, a veterinary surgeon, drummed up a solution. As the story goes, he took a piece of rubber hose, filled it with compressed air, and glued it to his son's tricycle. The pneumatic tube, ensuring a faster and more cushioned ride, went into production shortly thereafter. For the same effort, on the same bike, a racer on pneumatic tubes went about a third faster. "If you want to come as near to flying as we are likely to get in this generation, learn to ride a pneumatic bicycle,'" cheered a *Scribner's* writer.

The combination of Starling's and Dunlop's creations, first paired together in Rover's 1890 model, was something special: comfortably undiluted speed. When an American and European community of mechanics began tinkering even more—trimming off excess weight, adding more speed-producing gears, experimenting with the geometry of frames and forks, creating round, expertly machined ball bearings to keep wheels rotating without friction or wobble—the result was a true racing bicycle capable, it seemed, of almost anything. Speed records fell at a faster rate than ever before. Britain's W. C. Jones reduced the mile mark another ten seconds, and he and others were now contemplating the once unthinkable: the 2-minute barrier.

In the days of the high-mount, young American boys Taylor and McFarland's age had fantasized of a future in trick riding. Every boy did. A cartoon at the time depicts a grade-schooler contemplating a career either fighting hatchet-wielding Indians or performing acrobatic stunts on the bicycle. Trick riding, in the absence of fast roads and swift, lightweight bikes, was the most adventurous and interesting thing on two wheels. But now the thing was speed, and in the places where Taylor and McFarland grew up—each claimed the nickname "Speed City"—it had finally come of age. The world, and the United States especially, was ready to explore new boundaries.

The quest for speed would soon consume everyone and everything. Darkness was falling to light, with incandescent bulbs—"little spoonfuls of captured sunshine," a 19th-century writer observed—strung from coast to coast. New tabulating machines reduced the tedious census process from years to months. America was seeing a faster, more accurate picture of itself than ever before. The race was on.

CHAPTER 2

Flight

NOVEMBER 1878
NORTH INDIANAPOLIS, INDIANA

It is poor economic policy to spoil a good machinist
to make a poor coachman, or to force a natural
born compositor into a table waiter.
—*The Freeman*,
ON LATE-19TH-CENTURY
DISCRIMINATORY PRACTICES IN INDIANAPOLIS

IN THE EARLY 1870S GILBERT TAYLOR, his wife, Saphronia, and their three toddler-aged children, Lizzie, Alice, and
William, got moving. They crossed from the Kentucky side of the
Ohio River—the broad dusky river course that had long separated
slavery and liberty—and joined the steady stream of travelers pouring into Indiana along the northward Michigan Road. The Taylors
stopped in Indianapolis, where a new skyline of smokestacks rose
from beside the White River. The wind-bent columns of acrid black
smoke spilled out like a totem of hope.

Most of the black migrants settled on the West Side or in Bucktown, but those with a small stake headed for North Indianapolis,
where a newly platted grid of farms was bounded by the incomplete
Central Canal and Michigan Road. Most of the black farms were

small, about fifty acres on average, while the typical farm worked by
a white man was nearly twice as large. The smooth towpath along the
canal, a popular cycling route in the years to come, meant they could
easily haul produce to the city; the canal itself, though unconnected and
only eight miles long, was a local avenue of commerce and recreation.
Ice was packed out in the winter, smallmouth bass in the summer.

The promise that the canal would someday be finished brought
the beltway railroad and major industry; roads were proudly named
for Paris, Berlin, and London. Near the skyline of White River smokestacks, along Addison and Udell, the modest beginnings of a downtown sprouted up: grocers, shoemakers, and barbers put up shingles.
Members of a pioneer "prayer band" gathered in one another's homes
each Sunday, praying hard for their own church and a full-time pastor to guide them.

But the growth sputtered. Against the heaving national markets,
the speculators who had seized on the promise of Indianapolis raced
for cover. Panic struck. Men and their families were shaken off the
farmland before they'd even gotten a chance to dig in. They flooded
downtown and took the jobs they could get. Like dozens of other
independent black farmers and laborers from North Indianapolis,
Gilbert Taylor took a job as a coachman servicing a rich white railroad family.

His wartime dream of being his own boss had failed. His ambition never again approached what it had been the day he came to
Indianapolis, and perhaps he regretted his decision to push the family
north in the first place. A satirical cover illustration in *Harper's
Weekly* gave an inkling of Gilbert Taylor's broken faith. Under the
headline "Out of Sight, Out of Mind," the drawing shows a bundled
coachman shivering on a windy, wintry evening as he awaits his missus' return. "I'll give you a quarter to go in that house and tell the
Lady the Chimneys on Fire," the coachman tells a stable boy. "My

missus has been there for Two Hours, talking Scandal, and I'm most
Froze to Death!"

MARSHALL WALTER TAYLOR was born November 26, 1878, an
entrance made notable by its nearness to Thanksgiving and the light-
swallowing, ink-black fullness of his skin. At the time the family was
still working on their stake, not at the service of others. Within weeks
Thomas Alva Edison announced to a stunned nation that he would,
in six weeks' time, be bringing electric lights into their darkened homes.
He had solved the greatest problem of the 19th century, producing
a clean, white household light that wouldn't asphyxiate or explode
or grime a bassinet with pitchy residue. The faith in the Wizard of
Menlo Park, and in miracles in general, was such that the bottom
dropped out of the gas market the next day. The Gilded Age, in a
phosphorescent shower of pinging subatomic particles, came into
view. An extraordinary time was about to dawn.

To a struggling family, Taylor's birth was connected, in a diffuse
way, to the same enrapturing elemental force. He was the first Taylor
child born in the North, what the old Negro spirituals saw as the territory of light. Gilbert and Saphronia, conversely, were products of
the slave South. At midcentury their native Louisville had been a
slave trade hub, rivaling New Orleans in economic importance to the
South. Kentucky became a Union state, but in the deal that brought it
to the Northern side President Lincoln agreed to exempt it from the
Emancipation Proclamation. Slavery was legally permissible throughout the Civil War. In Louisville, a large percentage of the black population didn't gain their freedom until long after their brethren
from neighboring states. That portion of the city's population never
appeared in the city or state's official records. No marriage certifi-
cates and no census information were kept for them. Many of those
who served in the Union army, such as Gilbert Taylor, went officially
unrecognized toward the end of the war when freedom-seeking

blacks enlisted in overwhelming, poorly accounted numbers. They were effectively nonexistent except in the Jefferson County tax rolls, where a column enumerated each landowner's total number of slaves.

Like the estimated quarter million black slaves in antebellum Kentucky, the Taylors left nothing on paper to recognize them as something other than property. Some years later the French impressionist Edgar Degas would describe blacks in late-19th-century modernist Paris as "walking silhouettes, forests of ebony." He meant his words to describe a kind of loneliness—the same terrifying anonymity that haunted southern-born blacks such as the Taylors.

The first official recognition of the family wouldn't come until after the war and the 1870 federal census. "Cannot read" was a box checked for both of Taylor's parents. Taylor said he was the grandson of slaves, but a well-regarded scholar at the Filson Historical Society in Louisville believes, after a review of the pertinent family documents, that he was more likely the son of them. Years later Taylor told a French reporter that his mother and father's ancestors came from the notorious West African slave trading empires of Dahomey and Senegal. The largest numbers of slaves transported to North America were brought over in the early 1800s. It's conceivable his ancestors earned their freedom from a kindly Virginia cotton farmer or the rare Kentucky abolitionist, just not probable.

It wouldn't have been unusual for Taylor to choose to obscure his family background. Like many men of his time, he feared he was diminished by his heritage, ashamed that his father wasn't in the records as one of Louisville's free coloreds. For the rest of his career Taylor seemed to be making up for what his father never had—a written history, a record that everybody from the town clerk to the president of the United States would remember.

Taylor's birth was followed in quick succession by those of three sisters and two brothers. He stayed close to his deeply religious Baptist mother, in part because he did what she did—take care of the children. "He was one of the fathers to his big family, and an excellent one he made," a family friend remembered. The "northern" half of the brood, including a lamed brother, were his responsibility. Years later his personal notebooks would be filled with lists of the gifts and cash he sent home: pairs of shoes for his younger brother John and younger sisters Eva and Gertie, a $25 railroad fare to Alice, and $55 for the family before Christmas.

A North Indianapolis grade school teacher recalled Taylor's sisters and a younger brother but not Marshall. For much of the time the Taylors were forced to survive like sharecroppers, shuttling between a series of temporary addresses up and down Michigan Road, the city's north-south artery. "My parents were poor," he once said. "All we had was just what we needed."

His mother couldn't provide much in the way of material things, but she instilled in him the unapologetic rules of Christendom, the hard boundaries of his future race. As a young boy he was introduced to the idea that life was a contest of stamina in a race against sin. He would lose, he knew that, but there was fairness in the evangelical dictum, with punishment in the hereafter applied equally to white and black sinners. There was no qualifier, no fuzzy scorekeeping, no gray line. There were winners and losers. In the North Indianapolis shanties where dimly lit living rooms were regularly transformed into makeshift churches, Taylor's extraordinary future philosophy began to form. As he once said in the lead-up to his duel against Floyd McFarland, "All to the winner, nothing to the loser."

His mother's influence, always forceful, grew stronger through each stage of Taylor's development. The older he got the more he sought her counsel and the harder he worked to bring the family around him the way it once had centered on her. In his racing prime at least three family members would come to live with him either in the Boston area or in the home he purchased for cash in Worcester—

his oldest brother, William, his youngest sister, Gertrude, and his aging father, Gilbert. He was the sun, they cold planets drawing strength and stability from his heat. Rather extraordinarily, he kept a rein on them all: his lamed brother, John; his widowed sisters, Alice and Lizzie; his day-laboring father.

His old scrapbooks, preserved at the Indiana State Museum, are dotted with a tantalizing but incomplete trail of his longing. There are clipped obituaries about former slaves who rose to greatness, about the ships that carried still more slaves but disappeared into the bottom of the ocean, about the native Maoris of New Zealand. "You will remember," he wrote a friend, "that this country was first inhabited by a colored race who are a beautiful race." On the border of those pages, and especially where there were blank yellowing gaps, there is the careful brushwork of a delicate female hand, that of the mysterious woman who would come along and change everything. Daisy Victoria Morris painstakingly inserted her drawings, soft flowing landscapes and patches of spring wildflowers, in a way that suggested she recognized the book's pattern, too. It was as if, as he was traveling around the world in the early 1900s, he was looking for something: a clue to the people who had delivered him and the mother who raised him, proof he wasn't alone but part of something bigger— an unbroken family, a resilient tribe, an indefatigable movement.

The people who filled his mother's home on Sunday, the southern-born Baptists who were too poor to build their own church, would've been a welcome sight to a young boy. The problem was something he never told Saphronia Taylor or anyone else about: a feeling of fierce superiority that sometimes came over him, anointing him when he played tag or raced on foot against the boys in the neighborhood. He had a jump, anybody could see that. There was a jolt and a dash of inexplicable power, as if he were wearing one of Edison's toy electrical belts or was one of the senators at the Capitol who in the

course of a burden-filled day descended to the basement to stick his
hand in a machine that dispensed a low-voltage pick-me-up.

Major Taylor's late-19th-century world wished to feel alive, to
speed up, to sizzle. A few fortunate sons were blessed with the
feeling.

BY THE 1880S THERE WERE, IT SEEMED, TWO types of people
in Indianapolis—railroad men and everyone else. Unlike the other,
the former had ample reason to believe anything was possible.
Gilbert Taylor's new boss, Albert Southard, was a railroad man.

He was superintendent for the Indianapolis, Peru, and Chicago
line, a hugely successful enterprise started by his uncle, the beloved
Hoosier pioneer David Macy. Macy and Southard oversaw IP&C's
growth from a small line to a major regional rail line linking Lake
Michigan, the Erie Canal, and Indianapolis. On its freight cars came
the lumber that planked downtown streets and drove the city's post–
Civil War building boom. He was one of the richest men in Indianapolis in the business that put the city on the map.

He and his kind had produced a city from scratch, transforming a
landlocked place full of stumps, ironweed, and topography as flat as
your hand into a crucial hub in the most advanced transportation
network the world had ever seen. In a country built upon rivers and
oceans, Indianapolis was a new urban species. In 1888, some sixteen
lines centered in Indianapolis; 116 trains arrived and departed daily.
Goods came from every major city in the country, making Indianapolis,
with nothing more than its shrewd midstate location and lattices of
steel rail, the city of the future.

Where the railroad men's vision ended was where the large numbers of blacks in their nearly perfect city began. The growing constituency of Bucktown, West Side, and North Indianapolis unsettled
the grand plan, the perfect grid. Indianapolis' post–Civil War black
population had ballooned, expanding from a mere 500 residents in

1860 to 6,500 in 1880. At the downtown YMCA, which offered
working-class Christians a pool, a gym, and the kind of morally
upstanding atmosphere that promised a better brand of employee,
the door was shut to blacks. As applications from blacks increased,
the YMCA moved to codify the racial ban in its bylaws. No place
said publicly what everyone knew privately: blacks weren't welcome
in the social circle of whites, not even working-class whites.

Of the myriad railroad men who engineered the startling rebirth
of Indianapolis, it is doubtful more than a few empathized with the
black underclass who lived in the desolate places outside the hum-
ming steel rails. Providentially for Marshall Taylor, Albert Southard,
his father's boss, was one.

Southard and his wife, Laura Brouse, were of the era a Harvard
historian characterized as the "golden age of interracial friendship."
Examples in antebellum America abounded, from Mary Todd Lincoln's
best friend, Elizabeth Keckley, to the openly amalgamated black and
white families on some southern plantations.

Albert Southard hailed from a family of pioneers whose rich line-
age could be traced from Wiltshire, England, to Nantucket to North
Carolina. Family members were said to uniquely possess the "soften-
ing" effects of a Carolinian upbringing combined with the "rugged-
ness" of the frontier. Laura Brouse was the daughter of Judge H. A.
Brouse, an uncommonly liberal jurist and a recognized friend to Indiana's black citizens. Every summer the black folk of Kokomo and
Indianapolis marched to Judge Brouse's heavenly grove with the
"e'er piercing life and soul stirring drum" to celebrate the 1870 ratifi-
cation of the Fifteenth Amendment, which guaranteed their right
to vote.

Though the Jim Crow era would curtail the interracial societal
trend, Mark Twain's best-selling *Adventures of Huckleberry Finn*
(published in 1885) was a reminder of earlier promise. When two
eight-year-olds, Marshall Taylor and Daniel Southard, met near the

family's stables—Taylor sometimes helped his father groom and shoe the carriage horses—their fast rapport and easy fellowship served as another reminder. When Daniel, her only son, began playing with Marshall, Laura Southard didn't hesitate to invite him in, barefoot and all. In time he stayed with them overnight, then over several days, then for good.

Born in the same year, the pair were treated as twins. They were tutored together, fed together, and "kept dressed just alike all the time." The image is almost farcical—two boys, one white, the other black, a no-nonsense nanny before them with a day's attire of pressed flannel britches, suspenders, and vests. Not even the race-conscious world of 19th-century fiction would have found the scene plausible enough to exploit. And yet it was all true. Taylor remembered a play-room "stacked with every kind of toy imaginable" and a workshop where he was "the happiest boy in the world." He and Dan Southard got along well, certain that the other was the lucky one. Taylor was one of many, never fussed over. Southard was an only child, never free from suffocating oversight.

Years later Southard would appear in a baseball team portrait as an eighteen-year-old undergrad at the University of Chicago, his eyes bright, a cocky, upturned grin on his face. A year later he was booted off the team for playing professionally during the summer. Big Dan, as his family would come to call him, exasperated his father to no end, married five times, and trended toward risk-laden entrepreneurial ventures, one of them being a Rolls-Royce dealership in boomtown Denver, Colorado. Even as a boy Big Dan was wildly impulsive and extroverted—traits the pint-sized, tight-lipped Taylor found as alien and fascinating as anything in his adoptive home. Years later the celebrity photographs of Taylor on a vaudeville stage or in a Parisian nightclub playing stride piano—incongruous moments of showmanship and panache—would strike Taylor's North Side sib-

Dan Southard, Taylor's boyhood friend, in a photograph taken in the late 1890s, when he attended the University of Chicago. *Source: Courtesy of Dan Southard III*

lings as false notes, as if they came from a person other than the one they knew. Which, in a sense, they did.

Taylor's three years in the Southard household earned him an education worthy of a young prince. He learned the etiquette of formal dinners and the dress code, mannerisms, and dialect of parlor visitors. He was exposed to science, math, and the city's burgeoning cultural scene. Late-1880s Indianapolis was suddenly home to ten libraries, a geological museum with "thousands of specimens" worth a total of $100,000, and four theaters. *Frank Leslie's Illustrated* and *Harper's Weekly* published special pictorial supplements describing a place that "has at last thrown off the quiet of the inland town and assumed the airs of a great city." Taylor saw the windblown bonfires that leapt from the new natural-gas streetlamps, the blue-eyed kids in britches peering into the Arcade, and the signs on Washington Street beckoning travelers to visit Chicago via "the great panhandle route."

He would've seen something else too—bicycles.

NATURALLY, A PAIR of bicycles came into the possession of Dan Southard and Taylor. Albert Southard purchased the first ones he could find and probably soon thereafter brought the boys to see Indianapolis' Prince Wells, an acrobatic stage rider who performed in light blue tights and black patent leather shoes and customarily concluded his show with a peculiar striptease in which he would progressively remove more and more critical-seeming parts of his bicycle until he was down to little more than his big, sky-scraping wheel.

Both the boys learned how to ride their bikes, but Taylor taught himself to ride backward, balance on his wheel's spokes, and pedal with his hands. "He sits on the wheel and keeps it motionless while he removes the handle bar, rides backward, stands on the seat and handle bar and rides it, or rides it without seat or handlebar," observed a reporter a few years later.

It pleased Taylor to do something others, even the reckless Big

Dan, weren't bold enough to try, but more crucially he adored the feeling of mastery. His intense rehearsals, what a present-day sports researcher would term "deliberate practice," ingrained a skill along with an intoxicating feeling. He could replicate an intricate, nearly impossible movement. He was manipulating great forces—precession, gravity, and centrifugal—because it was fun. Young athletic geniuses aren't born or made, say modern sports physiologists, but they share a set of conditions, which maybe more than anything come down to an exquisite level of desire, love of what they're doing, and luck. A blossoming young star in a beat-up gym, writes Daniel Coyle, "is not science . . . It's closer to what happens in a garden, a forgotten, run-down garden that somehow produces marvelous tomatoes, summer after summer." In other words, there's a scrap of nutrient-rich dirt, a gap in the tall buildings where the late-afternoon sun finds its way through, and one perfectly tenacious, opportunistic seed.

Given the legendary hostility of the bike to being tamed, Taylor proved to himself the value of perseverance and courage, and reveled in the sublime beauty of odds-against victory. Each new trick was like David slaying Goliath. There were questions and doubt, and then something happened he couldn't fully explain. Though only ten, he sensed his strength.

When Dan Southard, Taylor, and the rich white boys roared down Washington Street opposite the Statehouse, Taylor rode fastest. Even if he couldn't articulate what he felt in that scintillating moment, he knew as a ten-year-old that the bicycle bequeathed the one thing America promised but almost never delivered—freedom.

CHAPTER 3

Fire

JULY 1863
WIRT COUNTY, VIRGINIA

The Civil War is not ended: I question whether
any serious civil war ever does end.
—T. S. ELIOT

W IRT COUNTY IS ONE OF the smallest, least populated
counties in West Virginia, but for Scottish immigrants
who came in the 18th century it had the rugged, temper-
ate sweep of their homeland, and they burrowed in for the long
haul. The McFarland clan were among the earliest settlers to cross
the Alleghenies and farm the bottomland along the Little Kanawha
River, making their way into the county histories as a handful of
rough-and-ready pioneers. They weren't merely sturdy farmers but
an extraordinary brand of frontiersmen who left their mark on seemingly every visitor who stumbled into the mean wilderness where the
McFarlands chose to live.

In recalling his interlude with a patriarchal McFarland descendant, a traveler wrote: "The next morning we came down we found
the old farmer sitting on the porch reading a paper. On the table lay
Morse's Geography, The Beauty of the Stars, The Vicar of Wakefield,
and other good books. I enter into particulars in my description of
this family because we were then only five miles from the Gallatin,

where the people are too often represented as rough, uncultured, good for nothings . . . it is something to find a family such as this, living . . . [in] the mountains, 300 miles from the sea coast."

For some seventy-five years the McFarlands thrived in the hills, making a name for themselves and leaving an imprint of the Jacksonian ideal: self-made, rigorously educated, and undaunted by the travails of frontier life. Their composition was vastly different from the aristocratic slaveholding planters on the other side of the state; when people advocated for a new state and a different destiny, they saw the McFarland family as representative of an exemplary breed. Their attachment to the land seemed permanent. When West Virginia made its devil's bargain by siding with the Union to get its statehood—a minor move given that everyone expected the Civil War to be brief— the McFarlands and their neighbors in Wirt County had every right to celebrate a prosperity and affluence that their plantation brethren could only dream about.

In 1860, oil was discovered in Wirt County. It was the same year Fort Sumter was occupied by Union troops and the same year Thomas B. McFarland and Almira Moorehead had the first of what would be seven children. The big vein was at Burning Springs, where the gusher was found only a hundred feet below the plowed farmland. As in California a decade earlier, a metropolis sprang to life with a "swarming mass of humanity representing almost every nation on earth." A single well had enough gas to illuminate every city in America. A majestic hotel was erected, using the petroleum flooding beneath it to shine forth day and night. For a moment, little Wirt County was the richest place in the universe, and the father of Floyd McFarland had once more burnished the family legacy.

Then the war erupted and fractured West Virginia in half. In Wirt County, which, like the rest of western Virginia, was supposedly part of the Union, almost half the men joined the Confederate army. Families divided, and in the chaos and terror that ensued the boom

abated. It's unclear for whom Thomas McFarland served, or whether
he lost his fortune like so many others; the only thing that is sure is
that the war drove him from his dear ancestral stake and pushed him
west. Undoubtedly the catalyst was the event of May 9, 1863, when
a Confederate detachment under the command of General William
Jones ordered a devastating strike on the wells at Burning Springs. The
apocalyptic conflagration caused by the ignition of 100,000 barrels
of oil sent a tidal wave of black smoke rolling across the immediate
vicinity and sparked a plume of light visible all the way to Parkers-
burg, forty miles away. It was the biggest explosion anyone had ever
witnessed, and it convinced even the most rooted souls that heaven
had turned to hell and the future was elsewhere. Thomas B. McFarland left it all behind—the family stake and the West Virginian state
his ancestors had helped make—and slowly but surely headed as far
away as he could possibly get: California.

BORN ON JULY 9, 1878, FLOYD McFarland was the youngest
of Thomas and Almira's children. By the time he was four the family
had moved off the farm and was living in San Jose near the Normal
School in Washington Square. The land Thomas had purchased several years earlier—and had farmed when he first came to San Jose in
the early 1870s—was becoming more valuable by the day as San Jose
outgrew its status as a weak sister to San Francisco and became a
thriving city reachable by the mighty Southern Pacific. There were
neoclassical homes on palm-lined streets and a smattering of celebrity
residents, including the Shakespearean actor James Stark, naturalist
Andrew Jackson Grayson, and Eliza Poor Donner, a survivor of
the Donner Party tragedy. The 1870 census gives a picture of a thriving after-hours district as well, with 200 people listing their occu-
pations as either prostitute or gambler. By the late 1880s land sales
were averaging $2 million a day and Thomas McFarland, like every-
one else in San Jose, was a real estate impresario.

The orchard city bloomed, but unlike other railroad towns such as Indianapolis, there was an almost total absence of black citizens. Part of it was the deeds Thomas McFarland and other leading California real estate agents wrote, which prevented the transfer of title to black families. There were approximately 4,000 blacks in California circa 1870, with fewer than fifteen families sprinkled about the two northside wards of San Jose. The adults were bootblacks, barbers, or "keepers of house." (The far larger Asian population in San Jose were launderers, washmen, and strawberry and hops pickers.) When a young black woman moved to San Jose in the 1940s she was astonished to find no blacks in the cityscape. There were no black waiters, clerks, bank tellers, teachers, or officials. There were no classroom pictures of blacks. No black history. From the earliest ages young boys such as Floyd McFarland grew up accepting the lopsided racial balance in San Jose as the way things ought to be.

In the beginning, Floyd was overshadowed by his talented brothers and sisters. His sister Flora was one of the earliest graduates of the all-white San Jose state normal school and his brother Robert, only three years older than Floyd, was among the first students to attend Stanford when it opened in 1891. Like his Gallatin forbearer, Thomas McFarland's family was carving out a distinctive niche in early San Jose.

If a single word defined both the McFarlands' and San Jose's makeover, it was *speed*. Only a decade earlier the desolation of San Jose had been so profound as to cause an official to bemoan, "San Jose has nothing." By 1890 it had improved roads, sewers, and bridges and boasted a new city hall, a deluxe hotel, and, in true California fashion, a bustling saloon trade with no fewer than 120 establishments. Still, the real measure of a supercharged, overachieving American city was neither barrooms nor towers of electric light but a train-delivered cargo of revolutionary English-made, low-mount bicycles. San Jose received its in the summer of 1890. Floyd McFarland, wishing to make his own way in the McFarland pantheon and stand out in a crowd of siblings, saw his future in being a kind of pioneer his ancestors wouldn't have recognized but a pioneer nonetheless. He wanted to be the fastest man in the world.

The gangly adolescent began his rapid cycling ascendancy as a carrier for the *Mercury News*. Every day he lugged seventy-five pounds of newspapers the thirty upgrade miles between San Jose and Gilroy. The rest of the time he hung around the bicycle shops sprouting throughout San Jose. In 1892 the East San Jose track opened— the first in California—while time trial specialists paced by the Hayward electric cars roared down the roadway between Fruitville, Oakland, and the city center, attempting records. In August 1894 native son Otto Ziegler won every sprint distance from a quarter mile to two miles at the national championships in Denver, earning the sobriquet "little demon from San Jose." On his return the entire city turned out to welcome their newfound hero, with all three of the city's cycling clubs and Parkman's Band forming a parade column stretching more than a mile. Ziegler, like a conquering emperor, rode in a carriage drawn by four white horses, his little round face aglow as his adoring supporters chanted, "Ziegler! Ziegler! Cycling star! San Jose Road Club! Zip! Boom! Ah!"

The experience left an indelible mark on McFarland, who that same year had won his first major amateur championship in San Francisco. Standing on the periphery of the celebration, he was like the young unsung bicycle racer from the hill country of Texas who gets to touch the hand of Lance Armstrong on his return from his Tour de France victory. There is something electric in the moment, something affirming, and something that he wants. McFarland did not seek guidance from Ziegler or fantasize about meeting and befriending the San Jose hero. He was already a creature of competition and of the well-nurtured grudge. Moreover, Ziegler hailed from the cycling club that was his own Garden City Club's biggest rival. To become the foremost racer on the Pacific Coast, McFarland knew what he had to do.

In the coming years he began the long march up the ladder of riders who stood between him and Ziegler. "McFarland loved the game," recalled a well-known local trainer named Jack Dermody in a column years later. "Not satisfied with a 60 mile ride before breakfast, he would come home, rest up until noon, and soon after lunch would go out to the track and tear off a bunch of miles." He would beat everyone in California, but when he finally pinned down Ziegler to a best two out of three on their hometown track, he crashed in the rubber match and watched from his backside as his adversary passed the finish post. He was dismayed but not discouraged. Unlike his fleeing father, he intended to defend his home territory before he moved on.

IT WOULD'VE GALLED FLOYD McFarland to know that Marshall Taylor, the son of a servant coachman, was his educational equal. But in the early 1890s it all changed for Taylor when the Southard family left Indianapolis and he stayed behind. Albert Southard had decided to take a job in Chicago, and though Taylor was extended an invitation to go with them, Saphronia Taylor told her eleven-year-old son no. Taylor glumly recalled that he "went from the happy life of a millionaire kid to that of a common errand boy, all within a few weeks." For the rest of his life he knew something that would both bless and haunt him: how it would be not to have black skin.

A year earlier he had been turned away from the city's whites-only YMCA, even with the persuasive support of the Southards. Without them, he returned to a separate and unequal community of black schools, clubs, and churches. He couldn't make eye contact with white people the same way, or have something a white man wanted—a job, a bicycle, a speed record—without worrying about what the consequences might be. The black-run newspaper depicted the worsening struggle with a front-page illustration in which the "negro" as Hercules is shown shouldering a planet of burdens—an ocean of opposition, continental landmasses of ignorance, race hatred, poverty, and prejudice. In Jim Crow Indianapolis he could take the trolley cars, but only if he sat in the last three seats. Indianapolis set the tone for Cypress, California, a century later, where a five-year-old was tied up, stoned, and spray-painted with the word *nigger*. That boy's name was Tiger Woods.

Taylor's salvation was the bicycle. Like McFarland, he pedaled a paper route. He made $5 a week and developed a reputation for reliability and durability, much like the new bike itself. In the summer of 1891 Tom Hay of the Hay and Willits bike shop offered Taylor a $35 bike and $6 a week to "sweep and dust" and perform "homemade tricks" in front of his Bicycle Row shop. At 4:00 P.M. daily large crowds amassed on the sidewalk in front of Hay and Willits. Taylor wore an officer's uniform, with Hay billing him as the trick-riding "major." A white laundry owner on North Meridian named Major Taylor threatened a lawsuit because he didn't appreciate a black boy appropriating his name, but the nickname stuck: Major.

Months later Hay and Willits sponsored a 10-mile handicap race for, what Taylor recalled, were the cream of amateur riders in Indiana. The event started near Bicycle Row and headed north up through Fairview Park to Crown Hill via the towpath. Taylor said there were hundreds of cyclists, but his memory was faulty. That would be the next year, at the club's inaugural race at the city fairgrounds. In 1891, the race was still looking to establish itself. When Hay saw Taylor near the start, he invited the thirteen-year-old boy to jump in and offered him a fifteen-minute head start on the field. Taylor said he didn't want to race, but Hay refused to take no for an answer. It was the hare-and-hound format with a twist—a black boy and a pursuing white mob. "Although the band was playing a lively tune and the crowd was cheering wildly I was crying," wrote Taylor in his autobiography. "When Mr. Hay saw that he started to lift me from my wheel, but stopped and whispered in my ear, 'I know you can't go the full distance but just ride up the road a little way, it will please the crowd, and you can come back as soon as you get tired.' " The pistol exploded and the chase began.

Around the same time an article about top-notch racers identified what the perfect bicycling man should look like: "The style of man to be chosen for bicycling should be one above medium height, with wide hips, long legs and powerful thighs, with a chest big enough to give full play to heart and lungs." Walter Marmon, the scratch man in the race (and a future automobile titan), was such a man (as would be the massive Floyd McFarland). The teenaged Taylor weighed less than 100 pounds and had twigs for legs. In his own description of the race he says he was driven on by all those, like the shop owner Hay, who didn't think he could finish. The desire to prove someone wrong isn't an unusual athletic motivation, but his was probably stronger than average. A participant who didn't finish wouldn't appear in the published results. Taylor, like his father in the Civil War, would be a kind of ghost participant—there but not.

Taylor remembered his aching exhaustion at the halfway point and the desire to quit, but for reasons he didn't fully comprehend, "he rode like mad." In the final few hundred yards he could hear the adult Marmon bearing down on him—he crossed the line with less than three lengths to spare, avoiding, in the cyclist's parlance, the humiliating capture. Taylor was applauded for his pluck and awarded the gold medal that had obsessed him ever since it was put on display in the Hay and Willits store window. "My first thought," he wrote in his autobiography, "was to take it home and show it to my mother. Fast as I had ridden that race I rode with greater speed home."

Saphronia Taylor saw the bicycle as a gift, a sign of the Almighty's beneficent guiding hand. To his father, it was precisely the opposite. The bike—especially the fancy, eye-catching way his son liked to ride it—was bound to earn him the enmity of those who'd rather not see, hear, or be reminded of a black boy's gift. Gilbert Taylor, the coachman and the day laborer, had spent much of his life avoiding confrontations with whites; his son was doing precisely the opposite. He was anointed, all right. God help him.

Taylor's victory and his additional amateur race wins throughout Indiana, Illinois, and Kentucky did get him noticed, bringing him into the strange, rarefied orbit of Indianapolis' latest cycling legend. Birdie Munger had moved to the city in the aftermath of his racing career's collapse in Chicago, and was intent on building a racing bicycle the likes of which had never been seen. Perhaps the pair met when Munger's Zig Zag Cycling Club was out on one of its regular training romps, zooming north along the canal towpath, slicing past Taylor's old neighborhood. Or maybe Taylor shadowed the famous record breaker, having overheard Tom Hay say that Munger had moved to town to set up shop and was building something fast and special.

In 1893 Munger hired the fifteen-year-old as a valet for what the papers called his "famous bachelor quarters." It was a quasi-clubhouse for prominent racers passing though the city. "During the race meets this coming summer the racing men will again be asked to partake of the good things at the Bachelor's home, this home . . . is unique in many ways," a columnist recounted. "There is no woman needed to do the housework, a young man by the name of 'Major' Taylor doing all the work . . . 'Maje' is a character, and thoroughly understands the eccentricities of his employers. A meal with [the riders] and Maje to wait on the table, is an experience that once enjoyed will never be forgotten."

Taylor had leapt at the chance to be the "general man of all work," knowing the storied reputation of his boss, the "watch charm" bicycle he was in the midst of creating, and the wheelmen he entertained. In 1893 and 1894 they all passed through, including Arthur

Zimmerman, the first American racer to be deemed good enough to be asked to race in Europe. Taylor was like a teenage boy who loves baseball more than life itself staying each summer with an uncle who is training the major leagues' leading fastball hurlers. The men tell stories, share secrets, and pop the ball into the uncle's glove with a thwap that is deafening. The teen tags along, studying, listening, marveling.

Taylor was working as an errand boy, competing in boys' races, and rubbing shoulders with the men he read about in the *Wheelmen's Gazette*. What's clear, and what's surprising, is that the teenager had a *plan*. At some point, according to Birdie's memory, Taylor persuaded him to loan him one of his bicycles; at another, he persuaded him to come to the track to watch him race with it.

Taylor wasn't handed the stage, he seized it. When Walter Sanger, a powerful six-foot-three, 200-pound Chicagoan, was to make a run at the mile record, the sixteen-year-old Taylor scripted a plan to better him. Only moments after the veteran had completed his victory lap at the Capital City track—he had indeed set a new track record—Taylor snuck in with his own bike, a fourteen-pound Munger. Before the crowd got a chance to file out, he began whirling around the fifth-of-a-mile oval, clearly with intent. The record attempt was surprisingly well orchestrated, with pacers, timers, and a veritable squadron of accomplices culled from the local clubs. He easily eclipsed Sanger's minutes-old record, lopping off a whopping seven seconds from his 2:18 time.

Birdie had often envisioned the racer who would blaze a record path on his bike—"It's coming . . . the Munger," the adverts read. Now he saw Taylor, the fastest, "most game" rider he'd ever seen, as the perfect complement to his perfect bike. He had, in one brassy evening, taken on two opponents: the time record and the color line. Though several adult racers threatened him for upstaging Sanger, he stuck to his plan. The spirited Taylor reminded Munger of that

long-ago teenager stuck in an airless blind-making factory. Taylor
was desperate to be noticed and refused to give up. He loved the
game. Munger bound himself to an ideal, for better or worse, like
lugs fastening to steel beneath a blowtorch's flame. Birdie didn't
dwell on the obvious: Taylor was black.

Shortly after the Capital City stunt, which resulted in his ban
from Indy tracks, Taylor snuck into the seventy-five-mile Indianapolis-
to-Matthews road race, again arriving as a rogue entry. Moments
after the starter's pistol, and with the cooperation of the sympathetic
race director, Taylor jumped from his hiding place and "started in
hot pursuit of the fifty odd riders who were pedaling for all they were
worth." Taylor caught and passed them, guaranteeing his large winning gap when he put on a massive spurt along a thinly inhabited
stretch of road, with weeping willows on one side and a cemetery
opposite. "I decided that if my time had come I might just as well die
trying to keep ahead of the bunch of riders, so I jumped," he recalled.

The Matthews victory ensured Taylor's reputation as the foremost racer in the state. "Marshall Taylor, better known as Major
Taylor, is one of the best colored racers in the State," a paper reported.
"He is the boy who won the road race to Matthews last Sunday."
Taylor wrote in his book account that he didn't tell his mother he
was going to race because she would've worried the distance was too
far. In truth, she would have forbidden it because of the race's Sabbath start.

Taylor's derring-do was impressive—a trait often overlooked by
those who later mistook him as conservative and fastidious—but it
also doomed him. With his brazen record-making reputation, it was
impossible to sneak him onto any Indiana track. Before Chicago's
Pullman road race, the region's most prestigious event, Taylor, with
Munger's assistance, attempted to bleach his skin white. The specific
solution they used is unknown, though the Indianapolis black newspaper the *Freeman* was then running ads for "black skin remover."

The Virginia doctor who invented the product promised results in forty-eight hours. "For days and days we poured it on the lad," related Munger in a later newspaper story. "His hair turned a sort of red and his skin did seem to be turning whiter and whiter . . . [but] the mixture was poisonous in the extreme and we had to stop it." Unable to compete on Memorial Day weekend 1895, Taylor saw Homer Fairmon, a second-rater, take the first prize and the glory of the next-great-racer tag that went with it.

As the 1895 race season got under way it was difficult to say which was more unusual—the sixteen-year-old, the son of a coachman, in defiance of the understood way of things, or the thirty-year-old Munger, an established cycling legend, enigmatically standing with him. "Mr. Munger became closer and closer attached to me as time went on," Taylor wrote in his autobiography. Unfortunately, the proverbial noose was tightening around the black population in Indianapolis. "There are too many Negroes up here; they hurt the city," a white resident told a newspaper reporter, echoing a popular sentiment that would soon lead to racially motivated gang attacks. At the Munger Bicycle Manufacturing building on East Street colleagues confronted Birdie, asking him why he "bothered with that little darkey." In the early spring Munger, for reasons he never fully explained, exited the factory, though his specially designed, one-of-a-kind racing bicycle was only weeks old.

Taylor was certain, he later wrote, that Munger left his job, or was forced out, because he had teamed with a black racer. The cycling historian Andrew Ritchie isn't sure Taylor's understanding was accurate, citing other manufacturing factors, but his clinical assessment misses the point. Taylor thought he was responsible and felt deeply indebted to the sacrifices Munger made. Their bond cured.

In the summer of 1895 Munger and Taylor departed Indianapolis for the Northeast, specifically Worcester, Massachusetts. The industry and interest were in place for Munger to resume work on his perfect bike; the races were available for Taylor to showcase it. If there was any question whether times had changed and a new era was upon them, it was answered that same year. E. F. Leonert bicycled a mile in 1 minute and 35 seconds. The time was impressive—the 2-minute barrier had been broken only a few years earlier—but what set it apart was that it was a half second faster than the record time held by the legendary racehorse Salvador. In the small window of time before motorcycles, automobiles, and airplanes, bicycles and the select, tautly muscled men upon them combined to become the single fastest form on the planet. A bike was now likened to the bones of the wind itself.

You could almost hear in the whooshing sound four magic words: "It's coming . . . the Munger!"

CHAPTER 4

Six Days

DECEMBER 1896

MADISON SQUARE GARDEN

NEW YORK CITY

The Lord is always good to the honest gambler.
— BILLY BRADY,
PROMOTER AND FUTURE TAYLOR MANAGER

THERE HAD BEEN MAGIC in Pierre Lallement's bag after all. The wrought-iron bicycle parts were reconfigured, rethought, and vastly improved from the ocean-crossing boneshaker, but the beauty behind his two-wheeled premise was borne out. In 1896 you could go anywhere in America and feel the apostle's excitement he'd felt thirty years earlier when he mounted his contraption and rode the elm-lined streets of New Haven, Connecticut.

What the bicycle did, which nobody really foresaw, was democratize transport. In doing so, it changed society itself. Laborers could live in the country and work in the city. Women could escape the house to recreate, ruminate, or, as Margaret LeLong did, cycle alone from Chicago to San Francisco "packing a powder-box and a pistol," wrote the bicycle historian David Herlihy. Young people could ride out to tryst in the privacy of a wooded hollow. There were no laws about who could and couldn't ride, who could and couldn't own.

The price of a bicycle, once a prohibitive $300, was rapidly falling. In 1893 Pope offered a $125 Columbia model; two years later it was $100. The steady advances in producing lighter pneumatic safety bicycles led to annual trade-ins, which in turn begat a brisk second-ary market in which last year's models could be had for half the cost of a new one. The bicycle was the future, and the future was about getting to a place you'd never been: the country, or the city, or a pro-fessional racetrack.

But the racing arena was where the new freedoms ended, at least for Munger and Taylor. In Indianapolis, Louisville, Savannah, and most other late-19th-century U.S. cities, a black man couldn't com-pete against a white one. He couldn't box or bat a ball against a white man, or play his instrument opposite white musicians in a Broadway pit band. Segregation was uniformly in place, whether by law or by popular understanding, and few dared to experiment or be unpleasantly surprised by the one thing that titillated the popular imagination: the outcome of a black man in competition against a white counterpart. White prizefighters easily avoided black challengers, claiming the impropriety of sharing a ring with someone who was so plainly an inferior. Peter Jackson, called the "black prince" and recently crowned the Australian heavyweight champion, would go down in the sporting annals as the greatest fighter never to get a title shot as first John L. Sullivan and later Gentleman Jim Corbett ducked him. "All fighters—first come, first served—who are white," Sullivan famously offered his challengers. "I will not fight a negro. I never have and never shall." And he never did.

It hadn't always been this way. Some ten years earlier the bare-handed catcher Moses Fleetwood Walker, playing for the Toledo Blue Stockings, had broken the color line to become the first black player in the major leagues. In horse racing, colored jockeys had dominated the sport for the better part of a century. Today's richest trophy—the four-foot-high cast-silver Woodlawn Vase, made by the New York jewelers Tiffany in the 1860s—is topped by images of what was then the world's greatest racehorse, Lexington, and the most famous jockey, the colored Isaac Murphy. In 1891, Murphy became the first back-to-back Kentucky Derby winner, finishing his career the next year with a record 628 wins.

But as sports came to be a larger, more middle-class kind of fascination and racial tension in the country escalated, the color in professional sports was rapidly scrubbed away. What would be the last Negro baseball player in either the major or minor leagues for more than half a century was drummed out of the sport in the spring of 1896, and with Isaac Murphy's death that same summer, the nation's black jockeys found themselves increasingly denied competitive mounts; by the turn of the century most had left the country to compete in France, England, or czarist Russia. Peter Jackson, his career in ruins, took to the bottle and toured as an actor in *Uncle Tom's Cabin*.

In 1896, the *Plessy v. Ferguson* Supreme Court decision would put into law what was already established in practice: "separate but equal." A veiled apartheid system replaced the blue-sky freedoms of the immediate postwar years. Black athletes were confined to shabby playing fields, ramshackle racetracks, and basement-dwelling boxing rings. In satirizing a black bicycle race, a southern newspaper reflected how little the white world thought of the "separate but equal" colored sportsman. It showed a saucer-lipped, dim-witted competitor lazily reclining on the side of a road, having happily quit the ongoing competition, unable to resist a field of ripening watermelons.

It had come to this.

But in a country in the hasty process of dividing, New York City was the sometime exception. It was unapologetically hedonistic, libertine, and unbound by convention. Anything went, as long as it served the cause of entertainment. In New York, the shock wasn't that a black boy would get to start the biggest bicycle race of the year. The shock was what he did in that race.

IT WAS MIDNIGHT ON DECEMBER 10 when the twenty-eight cyclists emerged from the easternmost portico like modern-day gladiators. They were wrapped in their old country colors, swaddled in velvety robes, buttressed by smiling, fist-pumping entourages. The native diehards catcalled the green-as-grass Irishman, Teddy Hale, but the near capacity crowd of 5,000 practically stood as one in mock salute as Brooklyn's Charles Murphy waltzed before them in a dazzling racing suit of stars and stripes. The roar continued for Frank "Flying Dutchman" Waller, Peter "Stayer" Golden, and a rosy-cheeked lad named George Van Emburgh, whom the faithful had dubbed "Boy Wonder" for his stalwart debut performance at the same Madison Square Garden Six-Day race three years earlier.

Eighteen-year-old Marshall Walter Taylor and manager Birdie Munger stepped haltingly into the Garden spotlight. They had no natural constituency, of course—a black racer and a white trainer, after all! The Garden crowd reacted as promoters had known they would: nudging one another, whispering, titillated by the delicious possibilities of a black racer in a rare sanctioned competition against white rivals. The newly installed electrical lights hung down from the high girders and bathed the tiny wooden track in celestial light, looming over the Irishman's heavy brow, the German's stiff jaw line, and in Taylor's case his oil-black skin. He never got back "his old blackness," Munger used to say when he discussed their experiments with black-skin remover, but you wouldn't have known there was even the slightest diminishment next to a cavalry of Caucasian faces. Taylor was clearly a boy, not a man: blade-thin shoulders, an anxious look of uncertainty as he gazed straight ahead. He stood five foot six and weighed little more than 130 pounds for his first professional race.

He was virtually unknown in New York, but in a half-mile curtain-raising exhibition on Saturday night at the Garden he had whipped the reigning American sprint champion, Eddie "Cannon" Bald. "Round and round the track whirled the colored rider, pedaling away like a steam engine," described a reporter. "Once or twice he looked back, and although he was going on the bunch he kept on going like a scared rabbit. Eddie Bald was straining every nerve to catch the runaway African." The majority of newspaper reporters were disinclined to give Taylor much credit, saying that Bald was "quite lame" after a crash earlier in the evening, but the capacity crowd enjoyed the upset, especially the South Brooklyn contingent, which referred to Taylor as their "dark secret from Gowanus." The tie-in with the fast-rising stars of the South Brooklyn Club had been arranged with Munger's help.

Taylor was so excited, and green, he didn't hear the bell for the last lap against Bald and raced five more laps than he needed to, each a little faster than the last. The touts dubbed him the "colored cyclone." His brother William, ten years older than Major and helping to take care of him, was likely watching from trackside, screaming for Taylor to keep his wheel on the innermost line separating the track from the apron and to stop looking behind him. Taylor's crew couldn't believe what they saw and heard: thousands wildly applauding.

Billy Brady, a boom-and-bust prizefight promoter, witnessed Taylor's Saturday night debut, too, and returned twenty-four hours later for the spectacle of the introductions for the Six-Day race. Brady dressed according to the showman's convention of the times: white suit, red carnation, blue spats. He arranged his slicked-back brown hair with a conspicuous center part and filled his lungs with smells he adored: damp wood, smoky tobacco, and the pungent mix created from sweat and fear. He was thirty-three and newly widowed, and already he seemed to have lived several lifetimes. His wife, the Parisian-born dancer Marie Rose Rene, had died only a few months earlier, a loss that was barely conceivable given that he'd had to bury his firstborn son only a few years prior.

Brady would never forget the night. The Six-Day race was the start of his personal and professional rebirth. For the next several years, he would come at cycling like a hurtling freight train—fast, loud, and impossible to ignore. Beginning shortly after the Six-Day he would get races for Taylor that no other man could've arranged; he would cajole, bait, and humble the obstructionists in the sport until they had no recourse but to meet his demands for a match race. He backed down against no one, no matter the odds: he once challenged and won a $15,000 cut of cards against the notorious gambler Arnold Rothstein. When a coalition of southern cycling officials sought to ban Taylor from national competition, Brady merely built his own racetrack and started his own race series. The adrenaline-pumping game of risk and reward drove him to innovative heights. The idea that had come to him as the Six-Day unfolded—a black man, yes, a beautiful Adonis of a black man, as a national celebrity!—gave him goose bumps.

Night after successive night he kept one eye on the track and another on the crowd. At a subsequent Madison Square Garden Six-Day event, Brady would meet and fall in love with the ravishing young actress Grace George. Brady wrote about how he introduced himself to his future wife but, perhaps out of courtesy to that dramatic moment, he refrained from any details of his other equally electric meeting at the first Six-Day. He shook Taylor's small hand as though he would never let go. Within a year, "I signed up with Brady," Taylor wrote.

In the cyclist Taylor and in his future wife, Grace George, Brady had chanced upon a pair that would change his life.

WHEN MUNGER AND TAYLOR ARRIVED at the Garden Six-Day, they had been training together for two years, beginning first in

A young William "Billy" Brady, the fast-talking, pioneering promoter who helped Taylor break the color line. *Source: Billy Rose Theatre Collection, New York Public Library*

Indianapolis and more recently in Worcester. Taylor was competing in road races and on the New England tracks, where he was popularly known as Munger's protégé, or the "negro champion" (an ill-defined title that he brought with him from his dominant showings in the "colored-only" races of the Midwest). He was also working as a machinist in the Worcester Cycle Manufacturing Company. Of late they spent increasing amounts of time in Brooklyn as Munger prepared to unveil his latest bikes, the Boyd and the Birdie Special, at the popular wintertime trade shows.

They had spent countless hours together; still, Munger wasn't 100 percent sure about him. Taylor had fared well in the amateur sprint contests in Indiana and New England, but the professional endurance world was a far different arena. The Six-Day marathoners were hard men—lumpers, diggers, and barroom-brawling seamen. Munger wondered if Taylor was too nice, too accustomed to taking notice and care of others—he worried so much about his mother and a younger sister and brother. He'd barely won his exhibition against

Bald when he wired the entire $200 prize home. He was strangely trusting, as if he didn't recognize the limited, instigator role he was meant to play. What would happen, Munger wondered, when the crowd started to taunt him, baiting him with crude monkey noises and racial slurs? He had a quiet fire, which Munger could vouch for, but he wasn't sure where Taylor's threshold lay, or how he would respond when things got hard.

The Six-Day marathon wasn't about athleticism; it was about pain and the will to withstand it. One doctor wrote that a single race took ten years off an athlete's life. Sprinters such as Taylor were often the first to be destroyed. In fact, he was the only sprinter in the race and he was absurdly young, a full decade junior to the seasoned favorites. At the South Brooklyn clubhouse on Ninth Street in what is today the Park Slope section, he was known as a mascot, the kid who assisted and repaired the others' bikes. The *Brooklyn Eagle* offered perhaps the most complete prerace description: "He's taken care of by his brother and two South Brooklyn wheelmen—Bob Ellingham and W. F. Sibley, and it is due to the fact that he obeys their instructions implicitly that he is in such good condition. While his friends think that he has an excellent chance for a good position at the finish the general opinion is that he doesn't."

Part of Munger's thinking for introducing Taylor in a race he couldn't win was simple: it was New York. The city was the self-declared hub of the cycling craze. On a given Saturday night at the Michaux Cycling Club in New York City, Cornelius "Commodore" Vanderbilt, John D. Rockefeller, and Diamond Jim Brady might trot out their Columbia "light roadsters" to George Rosey's ragtime composition "The Scorcher." The club was housed in a three-story brownstone with a balcony overlook where the society swells could gaze upon the well-lit, smooth-floored riding rink. The women riders—in bloomers, unbound from corsets and bustles—stirred particular interest.

Not all were happy about the rapid turn of events. Some preach-
ers decried the immodesty promoted by the act of riding and how a
woman's indelicate position aboard a bumping, bouncing thump-a-
thump seat likely "fosters the habit of masturbation." Yet other
churchmen proved as vulnerable as the fairer sex. Rev. D. H. Chris-
tiansen, defying church policy, was dismissed for a-wheeling in the
warm city streets.

Simply put, all other activities in the year 1896 paled in comparison to "wheeling." Theatergoing, book buying, and piano playing—
to name a few avocations—would plummet in popularity as both
New York and America's obsession approached its peak. "In America
the point now is reached where rather than to say as a people that
cycling is in our midst, it is more expressive of the conditions to state
that we are in the midst of cycling—fairly launched into an era of
self-propulsion," began a special cycling pages section in the *New York
Times*. "The wheel is triumphant."

Tiffany announced a silver-plated bicycle frame, and Thomas
Edison was busily planning an electric tricycle. Another less sanguine
development was the rash of accidents between speed-obsessed riders
and everything else on the congested streets. Bikes and the people on
them hit trains, grip cars, trolleys, carriages, produce carts, and other
cyclists. Samuel Clemens—eight hours of lessons notwithstanding—
broadsided a cabbage-laden wagon on the streets of Hartford and
lived to write about it. "Robert Whittemore dashes headlong into a
buggy," a typical weekly headline read, "the youth's family waiting
dinner two blocks away and he hurrying home—the wheel unhurt."
New York City recorded more cycling-related deaths than ever before.

One wire service story reported a man arrested for stealing his
mother's wheel. When police asked the woman if she was satisfied
with the recovery of her bicycle, she said no and insisted on the pros-
ecution of her son for the "benefit of other wheelwomen." Wrote a
wise-guy editorialist: "Even maternal affection, which forgives many

things, draws the line at stealing bicycles, so the wheeling instinct can now justly claim to be the strongest in human nature, as it has conquered the only one supposed to be invincible."

In Paris a scientist named Dr. Tissle published an academic paper attempting to explain the joy of fast riding. It was an effort, he wrote, to secure equilibrium, a steady state in the imperfect, imbalanced, and oft-tormented human mind. "The effect produced by the motion," penned Dr. Tissle, "is the exaltation of all the faculties of the physical activity: these are the new conditions that provide the sensation of pleasure. Thus it is possible for the entire character to change. Talkative people become taciturn and taciturn become talkative." Servant boys, he might've added, could become world champions.

Nationally, more than 300 U.S. manufacturers produced bicycles. Industries that had made armaments during the war or sewing machines after the war retooled to make bicycles. The League of American Wheelmen counted 75,000 dues-paying members—there were chapters for those over age sixty, all-women divisions, and members who occupied the highest offices in the land (Chief Justice Edward White being one, the industrialist John D. Rockefeller another). The vast lovely landscape of consumers stretched from sea to shining sea, from farms to city mills, from the gilded society of Madison Avenue to the rocky coast of Maine.

Gear information was circulated through the ascendant newspaper and magazine trade. Companies vied with one another with zesty tenacity, commissioning rich illustrations and spicy ad copy. There were goddesses riding bicycles, nuzzling couples on tandems. The bike was associated with freedom, health, and sex. The handsome "circuit racers"—akin to today's NASCAR racecar drivers— were offered salaries to ride and promote the newest models. When they gusted around a track to set a speed record, the companies took out full-page ads. The pro riders and the bicycle companies rose together, each integral to the other. It was the beginning of modern professional sport and the end of amateurism. It was Michael Jordan and Nike and ESPN. It was New York City.

FOR A BRIEF TIME THERE was no more popular form of pro bicycle entertainment than the Garden Six-Day. The Garden itself was part of the allure. Beautiful people collected in beautiful enclaves around the city, and nothing at the moment matched the block-long Madison Square Garden, with its Sevillian architectural flourishes and its leisure-class opulence. There was an opera house, a ballroom, and a rooftop garden for cabaret productions. These classical, cultural affectations were a nice touch but the Garden was truly built for wheeling.

Commodore Vanderbilt, whose money built the building, loved the sport's whirring speed, risk-taking sprints, and bone-snapping collisions. His arena was a grand sporting palace with fast-talking touts, glittering women, and stripped-down racers who swooped past, their brashly exposed muscles pleasingly accentuated by tight shorts and slender-cut tanks.

For all those reasons and more, the 1896 Six-Day was a promoter's dream, full of the things that drove American audiences wild. A step beyond a mere horse race, it was an event that promised a kind of agony and suffering that perhaps was available only on the battlefield. The riders rode as continuously as possible for six days and six nights; the winner was the rider who at midnight on Saturday had covered the greatest distance. So extraordinary was the physical output that Professor Wilbur O. Atwater, a New England–based pioneer in nutritional science, was on hand with staff members to inventory and analyze the food intake of various athletes.

*   *   *

WHEN THE GUN BLAST signaled the start of the event, Taylor had never ridden a race more than 75 miles long. The beginning was marked, as everyone knew it would be, by high-speed pileups. Unaccustomed to the tight, steeply banked track, the racers flew over handlebars and crash-landed either on the wooden track (where they were trampled by others) or in the rows of high-paying dignitaries seated an exhilarating few inches from the outer edge of the track. The crowd howled for more of the same. Noses were broken, spleens punctured, and legs gored by the hard steel parts of a bike that became weaponry when airborne and aimless. The Flying Dutchman and Boy Wonder were forced to retire within the first two hours, the former trampling the latter as he laid prone and unconscious. "It is thought the little fellow is injured internally," the papers updated.

As minutes turned to hours there were other novelties to keep the customers happy: bands playing, Coney Island–style concessions, and vaudeville acts in the infield. Side bets proliferated. A former rider turned industrialist offered $50 to the scorcher who could beat his record of 236 miles 800 yards without dismounting. Ned Reading, a soldier from Nebraska, turned the trick. Naturally, the most intriguing novelty, the one avidly charted in the papers in the succeeding days, was the progress of the mascot Negro rider.

After day one Taylor was vying for first place, having amassed a staggering 300 miles in the first twenty-four-hour period. He needed more sleep than the other racers—roughly an hour for every eight of racing—but when he rode he rode sensationally fast. Taylor kept pace for two days, but after three he quarreled with Munger, complaining of fatigue and the need to rest. Munger gave him fifteen minutes and told him to drink a glass of water mixed with a special powder. Though Taylor said the special powder was a cheap ruse— bicarbonate of soda, not the strychnine- or cocaine-based pick-meups other riders resorted to—he rode the next eighteen consecutive hours without pause. After seventy-two hours he was ninth, only a hundred miles behind the leader, Hale. "His popularity grows every minute," wrote a *New York Times* reporter. "He really thinks he will finish."

After the fourth day his mind wandered and he fought an almost insatiable hunger. At one break he devoured "two fried chickens and four and half pounds of meat" and was still unsatisfied. Several cyclists had dropped out, and those that remained were hallucinating, a procession of the living dead. The wafting smell of grilled meats was overwhelmed by noxious salves slathered on knotted leg muscles and spasming backs. The stadium, its crowds waxing and waning in the days previous, was now jammed full. The irresistible spectacle rivaled the Bowery dime museums with their dwarfs and dog-faced boys and bearded ladies. The opening-night fifty-cent admission ticket doubled to a dollar.

On day six Taylor erupted in several tantrums and begged to quit, first chiding Munger for being devious and trying to torture him and next complaining that he was being chased around the ring by a man with a knife in his hand. Munger couldn't reason with him. Instead Taylor wandered away drunkenly, stumbled next to the low rail, and seemingly before he hit the ground was asleep. Thousands screamed for him to wake and an assortment of stadium personnel rushed at him. When he got on his bike he unaccountably raced "like a streak," all as if nothing had happened. The word circulated through the grandstand and onto busy Twenty-sixth Street. The refined Italian Renaissance arches of the Garden's façade were a bit of the Old World amidst the decidedly New World pandemonium. The rush to get inside continued unabated day and night. Major Taylor was "the wonder of the race," the papers trumpeted.

*   *   *

WITH TWENTY-FOUR HOURS TO GO, fifteen of the original twenty-eight riders remained, Taylor among them. The crowd, much to Brady's interest, had built to 12,000, roughly one and half times the Garden's intended capacity. Spectators were jammed between seats, in aisles, and along the supposedly off-limits spaces of the track's infield. The riders were more dead than alive in the last few hours, which made the viewing particularly invigorating. Joe Rice, a coal miner from Wilkes-Barre, had vowed not a minute's sleep until he passed a thousand miles. Earlier in the race he had been urged on by a legion of friends and a night's worth of songs ending,

> *Once, twice, thrice,*
> *R-i-c-e, Rice.*
> *Who are we?*
> *Who are we?*
> *Rice's friends from Wilkes-Barre.*

At mile 968 he collapsed in a heap. Thousands of dollars changed hands. That was days ago. Now he looked over his shoulder constantly and dismounted in fits of panic, convinced that the rest of the riders were armed with bricks and sticks and preparing to murder him.

In truth, the others were semiconscious and moving so haltingly they often fell at each rise in the track, unable to maintain any sense of equilibrium. Food handoffs had long since become too difficult due to their impaired coordination. Laps that had taken seconds days earlier now took minutes and sometimes hours. The riders looked like corpses, skeletal, hollow-eyed, and bloodless. As per tradition the fans offered tribute in the final agonizing stages with grand bouquets of flowers. The florist's buggy deposited fresh arrangements for most of the riders, including floral harps sent by the Dublin Club for the leader, Hale. Though Taylor got nothing, he doubtless didn't notice. He had collided with other riders twice in the final twenty-four hours. The first time a wild sprint resulted in a twenty-foot skin-to-lumber skid on the Fourth Avenue turn. His second crash, hours before the race's close, was unrecoverable and his helpers, presumably his brother William included, scraped him off the track and into the dressing room. He was unconscious; his condition was such that the following day's paper would duly announce that he probably wouldn't survive.

At 9:58 P.M., the pedaling stopped and a winner was crowned. Teddy Hale, the charismatic Irishman who smoked a cigarette while riding a day or two before, had amassed 1,910 miles, eclipsing the previous Six-Day record by more than 300 miles. Taylor, the eighth-place finisher, had also bested the record with his 1,732 miles. In the next day's paper Billy Brady noted how Taylor's game riding "won for him many friends among people ordinarily opposed to the colored race." It turned out that Brady was, in part, talking about himself.

Another man would've laughed at Munger's grand plans for Taylor—to make him the American champion—but Brady was conditioned to long odds, even spurred by them. Despite Taylor's youth and inexperience, there was something self-assured about him that attracted Brady. He couldn't figure out where a poor black kid had attained such class, but he knew it when he saw it. Perhaps, too, he identified with Taylor. Brady was Jewish and, as a contemporary recalled, a Jew was unwelcome in the top tier of the Manhattan social strata. For the longest time each would be pushing against the tide: the son of a slave and the orphan Jew. So maybe it wasn't surprising that a man recklessly attracted to a cut-of-the-cards gamble, and one with a Gibraltar-sized chip on his shoulder, would find the motivation to try something extraordinary. Shortly after the race Brady began the legwork that would soon have him breaking ground for a new seaside racetrack on Coney Island.

Taylor was nowhere near dead. He found himself recognized now; in fact, at the Amphion Wheelmen's Ball in Brooklyn an actor impersonated Taylor as part of the entertainment, re-creating his courageous Six-Day ride. In February, before thousands at the Madison Square Garden bicycle trade show, he promoted Munger's dream bike and displayed, like a piece of armament recovered from a Civil War battlefield, the rawhide chain he'd used in the Six-Day.

Some cycling writers questioned whether he'd recover to be the same sprinter who electrified the Garden on a Saturday night, but Munger was hopeful. He oversaw Taylor's recuperation after the race, bringing the boy back to his new home on Washington Street in Middletown, Connecticut. The old bachelor was newly married but no less involved. Running his own sprint with a new life and a demanding, high-risk business, Munger tried to think ahead. On the calendar he circled two Boston-area events in the spring and desperately hoped Taylor would be ready for the sprint race that America and the world was about to fall head over heels in love for—the flying mile.

Unlike foot racing, where the four-minute mile was already in place as a human threshold, bicycle racing had no such benchmark. The future was wide open; the limitations of a slender bike and a handsome flyer were as mysterious and alluring as the blank places on maps where men simply wrote, "Here be dragons."

CHAPTER 5

New Year

JANUARY 1, 1897
PASADENA, CALIFORNIA

> Fruit is destined to be the ultimate glory of California . . . such
> pears, peaches, apricots, nectarines, etc., as load the trees of
> this valley would stagger the faith of
> nine-tenths of my readers.
> — HORACE GREELEY, WRITING IN HIS
> *New York Tribune*

THREE THOUSAND miles away from a smoke-filled Madison
Square Garden, the sweet fragrance of red roses and lavender
perfumed the air. Southern California sunshine flooded down
from a high hazy sky and a flirtatious wind snuck up on fashionable
ladies, flicking dresses and sending wide-brimmed hats airborne. The
Tournament of Roses parade—a floral come-hither to the entrenched
East—was nearing start time. The line of the parade route teemed
with Pasadena's finest and not so finest, all of the same mind as they
awoke to the first day of the New Year. It was their showcase day, a
moment in the sun, as it were—a few hours to highlight their special
place, where "January was June" and the normal rules of engagement with Mother Earth were suspended. There was no struggle, no
starving winter, no dead brown earth hardening into bluntness. Fruit
and flowers filled the trees, waves of birdsong came in the predawn,

and life flourished uninterrupted—without need for prayer, or even much effort, it sometimes seemed.

Floyd McFarland, newly home after a long and successful racing schedule in the East, was near the front of the procession, leading out lily- and marguerite-cloaked six-in-hand coaches, a bicycle-riding barbershop quartet, and 500 others. Like Pasadena, the nineteen-year-old McFarland was in a fierce rush to make a national name for himself. Now a gigantic six foot four, and 170 pounds, McFarland gave credence to the notion that San Jose's Electric Tower, absent any other function, was a 4,000-candlepower growth catalyst. He was almost a foot taller than most of his competitors and his voice was an octave or two deeper. But it was more than just his Amazonian size that entranced the 15,000 spectators as the parade wound its way toward the track off Lincoln Avenue. There was a sense they were viewing the next great champion. As a cycling historian would later write, "He was a commanding looking chap, a natural born leader."

Unfortunately, it was not to be one of the finer years for the Tournament of Roses. Sometime between the parade and the afternoon races the weather turned. The frolicsome wind of earlier in the day blew to near hurricane strength and scattered everything that wasn't nailed down—most notably bushels of white, red, and yellow flowers. They joined frothing plumes of fine confectionary dust in an airborne assault of winging petals, twigs, and vines, a perversely jumbled-together floral storm of color and aroma and rotting vegetation ripping through the Queen City. Tomatoes fell from green-stemmed vines at the height of their fullness. The grandstand creaked like it was about to fracture.

Apparently there was no consideration of postponing the race between McFarland and the popular California champion Walter Foster. Foster, like Ziegler, had made a name for himself long ago at the national championships in Denver. The challenger McFarland wore a skintight, almost sleeveless shirt that accentuated the length of his sinewy arms and the hard turn of his elbow. His brown hair was short, middle-parted, and curled near the temple. Confidently striding out of the freakishly swirling tempest, he was vigorously greeted with cries of "Little Zimmy," a nicknamed he'd earned for his similarity in looks to the reigning world champion, Arthur Zimmerman. He was distinctly at ease amidst the chaos, as if his immense physical stature better rooted him to the ground.

This was McFarland's proving day, but he'd been discovered exactly a year earlier, in the winter of 1895, when the top racing men made their first-ever pass through California. The "circuit riders" had come 3,000 miles to entertain the crowds and use up the fair weather. The magazines seized on the momentous occasion with spreads designed to look like family photo albums. "We are New Yorkers, you bet we're corkers," read a caption beneath a photo of the arriving racing men. "Snapshots from California," a weekly feature, showed the glamorous "Western Pilgrims" splashing on Pacific beaches, mugging in swim trunks at the Mojave Desert, and staring gap-mouthed at bursting orange trees in a massive Santa Clara grove. They were mischievous boys on a grand adventure, their arrival in the Golden State playing like the Beatles setting down in America for the first time.

The national sporting scene had always been a finite sphere, starting and ending in New York, or Chicago at the farthest, but in California there was a giddy sense among the cracks that they were looking at the future, or as one exuberant headline crowed, "a center of cycling speed in the land of cloudless sky." What was once a nickel-and-dime racing circuit where men contested for pewter pots and dinner plates now boasted cash prizes and fine, sun-stroked stadium venues stretching the length and breadth of the country. In California the warmth of celebrity fell upon the newcomers—the fruit, the flowers, the fair women of the Golden State, the local racers who idolized them from afar. McFarland was one of the last group, though he never let it show. In his first race against eastern top-notchers such as Tom Cooper and Earl Kiser he captured a first; in subsequent events he won twice more, including a victory in the hotly contested mile open at Santa Ana.

Uplifted by his debut performances, McFarland immediately turned professional and embarked on an impetuous journey east, an odyssey really, in which he and San Jose native Orlando Stevens criss-crossed Canada, the United States, and parts of Mexico in search of fame and fortune. Kalamazoo, Peoria, Montreal, Racine, Memphis, St. Augustine, Galveston, and Mexico City . . . the "crack boys in blue," as he and Stevens called themselves, made up a formidable team, starting twice as many races as anyone else in 1896. They worked with each other and more often than not found others to work with them as well—a "teaming" strategy that was both effective and con-troversially their own. McFarland had a knack for getting people to do what he wanted. Those who knew the family saw a lot of his father in him. During an auction, Thomas McFarland's eyes darted everywhere with the opening bid but he understood where his quarry was and how the capture would happen. He'd push, then ease off; charm, then challenge. His son learned well. In Foster's case, Floyd focused on him the way his father did a vulnerable bidder. He would engage him, play him, then own him.

McFarland had been back in his home state only a few weeks when he read about the results of the historic Garden Six-Day, including Major Taylor's news-making role. A black boy from Indi-anapolis had, in one race, usurped McFarland's 40,000-mile, coast-to-coast season. Taylor had defeated the great Eddie Bald in New York City; he was the "flying son of Africa," the "black comet," like nothing anyone had seen before. *He* was the exotic, not the Californian McFarland, who had wowed the cracks, too, but in a way that had reminded them of something they'd seen before. It both-ered McFarland to be compared to anybody else, even the great

Zimmerman. He envied Taylor's exoticness and soon came to hate him for it. But for now, McFarland would have to use up his fury on another.

McFarland's set-to with Foster was the last event in the afternoon's long program. Observers thought he cheated the starter's pistol in the first race and were sure he did so in the second. He'd blasted off like he was shot from a cannon, benefiting from an aggressive push and the cracking tailwind. In the noise and fury of the heaving winds and foot-stomping crowd in the grandstand, the race officials who hollered for a false start were either unheard or ignored. Before the race was under way he had a four-yard lead. On the last turn Foster bravely made up the gap and rapidly closed McFarland down. McFarland seemed to let him take the inside but at the last moment he leaned into his opponent's path and snapped an elbow into Foster's tucked head. Foster's cadence, strong and smooth, faltered. One moment he was accelerating on a following sea, the next he was out of control, driven into the shoals of the racetrack infield. McFarland, with hands raised, steamed across the line in first.

McFARLAND'S RUTHLESSNESS was an eye-opener for his colleagues. A few months later, this time in San Francisco, McFarland took the Pacific Coast crown outright when he defeated Otto Ziegler at the Pavilion. His scorched-earth approach to racing—in the Ziegler match McFarland fended the "little demon" into the barricade—put an abrupt end to comparisons with the breezy Zimmerman; it also demarcated an era.

Zimmerman, the Jersey skeeter, was an easygoing lad more amateur in spirit than professional. He was an untouchable glider, a natural pedaler with a stroke so slick he could use half the gearing of his opponent and still win. He won a record 103 races in 1893, including the one-mile world championship. His reign had helped the sport blossom and had brought American cycling to the attention of Europe,

Australia, and California. He seemed to view racing the way a bounding creature might look at a ridge run in the woods. It was freedom that propelled him, not anger; it was the soaring, sun-drenched vista that opened when he leaned into a corner fast and came out of it even faster. He was the last amateur, at least in sensibil-ity, and he was the reason Baron Pierre de Coubertin, the Frenchman who revived the Olympic Games in 1896 in Athens, saw cyclists as potentially Hellenic. He granted the sport Olympic recognition on the gentlemanly promise they offered; Zimmy was part of that prom-ise, a benevolent dictator from whom the entire tour took shape— and flight.

But his career was destined to end prematurely. On a tour of Australia, the first by an American racer, he contracted malaria. For weeks he wasted away in a fevered state. Late in the winter he announced he would have to sit on the sidelines in 1897, leaving a void at the center of the peaking sport.

McFarland rushed into the void. Though just nineteen, he was the consensus heir apparent. His California birthright didn't hurt, nor did his ability to ride day after day. He raced more races harder than anyone had ever seen. Moreover, he had the strength and will to direct others. Every sport needed a boss.

Years later when the Tour de France caught fire, the same struc-tural blueprint would be followed. The French called him "Le Patron." The best-known example was the Belgian Eddy Merckx, the road racing champion in the 1970s whose nickname was "the Cannibal." He was feared, attended to. His leadership extended into every race he competed in, from the Tour de France, which he won five times, to the spring one-day classics like Paris-Roubaix and Liège-Bastogne-Liège. From Le Patron everyone took their cue. When an unknown rebel broke away and threatened to upset the hierarchical order, he instructed the pack to give chase and overtake him. When his own teammate, perhaps out of the money for a stretch, took off, he might tell the pack to let him go. "Easy" he'd caution, "Easy." The others listened because he was strong and because he would get everyone their share. Doing what one was told was a form of self-protection. Le Patron made sure the spoils were spread around, as long as the others honored the pecking order. The boss came first.

Taylor was now foreseen as part of the national race circuit mix, an intriguing side element to the circus for everybody except Billy Brady and Birdie Munger. Nobody could've predicted the dark turn things would take. As far as anybody knew, it would be as always: when the Pullman cars arrived in Peoria or Savannah or Ottumwa, Iowa, to deliver the racing men for a weekend's worth of entertainment, the spectators would charge up to the rail, believing that anything might happen, that the fix wasn't in, and that a young local boy with broad legs and a focused rage might just crash the finish tape first.

Together

MAY 29, 1897

CHARLES RIVER TRACK

CAMBRIDGE, MASSACHUSETTS

And while the law of competition may be sometimes
hard for the individual, it is best for the race because it
insures the survival of the fittest.
— ANDREW CARNEGIE,
FROM THE *Gospel of Wealth*

A S MAJOR TAYLOR WARMED UP at the Charles River
track, the site of his first professional sprint race, he looked
like a different person. Over the winter he had trained relent-
lessly to redraft his slight frame into something far more robust. In the
training quarters the others had noticed: the baby fat was gone, his
upper body chiseled. His body fueled a steely confidence that was
unmistakable: he had entered the Six-Day as a boy and exited a man.
Taylor expected a record day.

Though the League of American Wheelmen barred blacks from
club membership, its Racing Board made no serious attempt to prevent Taylor from registering on the professional circuit. Where there
might be problems were the tracks run by the powerful racist managers of Taylor's competitors. The Charles River track in Cambridge,
however, wasn't one of those.

The Charles was a stunning achievement: only one year old, banked, with "compound curves" in the turns, surfaced with granolithic blocks, and shielded from the easterlies with high walls on the backstretch. "It will undoubtedly be the fastest track in the country," the papers wrote when the facility opened in 1896. On the track's first weekend the seventy-three-year-old inventor Sylvester Roper seemed to back up the claims when he flew around the track at 40 mph in a steam-engine-propelled bicycle. He had intended to stop after a couple of laps but was so "elated" at his time that he continued to "scorch around the track." To the crowd's horror the bicycle began to visibly wobble, then toppled over. The inventor's machinery had worked to perfection, but Roper, doctors said, had been overwhelmed—a case of speed-induced cardiac arrest. "Died in the Saddle," the *Globe* headline read.

Rather than keep the riders away, Roper's last ride acted as a magnet to would-be record breakers. Charles River's manager, a highly regarded ex-rider named Billy Corcoran, fed the fire. He continued to refine the track for maximum speeds and invited the nascent filmmakers from the American Mutoscope Company to set up on his backstretch for a series of silent films on Boston's speed mavens. In the final preparations for the 1897 season the Charles was upgraded with an unrivaled electric light system, heightening the venue's gorgeous setting on the Cambridge side of the Charles River, only minutes from the heart of Boston. There was seating for 15,000 spectators, making it the largest racing stadium in the East. The dressing quarters adjacent to the massive double-tiered grandstand offered showers, baths, and toilet rooms.

When Corcoran, who had famously discovered Arthur Zimmerman, promised next-generation superstars in McFarland, Stevens, and Boston-based Eddie McDuffee, the paying public believed him. On the May 29 season-opening holiday weekend, cycle racing anchored a slate that included balloon ascensions, midget trick-riding displays, and the "greatest athletic novelty of the century," a broadsword combat featuring the actress-turned-swordswoman Jaguarina and Sergeant Major John Swift, formerly of the British army's First Royal Dragoons. "Soon, record smashers will begin to congregate as thick as robins in the early springtime," said Corcoran with a wink, his Irish brogue as flush as his handlebar moustache.

In his debut race Saturday afternoon, Taylor placed a respectable third in the mile open, betraying a few jitters against the all-star field. In his next race, under the lights (in what Corcoran immodestly described as the "greatest bicycle tournament ever given"), he was the narrow runner-up to H. R. Steenson in the ⅓-mile dash. The pair's driving, dead-heat finish, coupled with the narcotic sensation of seeing a bending fireball accelerate through a still night, brought the ruddy-faced customers to their collective feet. The forty-two seconds it took the men to cover 600 yards—a second faster than the 1895 world record—seemed like four seconds. Over the next two weeks, with much of the racing centered in Cambridge and other Boston-area tracks, Taylor did well, apparently putting to rest all the talk of the Six-Day crippling his sprint. "There is every indication that he will keep some of the big men a-moving," wrote a *Globe* correspondent. McFarland also excelled, helping to bring into focus for the first time the nature of the dual to come.

McFarland was different from Taylor, and not just in the obvious ways. He was a "made rider," in the fraternity's parlance. He had an unmatchable capacity for work, not speed. He was already well into a campaign he would maintain for the rest of his career, a tireless, year-round program of racing. He often competed in three or four separate heats a day, three to four days a week. In later years he would get off a ship after a month's worth of brutal transoceanic travel and race as though he'd never been interrupted. It was as if his competitiveness willed his body to do things that shouldn't be possible. McFarland simply couldn't stand to watch another racer in front of him. When promoters first saw him chase others down they recognized he was the perfect handicap rider. Give the other riders a 20-yard head start, or 30, or even 50, as they would in the prime of his career, and McFarland would bring them back. Of his 1,000 career victories, the majority of them began with him looking up the track toward a handful of men he had less than two minutes to catch. He was the prototypical "scratch" racer, meaning he was acknowledged as the fastest man in the field and the handicapper's baseline upon which all others were measured. His nickname was the "Human Engine."

Taylor was an explosive flyer. He didn't incrementally build momentum the way McFarland did; instead he waited and waited until he saw the sliver of an opening or a shiver of weakness, and then he pounced. The break was clean and smooth, an aesthetic crowd-pleaser. Part of the reason the Garden onlookers had found him appealing was the sprint. In a race where the immense duration meant that nobody had to sprint, he did so anyway. He couldn't help going fast.

The interesting and unanswered question for the sport's cognoscenti was which entity—the flyer or the racer—was more dominant at winning. For the rest of the fans, the outstanding general-purpose question was racial: black or white? The mile-distance events of the first month of racing showed what the fans had to look forward to. In Boston, Taylor would emerge from the dressing room as the band played "The Warmest Babe in the Bunch." His white rival heard strains of "All Coons Look Alike to Me." Night after night, in packed grandstands, the racial scorecard was kept, charted, and talked about. As thousands of glossy buttons would soon read, it was black versus white. It wasn't theoretical, wasn't comparing the size of brain cavities in a laboratory or watching sullen tribesmen rounded up for a World's Fair; it was real—black versus white in hot lovely scrutiny night after night after night.

*   *   *

THE PLANNED STOPS on the championship tour in 1897 included
New York, Boston, Buffalo, Detroit, Indianapolis, Philadelphia,
Springfield, Peoria, Louisville, and Galveston. Almost all of the cities
boasted new stadium venues with newly designed tracks vying for the
title of world's fastest. On the so-called two-minute track "wheels
would stand at right angles with the track when the bicycle was traveling a speed of a mile in two minutes." As the racers got faster the
tracks got steeper. Engineers called for the hard and fast Baltic pine
of northern Europe and crunched formulas with speed and banking
angles to determine the safety net of centrifugal force. Speed was
corralled and channeled forward in death-defying fifty-two-degree
banked turns in New Jersey. In Salt Lake City, like Cambridge and
other places, electric lights were strung overhead for night races.

The pros had well-known weaknesses and strengths—all played
out daily in the newspaper columns—but also a measure of unpre-
dictability. They were a colorful lot, a mixture of sprinters and
middle-distance specialists such as Eddie Bald and Jimmy Michael,
who were known by their nicknames: "Cannon" Bald and "Midget"
Michael. They represented a cross section of the country: fresh-off-
the-boat immigrants looking to make a name, cold-eyed nativists
looking to protect what were theirs, and everyone in between, from
Boston Irishmen to Pennsylvania Dutch. Bald, the son of a Buffalo
butcher, had an operatic voice. Bostonian Eddie Root insisted on
wearing the number 13, his peculiar superstition being the necessity
of showing he wasn't superstitious.

In Trenton or Springfield, they arrived for their qualifying rounds
in dark suits and bowlers, with trainers and bicycles in tow. No matter the event—often a handicap or pursuit-style race was on the
card—the matchups reeked of pleasing contrasts. The big men relied
on strength and enormous gears; the pint-sized riders used smarts
and a lightly geared setup to exploit their quickness advantage.

Those who didn't have an explosive jump tried to wear the field down, draining the fast finishers so that they had nothing left in the final straightaway. In the thick of the pack there would be jostling or a prolonged lean to take another rider wide in the turns. In desperate instances where a rider was boxed in he might slap his front wheel against the outside of a blocker's rear one, anticipating an overreaction to the outside. In a flash the rider would dive to freedom along the rail.

As the favored top cracks advanced to the evening's final-round heat, the intensity increased. Nervously, the riders sat poised on their bikes, held by their handlers at the start line, glancing at the gear teeth on their opponents' bikes and wondering who might be helping whom and when that help might be revealed. Then the starter's pistol cracked and they flew at one another. Theirs wasn't an activity like golf or baseball, where the athletic engagement was comparatively civil. They were involved in a power discipline where a half dozen bodies scrapped for position while revving to the top end, where the musculature screamed to maximum exertion, where moody hormones swelled into the bloodstream. Not surprisingly, arguments and fistfights routinely punctuated the program. Around the same time as the Charles River races, at a Chicago track, a racer stabbed another for cutting across his line. Afterward, amidst the ambulance siren and police reports and the threat of jail time, neither combatant seemed to understand the fuss. A violent passion and the inevitable clashes to arise from it were part of the sport, part of life.

The best part was that at night's end an immediate accounting could be made. Statistics were kept, wins and losses tallied. A separate percentage formula was calculated to show how successful the top racers were in head-to-head matches against each other. Much like a baseball player's batting average, the chances for wins were compared to actual victories. A second table tabulated the points and prize money leaders. Up to six points were awarded for a first-place finish in a national circuit race, and at season's end (after the points were totaled) an American champion would be declared. After the first month it was a hot Tom Cooper in the lead. By midseason, Bald stood atop the standings with an .859 winning percentage, sixty-nine points in thirty starts, and $1,732 in prize and cash earnings. Taylor and McFarland were both in the top ten.

The newly emergent pro sport was different in one obvious way— the chance to win prize money. For years cycling's promoters, not willing to risk the backlash from the powerful figures who favored gentlemanly, amateur-only competition, had attempted to tiptoe around the issue. Instead of cash, race winners were offered prizes. When Zimmerman dominated the race circuit in 1892, just five years earlier, the *New York Times* listed his take as follows: twenty-nine bicycles, several horses and carriages, half a dozen pianos, a house and a lot, furniture of all descriptions, and "enough silver plates, medals and jewelry to stock a jewelry store."

The sea change event was the Six-Day in New York, where Taylor and others received cash for prerace exhibitions and their Six-Day placing (in Taylor's case his eighth-place finish earned him $125). The cycling historian Peter Nye remarked that the winner, Hale, took home so much gold "he had to put it in his hat and carry it away with both hands." Purses of $100 gave way to $500, $1,000, and, by the time Taylor and McFarland met in Australia at the peak of their careers, $10,000. In a land-rich, cash-poor world the inflated purses caught everyone's attention. At the same time major-league baseball had capped salaries for pro ballplayers at $240, Taylor had earned nearly that in a single two-minute-long exhibition race at Madison Square Garden. Fred Titus achieved headlines late in the season for winning $1,000 in a week, the equivalent of $20,000 in modern dollars and twice the average workingman's annual wage. A top-ten cyclist, if he raced enough, could expect to make $2,000 in prize earnings, or about $40,000 in 2007 dollars.

As the season progressed, new-style events brought still more money to the game. Promoters began to think in terms of duels, seeking out the racers who either because of past history or future promise made for delicious, spectator-drawing pairings. The match race was a perfect headline event, taking the two most prominent racers of the moment and pairing them together for a highly charged best-of-three showdown, usually at a mile distance. The first of them occurred in June at the Charles River track when Michael faced Eddie McDuffee for a winner-take-all $1,500. A thousand dollars was put up by the racetrack, $500 by the riders' managers.

The bigger stakes made for instant excitement, but there was an obvious downside. Winning was acutely important. As the races continued through the summer, sabotage was increasingly part of the game. Racers on the circuit who didn't cotton to the game plan (oftentimes racers would conspire to split the larger purses) found themselves subject to a range of punitive measures. Some, after an inexplicably slow performance, discovered emery powder in their wheel bearings. Others reported their chains tampered with, a link having been replaced by a piece of wire, which invariably gave way, disabling the bicycle. There were reports of doped food and tainted liniment. The latter, rubbed onto a rider before a race, would produce a violent skin reaction, causing widespread blistering. More annoying still, riders' shoes would be stolen. "All know that a racing man is superstitious to some degree," wrote a cycling columnist about the dirty tricks, "and the loss of shoes in which race after race has been won is a misfortune."

The League of American Wheelmen (LAW), which sanctioned the national slate of races, looked at the money-chasing trend and didn't like what it saw. The aristocrats who had formed LAW twenty years earlier saw the bicycle as a signature item of elite stature. The racing game represented a lowering of their noble activity, ushering in the sort of riffraff that wasn't welcome at the private clubs where their leadership convened. The league's constituency was made up of the Vanderbilts and the sons of Vanderbilts who could pursue amateur sport without the indignity of needing money.

Racers were necessary evils, as were the myriad hoi polloi who admired them. LAW, with its membership approaching 100,000, wanted to control the ragtag element but not endorse it. They refused the racers membership, which made them understand their place, yet taxed them $2 for registration. A racer was a second-class LAW citizen, much like a Negro. McFarland, among others, bristled at the treatment.

It wasn't that LAW didn't have legitimate concerns. Fixing was a problem in all sports. Gambling was and always would be the real American pastime, bigger than even cycling at its most popular. If anything seemed fundamental to American human nature, it was the urge to wager. Sporting events had usurped the lotteries of old. More interesting still, the gamblers weren't seedy whiskey-nippers but the best and brightest, the stewards of the nation's future, the educated elite. "At a recent intercollegiate football match it was rumored, and I have not heard it denied, that over $40,000 was staked upon the result of the game by the collegians themselves," wrote an indignant John Bigelow in *Harper's New Monthly.* An estimated $1 million was bet in New York on the outcome of the 1892 presidential election. Four years later the take doubled with four-to-one odds posted on McKinley. Bieglow lamented that gambling seemed the one force in turn-of-the century America impervious to change. "Civilization seems thus far to have exerted no more influence in arresting its ravages than in taming the leopard, or in converting the hole of the asp into a repair for children; and reformers of all denominations have agitated, legislated, and denounced it for centuries, but with as little apparent influence upon it as upon the weather."

Promoters, handicappers, and riders were all brushing up against a force greater than themselves. A race could be thrown a dozen different ways. To most observers the litany of unfair maneuvers—such as muscling an accelerating rider off his line and forcing him up the track, or working in twos and threes to slow down some and release others, or chopping a racer by cutting across his path—were imperceptible. It was easy to hoodwink spectators and find a way to satisfy a meddlesome referee. Everyone could benefit, and the throngs that came could still be happy and none the wiser. What mattered, a young McFarland shrewdly recognized, was the perception of an honest race. A bicycle racer represented a glorious composite, part God's creature hurtling toward the finish line, a product of instinct and sinewy athleticism, and part gambler wagering on his own and others' outcomes. McFarland's oft-quoted motto was "Be honest but get the money, no matter what the sacrifice."

McFarland did just that. As the season proceeded he hovered near the top of the money-earning tables. He used his pluck, stamina, and ruthlessness to control and dominate. His specialty, handicap racing, was a thrilling crowd favorite, with the purses reflecting its popularity (at New York, he earned $250 for merely finishing second). As scratch man McFarland started up to fifty yards behind the lesser-quality racers to give them a fighting chance. He was slow to build pace but after a lap he dropped one rider and then another, his bike tearing through the field as if the others were standing still. Finally, the last racer in sight, McFarland flattened himself to his steel frame, barreling down the final fifty yards like a freight train, almost always edging out his rival at the line.

Spectators screamed their bloody lungs out and—win, lose, or draw—fell to their knees as if the Holy Ghost had passed through them.

AS GOOD AS MCFARLAND WAS, TAYLOR was a little better. He was virtually unbeatable in August, when he earned $475—a sum, pointed out a newspaper, any white man would be proud of. A few weeks earlier he helped anchor a Boston 5-mile pursuit team in a much-anticipated intercity match with Philadelphia. "The secret of it all is he is dangerous," a Boston newspaper reported. "The form he is displaying is higher than that of any of the other riders."

In early September, in the showcase mile event at the massively attended New Jersey State Fair, Taylor brought the crowd to its feet when he outraced a powerful field, winning by two feet. As observers noticed, he not only outsprinted his adversaries but outfoxed them. Several attempts to box him in and keep him from getting a clear path to the front failed. "Most of the men in the final had entered into combinations to help one another and freeze Taylor out," a paper wrote. "They did work together but the little bitty rider was tacking on at every opportunity and 'skinned' them all in the home-stretch." The betting favorite, McFarland, finished third.

Uncharacteristically, Taylor bowed out of the next final, the one-mile handicap, McFarland's specialty. Munger later explained that the white riders told Taylor they would knock him down and run him over if he raced to win. LAW officials ordered Taylor to start, but he rode without effort and with "his head bobbing from side to side to watch the other riders." In an interview several days later, and with a Taunton, Massachusetts, race upcoming, Taylor, nineteen, confessed, "I have a dread of injury every time I start in a race with the men who have been on the circuit this year. They have threatened to injure me and I expect that before the season is finished they will do so."

In September, *Bearings* magazine, alluding to Taylor's August performances, reported that "the position of the negro is a trying one, for every rider is anxious to top him, owing to his color." The *Wheel* wrote that ever since Taylor became prominent there had been reports of "efforts to 'do' him. That the white men who compete against him strain every nerve to 'beat the coon,' as they term him, is

"GIVING THE ELBOW" TO MAJOR TAYLOR

This illustration accompanied Howard Freeman's newspaper account on how he and other cyclists roughed up Major Taylor. *Source: From the Collection of the Indiana State Museum and Historic Sites*

an admitted fact. *The Wheel* has heard them so state." Tom Cooper, a Detroit racer who lost to Taylor, was typically blunt: "I would not care so much about the defeat by others, but that licking at the hands of a colored rider is too much, too much."

On September 22, three days after his remarks about a "dread of injury," Taylor decided to ignore the threats and race at Taunton. He was in strong contention for the overall points title, and he was considering an attempt to enter a series of races in the South if he won again.

It was a drizzly day, the cinder track slicked and dangerous. A large crowd of 25,000 had turned out at the county fairgrounds. The keenly awaited mile open went off as planned, with Tom Cooper (who was the favorite), Taylor, and the Philadelphian W. E. Becker bolting down the backstretch. Cooper nipped Taylor, with Becker taking third. Just as the applause died out, a sharp cry rose up out of the crowd and all turned to the fracas on the infield. Becker had come up from behind and ripped Taylor off his bike. With a knee in his chest, Becker proceeded to strangle him. By the time police dragged him off, Taylor was unconscious. He stayed that way for fifteen minutes, only coming to after Munger held an ammonia-soaked rag to his nose. On that day, Taylor wrote in his autobiography, "I found that the color prejudice was not confined to the South."

There was little sympathy for Taylor among the racers, but outside the fraternity the public's feelings were mixed. A *Globe* editorial pleaded for his fair treatment, "and if he does not get it, a Boston mob should not be blamed if it tears down the Crispus Attucks monument on the plea that it is a blatant inconsistency in granite and bronze." A rival publication, however, felt Becker's $50 fine was an outrage, citing Taylor's provoking habit of crowding in at the "pole no matter how narrow the opening."

There were a dozen more circuit events in southern cities, each of them offering points toward the overall national title. If Taylor wanted to contend for the championship, and he did, he had to go south. Few thought he would do it, however, given the unabashed hostility to integrated racing in the South. Perhaps he was hoping for the riders to come to his defense, or maybe he thought they wouldn't dare turn away a top points leader in the national standings. Whatever the case, he grossly miscalculated. Three weeks later, when Taylor arrived in Louisville for the southern extension opener, he was immediately informed he wouldn't be allowed to race. When he crossed the river to his native Indiana for a lesser-profile race he was also shown the color line, as "the southern riders who had entered refused to ride against Taylor, and openly threatened him with violence." The New Albany organizers, attempting to keep the gate and assuage the paying customers, hastily set up a match race between Taylor and a horse. The horse won.

Humiliated and understandably confused, Taylor announced afterward that, like the jockeys before him, he was contemplating self-exile. "I shall go to France," he said. "I can hold my own and will be thought something of, maybe."

His agonized soul-searching was one of the few times in his career Taylor would completely let his guard down. Almost every year for the remainder of his career he would threaten to retire, in part out of exasperation but also because he had established himself and could exact a bigger draw if he held out. He would become an adept businessman. But in New Albany, Indiana—the place where his parents had crossed into the state when fleeing postwar Kentucky—he openly displayed the wounds he had suffered. It wouldn't be a public airing he'd repeat. In later years his coolness and self-control would be perceived as brusque and businesslike, as if he didn't love the sport, only the money he earned from it. One hundred years later writers made a similar complaint about Shani Davis at the

2006 Winter Games—the first African American gold medal winner
in speed skating—after he showed no emotion on the medal stand.
He didn't appear to be moved or care, when in fact, like Taylor a century before, he had merely trained himself to keep his emotions at
bay; it was a matter of survival.

His rebuff in the South was a turning point. His fellow riders had openly attacked him, and he failed miserably to break
the southern color line. As the *Wheel* pointed out, Taylor has "suddenly reconsidered his determination to brave everything to keep a
place in the percentage table."

Munger hadn't made the trip; he was newly married and was desperately trying to succeed in his new bicycle manufacturing venture
in Worcester. He had barely bought his home in Connecticut when
the whole thing began crashing down. As early as the spring he knew
his company and his critically acclaimed bicycle were in trouble. The
high-end bicycle had appeared on the market at the very moment
there was a glut. Nobody was buying $150 bicycles, even ones that
were fairly billed as record-making "masterpieces of mechanism." A
perfectly decent Columbia was down to $80.

He had mistimed again. In a span of only a few months, the company's triumphant weekly ads, which once spanned the width of a
newspaper page, had all but vanished. In June, with the company
found to have $700,000 in liabilities, the sheriff's officers in Middle-
town and Worcester shuttered the plants and ushered in a new era:
bankruptcy.

Brady was also having problems of his own, with only mixed
results thus far in his bid to promote big-time bicycle races. Several
articles reported that Taylor was under Brady's aggressive manage-
ment—his fledgling organization was called the American Cycling
Racing Association—but the promoter's attempts to shake up the

cycling hierarchy had failed. "I will match Major Taylor against any man in America," Brady blustered, offering a $5,000 matching bet to a half dozen name racers. But the headliners ignored him, leaving the cash-starved Brady so adrift he temporarily returned to the fight game to get back on his feet. His normally insuperable instincts seemed to desert him. In one of his worst-ever ideas, a few months later he asked Taylor to go down to Savannah, Georgia, for winter training, presumably to show his mettle and win over the southern spectator. Taylor was promptly prohibited from using the city's wheelmen's track and forced onto the open road, where local racers harassed and threatened him. Two days after he had arrived he left, prompted by a note that warned he had "twenty four hours to get out of town." A departing Taylor fumed: "It is useless for a colored person to attempt to get along in the South. The feeling is so strong only a race war will settle it."

With both Brady and Munger either distracted or ineffective, Taylor was completely isolated. His soul-searching brought his mind back to his mother's funeral, which had taken place back in June. He had buried her amid the oak trees at Crown Hill Cemetery, not far from her North Indianapolis home. The Taylors had all returned home—his sister Alice from Minnesota, Lizzie and Gertie from Chicago, he and William from Boston. Saphronia Taylor had died at her home from heart disease, complicated by dropsy. Her death certificate said she was only forty-six, and declared that her spouse was unknown, an indication she and Gilbert were separated at the time. The lengthy service, coupled with the emotions surrounding her death, had started to kindle something dormant inside the most famous of Saphronia's progeny. In a notebook largely reserved for seasonal expenses he earnestly wrote down the readings from the service in a way that suggested he wished he had been familiar with them.

"Scripture lesson first," he noted. "Corinthians 15, 41, 58 . . .

Songs . . . Why should we start and Fear to die . . . Fade, fade each earthly joy . . . Sleep in Jesus blessed sleep . . . Text John 11, 25 . . . I am the resurrection."

Months later Munger noticed the black leather pocket Bible was his constant companion, one page folded to remind him of its place. The page itself was wrinkled as if moistened and dried repeatedly. It was Corinthians 15, about death and resurrection.

> Oh death, where is thy sting? O grace, where is thy
>   victory?
> The sting of death is sin; and the strength of sin is the law.
> But thanks be to God, which giveth us the victory through
>   our Lord Jesus Christ.
> Therefore my beloved brethren, be ye steadfast, unmovable,
>   always abounding in the
> Work of the Lord, forasmuch as ye know that your labour is
>   not in vain in the Lord.

In the same notebook he noted he had awakened to righteousness and "embraced religion." He also recorded a donation of $1,000 to the United Society of Christian Endeavor. A fast-growing, nondiscriminatory evangelist youth movement, the society espoused "the training of young converts for the duties of church membership." There was no one—no denomination, no race—who was not welcome. When President Herbert Hoover addressed the group's annual convention in 1931 he lauded "the principles it stands for . . . International peace . . . sobriety . . . character . . . righteousness and respect for the law." Spontaneously, as the president finished his speech, reported *Time* magazine, "the convention jumped to its feet, burst into the Doxology: 'Praise God from Whom All Blessings Flow!' "

The stipulation for inclusion was a doctrinaire Christian life in which the failure to read the Bible daily "is to break the Endeavorer's pledge." More specifically, the Christian Endeavor movement sought to prevent promising young Christians from sowing a "good crop of wild oats," from straying in youth and returning to God after the inevitable consequences. Perhaps Taylor felt he had already strayed by being in the constant company of "sports," men who were not known for their chivalrous character. The enormous sum he contributed—maybe the money felt dirty—represented practically all his race earnings to date.

The church would shape the rest of his life, with both the choices he made and those he didn't make. It provided him a decision-making framework and a much-needed bulwark against the chaos of the times and the devilish alliances mounting against him. The Endeavorers held particular reverence for the person who, though in the midst of temptation and surrounded with evil, "stays aloof and holds [his] ideals." He committed to never racing on Sundays, though he knew the racing in Europe was always on Sundays and that American race organizers were lobbying for the prohibition to end. As a Christian Endeavor pastor expressed, and Taylor evidently took to heart, "the sanctity of the Sabbath is the great dike between Christianity and infidelity and should be preserved." The Reverend D. Asa Blackburn added, as if looking the young racer in the eye, "It is impossible to serve God and skylark about on a bicycle." The flock pledged to "promise that I will ride my wheel on the Sabbath only as it will honor my Master, and as I believe He would like to have me do. I also promise to exert all possible influence to discourage others in the use of the Sunday wheels." When the Endeavorers held their national conventions in Washington, New York, and Boston, Taylor would've joined tens of thousands of others, all of them equally jubilant in their professed faith, many of them black. The only faintly comparable organization with the influence and numbers and power to transform a drab city into a joyous, spirited mecca was, ironically, the League of American Wheelmen. Their annual conventions drew roughly the same numbers: cycling and religion running neck and neck.

Taylor's awakening was prompted by personal tragedy but revealed itself to him in every subsequent race, just the way it had to Oxford miler Eric Liddell, of *Chariots of Fire* fame. Liddell elegantly explained how he was compelled to compete because he felt the grace of God with each brilliant stride, with each stirring finishing kick. His track was a holy place, an open-air church; the synchronous whir of arms and legs and the race of blood soaring through his veins was more levitating than the sweetest hymn. He felt the eyes of the Lord smiling upon him. Taylor came to sense the same. His cycling was an expression of something beautiful and true and honest in a world that was decidedly otherwise.

Taylor would never consent to say many of the things a bright and inquisitive man such as himself had to be thinking. He would never say that the pressures of being alone against everyone else, or being gifted in a way that put him in harm's way, led him to Jesus. He didn't say that his journey, the personal travails he had been through and would continue to go through, now made sense. He feared his enemies would use his feelings against him. He was naked and exposed on the bicycle, a purely physical entity for all the world to see, but what was inside was his. Taylor said only that there were things he would and wouldn't do now and that his sudden calling was a kind of family debt to his mother's memory. "I believe in the saying that 'a mother's prayers will last forever,'" he softly explained. When Saphronia Taylor died, his mission began.

In the midst of an unseasonably warm Boston winter, he discarded the idea of fleeing to France. Fueled by scriptural sustenance, he told Munger and Brady he was more ready than ever to compete at home in 1898 for a second season of pro racing. His goal was manifest: to fulfill Munger's prophecy and become the national sprint champion. In defeating the men arrayed against him, he would bring glory to himself, of course, but also to the Almighty.

MCFARLAND'S 1897 SEASON HAD A DIFFERENT set of disappointments. He was not quite the next Zimmy. The season, top honors and all, belonged to Eddie "Cannon" Bald, who seemed capable of defeating McFarland and anybody else whenever he felt like it. He won the national title, his third time in a row, and to add insult to McFarland's injury, he said the "darkie" was his biggest competitive worry. McFarland's low point came in October on the national circuit extension when a hitherto unknown racer, Dr. A. I. Brown, whipped him in a match race while setting a new record for the flying mile.

Brown was all the talk as the season ended, and Bald was the superstar entertaining lucrative offers for a trip to Europe and acting roles on Broadway. When McFarland returned to San Jose in early winter he was perhaps a bit adrift himself. In California, many of the top riders from the West were leaving the eastern-based national circuit to join a rebel western circuit that raced on Sundays. The renegades were banking on an untapped market and in so doing were defying the eastern establishment and LAW's unshakable devotion to a ban on Sunday racing. They believed California could secede and still succeed. It was an attitude that presaged the California way— better, bigger, and just fine on its own. Undoubtedly McFarland considered staying home in 1898. After such a promising start to the 1897 season, McFarland was no closer to being the boss of the sport than he'd been twelve months earlier.

At some point he, too, had a transformation. He didn't get religion, like Taylor, but something else. He all at once understood that it wasn't he that needed improving but the sport itself. He didn't simply want to win, he wanted to run the sport, and for that to happen a shake-up needed to occur. Over the winter he mapped it out.

A young Floyd McFarland pictured in his early San Jose racing days. *Source: Courtesy, History San Jose*

The riders needed to rid themselves of LAW—a meddling, unthankful, money-hungry middleman—and bid themselves out where and when they wanted to. The purses needed to be uncapped, the promoters unleashed. It was nothing less than the start of free agency and a sporting manifest destiny. It was Californian through and through.

Indeed, Floyd McFarland would be back in 1898. After all, a circuit run for riders, by riders, needed someone to keep order— a tough-talking, fast-riding union chief. Let Bald act and Brown set records; McFarland was moving with a lightning-like jump to control the biggest, best, and most prosperous sport in the world. Secession was for fools. He would return east and, as befit a McFarland, he would grab what he wanted and make it his own.

CHAPTER 7

Two Seconds

AUGUST 1898
INDIANAPOLIS, INDIANA

Is it any wonder that we are now a tribe of scorchers?
—*Cosmopolitan*, COMMENTING
ON THE URGENT DESIRE FOR SPEED

AS THE CENTURY DREW to a close, the art of training and peak performance was increasingly on people's minds. Everybody was interested. Even Thomas Edison, in his Edisonian way, got into the act when he invited a bodybuilder named Eugen Sandow to his Black Maria Studio in East Orange, New Jersey, so he could film him doing "muscle display performances." As the film rolled, Edison peppered the Prussian with questions about how he had engineered the most perfectly developed body in the world. What had once been a decidedly laissez-faire approach to athletic achievement—Arthur Zimmerman was renowned for his poor training habits—had changed dramatically. Science, logic, and ten years of race data were plumbed. Articles and books appeared with advice on diet, training regimens, cross training, and recovery. Photographs analyzed the rider's specialized sprint positions. Like the industry itself, which was becoming remarkably modern in appearance and overall marketing sophistication, training theorems followed suit.

Tom Eck, a contemporary of Munger's, produced a tidy pamphlet called *Training for Wheelmen* in which he preached base training, intervals, and more or less all the commonly understood principles of developing explosive power and quickness, the chief attributes of a top sprinter. At the same time the British champion W. Percy Furnival presented a paper to the Society of Cyclists in London on the sport's physiology. "The great muscular exertion required for cycling produces a large waste of the tissues of the body," he wrote. "The first question, therefore, is, what this loss consists of, and by what materials it can best be repaired." In warming up to his answer, Furnival explained that the average 154-pound adult possessed, among other things, 28 pounds of fat, 3 pounds of hair, and 7 pounds of blood. Furnival wasn't an oddity. Every cyclist who dreamed of speed was combing through the scientific literature, certain that enlightenment was ahead of him.

There was a seemingly unceasing comparison of riders' personal habits. Did a rider drink, smoke, and carry on late at night, and if so, in what exact proportions? "It is a tradition that has been handed down from olden times that an athlete should eat only beefsteak, mutton chops, and a little chicken now and then, and drink a bottle of bass ale for dinner every day to give proper strength," wrote Eck in his pamphlet, "but my theory is just the reverse." Furnival, not surprisingly, used roughly 1,000 words to detail what was necessary to replace "the waste of tissues." He talked about the benefits of cooking flesh-based products and the joy of simple, unexciting fruits and stale bread ("during mastication it can be more thoroughly broken up, so that the saliva can more freely penetrate and act on it. Remember, our bodies are nourished, not by what we eat, but by what we digest").

It wasn't just scorchers who were interested, either. Scientists and even theologians were drawn into the national discourse, each with their own agenda. At stake was not just the minute mile—something that the racing fraternity thought was within reach—but also a bulwark to intellectual thought, the concept scholars knew as vitalism. It was an ancient theory, first credited to no less than Aristotle, who held that there was something incalculable in the energy of the human being, a life force that could not be quantified and yet differentiated us and adorned us as a species. It was something akin to the soul. For centuries vitalism stayed intact, but as athletics came to the forefront and threshold-busting efforts continued to command attention it became clear that energy was being manipulated in the bodies of big-seated, thick-limbed men. Some had cups that runneth over, or that were made to runneth over through supplements and additives. Furnival's seemingly innocuous words about replenishing wasted tissues actually energized the debate. There was an ebb and flow, not a fixed reservoir of energy at a person's disposal. Scientists looked increasingly at what men and women put in their mouths.

Wilbur O. Atwater's published work—he had canvassed the Garden Six-Day racers to chart rations and sleep—drew widespread attention. Only a stone's throw from the Middletown, Connecticut, bicycle-making plant where Munger worked, Atwater had built a tomblike device at Wesleyan University that effectively took the wonderful world of bicycle racing and crammed it into a closet-sized contraption called the respiration calorimeter.

Student subjects lived, ate, drank, slept, and vigorously exercised within the chamber, with one series of diabolical experiments requiring cyclists to pedal a stationary bike for up to sixteen hours. Rectangular, airtight, and topped with Medusa-like coils that circulated water at a known temperature and volume, the calorimeter's water absorbed the heat thrown off by Atwater's sweaty exercisers. A change in water temperature related directly to an individual's energy metabolism. By charting precisely what they ate in the chamber, then charting their energy use, he could fix the values of food as fuel. There was nothing he didn't want to measure, from suet to cranberries.

In the case of the sixteen-hour riders he learned that the poor spaghetti-limbed students expended 10,000 kilocalories, the energy equivalent of a liter of gasoline. Though a crew of sixteen people manned controls and stood ready at the rescue, it wasn't all suffering. The Judd Hall calorimeter became known far and wide on the campus as being the one place you could drink alcoholic beverages and get paid to do so, all in the mighty cause of science. Naturally, Atwater's work caught the alarmed eyes of religious scholars, who saw sacrilege in the chamber of food and commanded their Christian brethren to rise up and write the Washington legislators who had put taxpayers' money in the hands of a sinful quack.

But the portly Atwater, the son of a Methodist minister and a chemist in training, was on to something. The results of his research into nutritional habits of boxers and cyclists provided a fascinating window to the world inside their unsung gut. It actually disproved the common belief that stimulants provided a pick-me-up to endurance athletes; in fact, the reverse was true, as it merely revved the metabolism momentarily to provide the illusion of benefit. His rigorous chemical analysis of different foods, his investigations of how cooking impacted their nutritional value, and his experiments into what amounts and types of nutrients were needed for the metabolism and respiration of a high-performing athlete would change sport forever.

There would be wider ripples, however. Like Darwinism, Atwater's bold experiments would prod a hot religious debate and force the reassessment of vitalism so that the world could find room for both the cell and the soul. It wasn't easy. Plain old food—inanimate, unemotional, and for the majority of 19th-century America fairly uninteresting—had an energy, a soul, as it were. The organic and the inorganic shared, at least in the infernal calorimeter, the storied gift of heat. It was almost more than an Aristotelian could take. But more importantly, and having nothing to do with sport or heat, Atwater claimed a social component to his research. Races were not fated to inferiority, he wrote; instead "the intellectual and moral condition and progress of men and women is largely regulated by their plane of living; that the plane of their intellectual and moral life depends upon how they are housed and clothed and fed."

A black man in America, an aborigine in Australia, a Malaysian in Indonesia—none was consigned to a dreary future because of the shape of his skull or the color of his skin. They were consigned to such because the other half chose them to be.

A YOUNG MAJOR TAYLOR had only the faintest grasp of what was going on in Professor Atwater's labs, but he had common sense. He once wrote, "Get out of the habit of smoking before you begin to train, for it is hard to leave off all of a sudden, and it might go hard with a man." Taylor was smart and attentive; more than a jewel, he was a coachable jewel. He had no vices, no adult distractions yet, and he hung on Birdie Munger's every word.

He was a product of the temperance age, a new believer in the idea that being the best racer came from being the best person he could be. Reward was the by-product of rigid self-discipline. In later years he would advise his wife, his daughter, and readers of his autobiography that there was one path to follow. In his book he repeated the dozen rules he said he faithfully practiced: don't use intoxicants, don't keep late hours, and so on. While his wife was enduring a difficult and ultimately unsuccessful pregnancy, he wrote to her, "Don't forget your [raw] eggs every morning, and you will be well and will pick up a lot by the time I get back." He was in Europe at the time, the start of a two-month absence from home. There was a certainty in himself and the way he prepared for races that carried over into daily life. His daughter once said that she wished he'd been able to loosen up and be less rigid about things, but it's hardly surprising that he was that way given the time and effort he spent in serious, hard-focused training.

Munger and Taylor began training for each season, including the upcoming 1898 campaign, in the early spring. He was early to the track, and usually arrived in a long swaddling robe. Munger brought Turkish towels, a rubbing board, blanket, sponges, and tools for breakdowns. He had a surgeon's sticking plaster and bandages for repairing blowouts. Taylor didn't try to match McFarland's macho workload but instead carved out an entirely novel approach based on perfectly prescribed bouts of quality, not quantity.

In April they started with five miles on the road in the morning and the same in the afternoon. During the second week they doubled the mileage but maintained a medium speed of four-minute miles. The current world record was roughly half that. In the ensuing weeks the mileage didn't change but each day Munger asked Taylor to cut his times five seconds; at a certain threshold the five seconds dictum was applied every other day. A month into training Taylor was routinely recording 2:40 miles.

With a sprinting base established, Munger began the delicate, more sculptural process of developing acceleration. He prescribed slow warm-up laps followed by a quarter mile at near all-out exertion. Following a rubdown, Taylor produced another all-out effort. Later, the mileage was extended to a half mile, then a mile. The first portion was paced by a fellow rider, while the second was all Taylor. Alone and flirting with the fitness threshold now known as the "red line," Taylor was expected to try for a personal best. The fragile balance of work and recovery was handled masterfully.

As described in *Serious Cycling,* a modern textbook for scientifically minded cyclists, power is how much force you can exert and how quickly you can exert it. Do too much work and the body shuts down, unable to summon the right biochemistry to improve. Do too little and the body isn't taught to acclimate to hard work, to master

"Majah" Taylor.

Around his twentieth birthday in 1898, Taylor would shock the world with his record speed trials in Philadelphia. *Source: From the Collection of the Indiana State Museum and Historic Sites*

the pain threshold and produce the witches' brew of chemicals that moderate the muscular burn. Taylor was born with the right genes and had an instinctual sense of what worked, but in Munger he had the perfect architect—competent, inquisitive, and motivated.

As the years passed, resulting in records and championships, Munger's work proved itself. On match race days Taylor always seemed on form, although the biggest events were often last-minute affairs where the riders had no time to customize their training. In high-stakes match races, which he competed in more frequently than any other U.S. racer, his record was an astounding 200 wins and twelve defeats. He reached peak sprint form more consistently for the simple reason he didn't overtrain; rather, he explored his physical threshold in training with incredible restraint. More athletes push it to remind themselves of their strength and because they are creatures of habit. Taylor, with Munger's oversight, learned not to need reminding. Yet Taylor's greatest gift from Munger wasn't a formula but his bull-dog example. Racers respected racers. What would never leave Taylor were the boyhood stories he read about Munger in the *Wheelmen's Gazette*. About the "cracking wheelman" who was toppled in races, only to get up. About the Munger who was seemingly exhausted on the penultimate turn, only to find a finishing kick. The lesson that stuck beyond all others was about good old-fashioned guts.

Unfortunately, Birdie Munger was burning the candle at both ends, training Taylor and trying to hustle up new investors to save the company making his next-generation bicycle. His elegant Birdie Special was a monumental commercial flop—it was fast and light and superbly designed for speed but came to the market a hair too late and was $50 too expensive. Dozens of creditors filed attachments against the company in 1897, followed by months of legal wrangling in state and federal courts. In 1898, the company officially ceased to exist. Within months the massive company grounds in Worcester was consumed by a new business, the Worcester Ice Company.

There are no Birdie Specials that survive, no pictures produced and published that might allow for a definitive autopsy. However, Munger built another bicycle around the same time that is on display in an art gallery at the Indiana State Museum in Indianapolis. The workmanship is exquisite: he was a man for whom creation was an end in itself. The bicycle features rims made from the finest lightweight ash, finished to a gleaming honey hue. The spokes, radiating in an ornate crosshatch pattern, are bamboo. The wooden ram's horn bars were tapered with grips bordered in black. A wafer-thin fender seemed to float over the rear wheel, suspended like a bridge with a geometric, interstitial pattern of matching black wire. In an age when corners were being cut to mass-produce the bicycle and make it affordable, he had built a customized masterpiece. It weighed a feathery twenty pounds. It had no horizontal top tube; it was a ladies' frame with a plunging V that conveniently allowed a modest woman to gracefully step over the bike. And yet any woman who mounted the bicycle would have, because of the radically downturned handlebars, found herself laid out like a human bullet. It was a ladies scorcher's bike, a model for which there was no buyer. It was as though Munger couldn't help himself.

He was sure he could produce a champion racer, just as he was sure he could produce a champion superbike. He had lost two highly touted businesses—the second, the papers reported, backed by the "largest trust in the country"—because of his distracting relationship with Taylor and his preoccupation with seeing him go a few miles per hour faster. There would be no exclusive Coney Island jolly bloomer balls with his wife, Emelie, where the men wore suits and ladies lace blouses and "snug fitting knickerbockers." Nor would there be moments of whimsical excess, such as when he built an exact replica of his Birdie Special sized for a friend's three-year-old boy. He had lost it all in 1898—everything except Taylor, a black racer who had barely survived his first pro season. Munger was, even his closest friends conceded, a hopeless dreamer.

*   *   *

BILLY BRADY WAS A WILD DREAMER HIMSELF. He and Taylor
had met at the Six-Day, then entered into a contractual relationship
soon thereafter. "I make no pretense at greatness," Brady wrote in his
memoirs, "unless that quality lie in the developing of greatness in
others." Brady offered experience, chutzpah, and feistiness. He had
come to Taylor's rescue around the time, Taylor wrote, when "there
was a plan on foot to bar me, as a colored racing cyclist, from future
racing on all tracks." Brady's dream wasn't the best bicycle or breaking
speed records but the biggest promotion the world had ever seen—a
star-studded promotion where the stadium would be full and noisy, the
betting frantic, and the reporters hanging on his every word. He wasn't
certain whether the event would be cycling, boxing, or even a Coney
Island stunt, only that it would be huge and he would be pulling the
strings. And when it was all over—he was still dreaming here—he
would walk away, go legitimate, and become an uptown guy.

Brady was born above a San Francisco saloon and became a
ward of the state before he turned fourteen. His theatrical sense came
from his mother, a singer and entertainer. His ability to charm and
cajole and his flair for inflaming the public's desires came from his
father, Terence Brady, a newspaper editor at one of the city's more
reckless, anti-Union tabloids. His childhood, he acknowledged, read
like the Bowery theatrical melodramas he later came to produce: a
tempestuous father, embroiled in a custody dispute with his separated wife, scoops up young Billy one day and flees town aboard a
Panama steamer, only to fall dead in a New York City street a few
years later, leaving the round-eyed child to fend for himself.

Brady worked the streets to stay afloat and hawked canned beef,
jellies, and mattresses on the transcontinental Southern Pacific between
Omaha and Red Wing, Nebraska. When he lost his entire stock of
goods in a card game, he was "summarily fired." Brady moved along
to the West Coast and scraped together a living entertaining, writing,

and acting in the theater. His entrepreneurial talents flowered in this setting, as he virtually invented the role of producer in the evolving theater business. His production of *After Dark* in 1889 represented the new era, with producer Brady pulling together all the elements: buying the play, hiring actors, renting a theater, and publicizing the show—all at great financial risk, of course, but also at terrific potential reward. His rousing popular success should've been a career maker, but the "honest gambler" in him had evidently overlooked the fact that the play was in fact someone else's property. He lost a plagiarism judgment and found himself temporarily banished to the bottom-dwelling world of sports promotion where, not yet thirty, he sought to remake himself yet again.

His first project, in the early 1890s, was an unheralded heavyweight boxer named James J. Corbett. In a tactic that he would soon perfect with Taylor, Brady issued a public challenge through his friends at the *Herald* and the *Sun* to the then reigning champ, John L. Sullivan. Brady said he'd put $1,000 on his man against the overwhelming favorite in a winner-take-all title match. Sullivan took the bait and Corbett took the title (which is fortunate, since Brady didn't have the money). His management of Corbett was truly masterly—Brady's ambitions were huge, their partnership stretching across a decade. He didn't just want Corbett to win the heavyweight title; he wanted to legitimize boxing and take it, as he said, from the "alleys into the royal suite." Thus Corbett wasn't just another boxer, but a gentleman who was charming, polite, and wholesome. It was Brady's idea to have him, once he won the title from Sullivan, resist painting the town red (as was the custom of every boxer before him). Instead, Brady directed his charge to go back to his hotel quarters and (as the photographers clicked away) celebrate with a tall glass of cold milk. In the ring Corbett had been coached to move and dance and jab, a style that was a hell of a lot more civilized than standing toe-to-toe and crudely slugging it out.

Brady's run in boxing ended when Bob Fitzsimmons dethroned Corbett at Carson City, California, in 1897. Brady tried unsuccessfully to insert himself into big-time Broadway by throwing his ring earnings around, but he backed off soon thereafter, keenly aware that he was still viewed as a low-class character "who worked with pugs." He was also bankrupt again. It was then he turned his sights to six-day racing and professional cycling, a comparatively virgin entertainment territory.

It was always all or nothing with Brady, and the Taylor association was no exception. Taylor's similarities with Corbett were obvious: underdog, well mannered, desperate for a championship shot. "I was like the fellow in The Jumping Frog who would bet on anything," Brady wrote sixty years later in his autobiography, *Showman*. "The public was having an orgy of freak contests. . . . I was one of the people who gave them whatever lunacy they happened to be craving at the moment." In time he would move beyond the confines of high-speed cycling and embrace motor racing, broadsword combats on horseback, a giant wrestler named Ismail Yousouf and nicknamed the "Terrible Turk," and virtually anything that involved "possible death." But until he saw Major Taylor he evidently never considered the best freak show of all: a black man versus a white mob.

Quickly Brady realized the scale was too broad, the tension too diffuse—that, as in boxing, the public needed two giants, each attractive in vastly different ways, each a different color, a standard-bearer for their race or class. He would explore different partners for headline-making matches with Taylor, but Floyd McFarland was in Brady's sights from the beginning. With a little time to build the suspense and a few choice words to his friends at the city newspapers, he foresaw the perfect match, perhaps the biggest one ever. He knew exactly what the people wanted. It would be a promoter's dream. "Never tackle anything but champions," Brady liked to say. In Taylor—and McFarland—he was following a perfect script.

*   *   *

PRECISELY WHAT BRADY HAD IN MIND for Taylor—and a
dress rehearsal of sorts for a Taylor-versus-McFarland showdown
race—would come to fruition late in the 1898 summer season. By
then he had built his Coney Island track at Manhattan Beach and figured out how to arrange five-star matches. Though he was probably
rebuffed in his attempts to get the top American racers such as
McFarland, who were holding the color line, he managed to land a
big one just the same: the Welshman Jimmy Michael.

To make the pairing, Brady had merely reprised the strategy he'd
made famous several years earlier with Sullivan and Corbett. As he
did with the prizefight, Brady took his case to the press. This time it
was the *New York Sun* and a public wager of $1,000 that none of the
top racers could defeat Taylor. It was one of the largest sums ever
offered in a U.S. race.

Michael in particular, with a large round head comically out
of proportion to his gnat-sized body, appealed to Brady's well-
developed sense of spectacle. He was a foreigner—good; was known
by the nickname "Midget"—better; and he hated blacks with undis-
guised vehemence. The date was August 27. The setup was a one-
mile, standing-start sprint, best two out of three. Each rider was to
be paced behind multicycles, a racing appliance in which a bicycle
was stretched to accommodate four or five pilots. Michael and Taylor would have to stay within inches of the hurtling machines, thus
benefiting from the windblock. A pace-aided race, Brady realized,
was the fastest and most exciting cycling race in the world. Instead
of one multicycle, Brady offered a new style of match racing featuring two. Each would take a portion of the mile course before giving
way to the other team. The extra pacers, by giving their all over
a shorter distance, ensured maximum speed. Taylor and Michael
would be the dot at the end of an *i*—just tucked in there, pedaling
like madmen.

The new cement track at Manhattan Beach, built by Brady and
his fellow investors for just this occasion, seemed to hang on the edge
of the world. Heavy sea air and swirling winds made it a difficult
place to set records—storms blew in and wiped out the boardwalk
stick frames periodically—but nothing could beat the ambience. Within
view was the extraordinary sight of the Coney Island amusement
park with the scream-making rides and incandescent spires of
Dreamland. Even the killjoys of the temperance and Sunday prohibi-
tionist world couldn't put a dent in the place. On a Sunday a month
earlier the police had sternly enforced a policy that prohibited bark-
ers outside the theaters. So men wore placards around their necks
and made *that* amusing. "Am struck dumb by the police, but will
talk tomorrow," read one. Fully 100,000 people visited Coney Island
that day.

On the eve of the race Brady promised nobody would leave disappointed. "The colored rider gets away very fast and the Welsh boy
is not negligent in this respect," he reported. "The battle between the
two will be the first of its kind ever staged in this country, and should
prove to be a heartbreaker."

For the day, the normal sideshows at the beach, the daylong fireworks, and the reenactment of the sinking of the *Merrimac* and the
"fall of Manila" weren't the headliners. In the grandstand, remembered Taylor, "was one of the greatest throngs that ever witnessed a
sporting event in this country." The weather, never a sure bet, was
perfect, with a light cooling breeze. Taylor wore a slender jersey that
read COMET (a nickname Brady liked). Michael was in all gray.
Brady, in a tux, introduced the combatants.

The scene inspired something approaching reverie for one newspaperman:

> Just as the sun went down, Bill Jones' friend climbed up behind the
> crowd in the grand stand, and looked around at the scenery. To the south

of him, railroad tracks, suburban trains, a great hotel and Manhattan Beach. Beyond, the ocean.

To the north, a confused, fading panorama of land, water, trees, houses. Beyond, Brooklyn.

To the west, Coney Island, Bay Ridge, lower New York bay, the battleships (invisible), Staten Island. Beyond, Old Sol, hot, red, glaring, sinking behind the sharply outlined hills of New Jersey.

To the east, racing men's quarters . . . and just below, a match bicycle race between a mite of a white man from Wales and a rubbery little Indiana coon.

Taylor lost the first race because of a problem with his pacing team but won the next easily, setting up the showdown race. Taylor took the pole position after winning the coin toss. At the start of the day he'd been a significant underdog, with the two-to-one betting line favoring the Midget. For the final heat it had narrowed to even money. Circling the track with the racers near the apron were the pacesetting multicycles, slow to build speed but getting there. At the gun the racers bolted, then settled into a steady pace. Michael wanted to conserve energy. When he told his pacesetters to take it easy, Taylor overheard and jumped. He won with ease, as if on a "pleasure jaunt with a comical grin spread all over his rather good natured face." With a full lap to go Michael gave up and coasted in.

Taylor was paraded around like a champion gladiator, his victory all the more celebrated when it was announced he'd broken the European-held world record for the prestigious one-mile distance. Four thousand fans witnessed the event, and the New York gamblers had a field day, the betting some of the most vigorous ever seen. The "pale as a corpse" Midget, a perennial New York favorite, was so distraught that he vanished from the U.S. cycling scene for the next two years. Almost goading his fellow money-chasing brethren, including McFarland, Taylor gave half his $1,000 prize to the riders who paced him, all of whom were white.

With Brady's chutzpah, Munger's preparation, and Taylor's legs, the trio had upset the balance of the racing world. The Michael face-off highlighted match racing's promise as a gate maker and established Taylor as a premier drawing card. Most importantly, Taylor's match notices brought him to the immediate attention of Harry Sanger, the manufacturer of a new kind of bicycle.

His "chainless" wheel, a dismal failure in a previous incarnation, was untested on the track. The shaft drive looked slick: the beveled gear, which spun when pedaled, was enclosed. It in turn powered the back wheel. By eliminating a chain, Sanger believed the public would come around to a cleaner and smoother system. Nobody disputed the smoothness of the system. The question was whether a chainless bicycle could match the power and speed of the chain-driven version. Most believed not. Sanger hoped Taylor would, in grandiose fashion, show the world that the chainless had come of age by setting a half dozen speed records.

The focus would be on the "flying start" mile, a crowd-pleasing variation in which the racer crossed the start line and began his record bid only after reaching full speed. To ensure he had gotten everybody's attention—and perhaps with public relations guidance from Brady—Sanger announced a $10,000 bonus if Taylor set a sub-1:30 mile.

In general, record-making camps had been terrible failures, sabotaged by the vagaries of weather and the imprecision of both man and gear. Taylor's effort was vastly different. The pacemaking appliances were tuned up to concert pitch. Four quintuplet teams were manned by crews selected from among some of America's most noted flyers. Taylor had a 23-pound bike and a 108-gear inch sprocket. He was being paid a salary—$100 per week—above and beyond a commission on each of his records. The frame was the latest design. In adapting to paced riding, where riders needed to tuck behind the big pacing machines, the front forks were made more vertical, with almost no curve or rake. For better aerodynamics and power, the saddle was put farther forward to redistribute body weight. The shift required bars with a radical forward curve. Shorter wheelbases meant less lateral instability, and smaller 26-inch wheels reduced friction. Cranks were lower to the ground, for better balance. From bottom bracket to seat, the bicycle geometry had been intelligently rethought before Taylor arrived at Woodside Park in Philadelphia, one of the fastest tracks in the country.

The camp was supposed to be the week of November 4, but because of the atrocious weather and various gear mishaps they were delayed. When on November 12 it didn't clear, Taylor decided he couldn't wait any longer. Time was money. Leasing the track, the top-drawer pacesetting teams, and the full-time employment of a mechanic was costing Sanger upwards of $5,000.

On the twelfth Taylor rode the mile in 1:32 flat, lowering the record three-fifths of a second. His average speed for the distance was 45 mph. He also twice lowered the half-mile mark to 45⅗. Two days later, Taylor lowered the ⅓-mile record from 30⅕ to 29⅘. The next day he rewrote the record books again, bettering his previous marks at every distance he attempted. He was deluged with congratulatory telegrams. Five days later, he smashed the 2-mile record by fifteen seconds.

Suddenly the record setting had become a serial drama. Newspapermen rushed in. Taylor promised 1:30. On November 16, with the weather deteriorating and Taylor experiencing pains up and down his thighs and across his hips, he tried a final time. The pacesetters were summoned from their huddle around a woodstove. Droplets of water seeping down the high banking of the planked track had collected near the base, freezing solid into one Saturn-like ring.

As before, the four quints began circling the track first, followed by the solitary Taylor. Raising his hand after several laps, Taylor streaked across the start line at 35 mph to several sets of stopwatches firing. Though his pacing teams seemed out of sync, Taylor was a marvel to behold. Midway through the record time, and sensing himself slowing, he blasted past his faltering pacing team to latch on to another one 25 yards up the track. Journalists who had never seen such a remarkable display of power and acceleration dubbed the moves a "flying pickup."

In the final quarter mile his pacing team couldn't or wouldn't maintain the speed Taylor needed. He screamed for more, but when he realized he wasn't going to get it, he passed them altogether in the final straightaway, finishing ahead of the five-person-powered bicycle by several lengths. The crowd was stunned. His failure to beat the 1:30 mark was outdone by what they'd seen: one man overtaking five of "America's most noted flyers." Later, some would suggest the pacesetters had been bribed to slow the pace and prevent Taylor from reaching the 1:30 milestone. Practically, it didn't matter. Taylor was a phenomenon, his performance described in dozens of newspapers as one of the greatest athletic accomplishments of all time. He had gone almost 46 mph. The automobile speed record in 1898 was 39 mph.

For the first time the prominent black newspapers put him on page one, calling him the wonder of the 19th century. The white press pointed out that the gentleman rider was a lovely anomaly: a black man with well-developed "white" character traits. Finally, the sporting journalists marveled not only that he had succeeded but that he had done so in wintry conditions. "It has been long a theory that neither man nor beast could exert his full speed powers while the weather was cold. . . . Either this belief is fallacious, or the dusky whirlwind with the military title is an extraordinary individual."

He had shown that the traditional method of building maximum speed—putting four men on a multicycle to block the wind and set pace for a draft-aided solo rider—was inadequate. Human pace, no matter how many men were put on a bike, couldn't keep ahead of Taylor. To fully explore the boundaries of speed, a man of Taylor's ilk would need something beyond human pace. He needed a motorized pacing apparatus. Munger was one of the first on it. He dashed off a letter to the Stanley brothers in Boston and anxiously awaited their reply. The evolving appliance would run through a host of names, but *motorcycle* would eventually stick.

The results at Philadelphia, said Taylor, cleared up any doubt about who was the fastest man in America. Not to all, however. Some questioned the accuracy of the timekeeping and the failure to keep intermediary splits. Others said he'd merely been the first to benefit from a well-financed and well-organized camp—thanks to his white manager, Munger—and that other racers would soon follow suit. Even his win against Michael was discounted since Michael wasn't a true sprinter but rather a middle-distance star. The country's top racer, Floyd McFarland, stood atop Taylor in the league standings.

Taylor and McFarland continued to be the stuff of great, beery debates. They represented not just opposite ends of the sprinter's spectrum but opposite ends of the moral spectrum. As a champion handicapper, McFarland required and demanded help. No matter his strength—and the Californian had plenty—he had to depend on the willingness of others to team with him and pace him back to the leaders. Without cooperation, he would have to do the work entirely himself to chase down the front men—a virtual impossibility even for somebody of McFarland's caliber. It wasn't considered cheating to team with others to pace back to the leaders, but often the race finishes had the air of inevitability, as if they'd been prearranged. McFarland was a marvelous athlete, but he wasn't a soloist. His brilliance was truly comprehensive: all-around strength, smarts, and audacity.

Taylor was a true sprinter, a soloist. He could race longer distances, but they weren't his forte. His gift, what they talked about at the track and the roadhouses after, was his explosiveness. His "jump" was genetic perfection, a freakish preponderance of fast-twitch muscle fibers, which favor explosive efforts and are part of the physiological profile of weight lifters, sprinters, and high-flying basketball dunkers. He was unbalanced to perfection: 75 percent fast-twitch muscle fibers to 25 percent slow-twitch fibers. By contrast, an endurance runner might have the reverse proportion. His body had the ability to instantaneously react—in scientific terms it responded to a stimulus, such as his opponent's move—because of the sheer speed of his nerve transmissions. Finally, he had a near-perfect anaerobic system, another attribute seen among the world's finest sprint athletes. Simply put, in the most intense efforts the body relies for its energy needs not on oxygen but on a high-test molecular fuel produced and stored by the muscles themselves. Sprinters are the only athletes, sports physiologists say, who don't need either heart or lungs to break world records. What they mean is the race is too swift, too intense for the comparatively balky fuel source of blood-supplied oxygen. The race is run at a higher domain. The fuel supply is found in the complex metabolic reactions taking place in muscle cells. For the rare few, the molecular fuel comes forth in comparative torrents, resynthesizing and circulating to muscle cells like Edisonian electrons.

The final few yards of a match sprint were riveting for the decision, but even more fascinating was how in those one or two seconds before the finish line—the jump—everything was compressed, how stored energy erupted with a violent but beautiful and unblemished synaptic precision. The power in those moments exceeded 2,000 watts, enough to run the millions of lights at Luna Park for hours upon hours: a Lance Armstrong would, by contrast, produce an average of 400 watts, rarely more, en route to a Tour de France victory. Leveraged by the long femur bone, the sprinter's legs bent into the pedals with tidal force and velocity. The torque erased the resistance of 100 gear inches—the equivalent of an eight-foot-diameter wheel—like a hammer on a tack.

There was no war whoop, no pain etched in skid marks across his face, but there was control. It was a conundrum: the absolute harnessing and unleashing of energy all at once. More than feeling supersonic, Taylor felt that everybody else had slowed down. He almost never tried to put into words what it meant to go so fast in those last seconds. Maybe he didn't want to acknowledge that he was motivated and bonded to those two seconds of a race, no more. Or maybe to do so was too hubristic, or too trivializing, as if he was attempting to explain the speed of light itself. To explain it was to diminish the sacredness of the interaction, or to jeopardize a tenuous relationship with the thing itself. Or maybe it was just scary to know the blunt force at his disposal and how it could only be parsed out in the right circumstances—on a pedal, through the bike, on a track. Violence but not violent.

There was a life force in those two seconds, a crystallization of pure energy, like the Holy Ghost rushing in to lay a revivalist out cold. It was a stimulant, but not in any recognizable form. It happened too fast, was gone too quick. A well-known modern sprinter, John Smith, once said, "There's a feeling, a vibration that is unique. It comes when you've never been in that space before." It was ethereal and addictive. Two seconds nobody else in the world possessed, two seconds to feel the universe pour through you. It was a conversion experience, a crossing to the other side. Something does happen. "They have this blankness—like an aura," Smith put it in an interview with Daniel Coyle. "Fear is released; they've walked into the unknown and let go. Maybe that's where the body understands what the speed of light is, what absolute zero is, what infinity is."

Perhaps Taylor's unshakable faith, his sacrifice, had to do with the two seconds as much as it had to do with a moral debt he owed someone or something. Those two seconds were his cathedral. It was a trade-off, a barter: for two seconds he felt at peace. His speed and power were tied to a spiritual force in ways that he couldn't possibly comprehend. His search for those two seconds was a holy grail, a mantra repeated. His dismay about McFarland wasn't from the latter's bigotry but from his arrogance, his belief that he stood apart and owed nothing to nobody. That somehow he derived his power from muscles and bones.

In those last two seconds Taylor made perfectly good racers look like they were stalled in sand. He didn't seem to have a threshold—or, like the majority of athletes, the fear of a threshold.

But there was one problem—he obviously did. He and McFarland *had* met in August at Indianapolis's month-old Newby Racing Oval. It wasn't a match race, with just the two of them facing off, but it did offer a preview of such a thing. Taylor, in his first return to his native Indianapolis in three years, was the overwhelming favorite. A record time was expected on the virgin track with steeply pitched turns built for speed. A section of the grandstands had been reserved by friends of Taylor's and his old See Saw Cycling Club, and the young black women of the city had vied for his attention during the week.

"Major Taylor, the colored champion, was the whole thing in colordom, Thursday night," an Indianapolis paper reported. "A reception in his honor, to which just 100 invitations were issued, was held in the criminal court room, and all 100 were there too. It was a brilliant affair, and showed the little colored rider that the townsmen of his own race are dutifully proud of their premier representative on the cycling turf." The highlight was the 100 Club's presentation to Taylor of a diamond shirt stud. Taylor was thrilled with the gesture but declined to make an address, saying he "could pump a bicycle" all right but he could not deliver a speech.

Taylor had returned to a city that was now considered "a great wheeling town." An estimated 50 percent of the population rode bicycles, led by the vigorously pro-cycling mayor, Thomas Taggert. Among the legislation Taggert had signed was a citywide ordinance making it illegal to throw anything in the streets that might cause a tire puncture. The dry-goods stores on Washington Street, not just the bicycle shops, offered a scorching uniform that included a shallow-brim, satin-lined cap, a sleeveless jersey, belt, hose, jockstraplike undergarments, and lightweight shoes made from the African Dongola goat. LAW's annual event, the biggest date on the cycling calendar, was the occasion to celebrate the city's growth and its association with speed. Indianapolis was a city built around the Herculean thrust of locomotives and what the YMCA had brilliantly characterized as "muscular Christianity." Fitness wasn't just an indulgence anymore but a virtuous display of sacrifice and moral grit. Speed was the Lord's work. The crack racer had gained popular acceptance; admirers were everywhere he looked.

As sure as a boy born in Indianapolis knew how to hunt, sit up straight in church, and lie motionless under a plum-red sunset, he knew and believed in the primacy of speed. Years later the winner of the Indianapolis 500 would further sanctify the union by kissing the track and guzzling a glass of milk in celebration. The instinct to go fast was in the nature of the boy and the nurture of a place. Speed had found a home.

The homecoming was also for Munger, who had raced in Indianapolis in the earliest days and who had spread the racing bug as a charter member of the Zig Zag Cycling Club (a free-spirited organization that spawned a number of automotive titans such as Barney Oldfield and Carl Fisher). He was returning with the prodigal son, an I-told-you-so grin stretching from ear to ear as he made his way through the mobs at the opening reception, held in the state capitol. "I cannot say whether Mr. Munger or myself was the happiest," Taylor remarked. Munger's crazy notion that he would steer the career of a black cyclist to the top of the white sporting world was coming true. He couldn't have been prouder or more eager to set himself up trackside for the coronation, scheduled for Saturday afternoon.

"Colored Boy Will Own City if He Only Wins," read the headline prior to Saturday's mile open, the signature event in a week of racing, countryside tours, and evening smokers. In accordance with the race's stature as the biggest event of the year, ten times as many points were given for the top five winners in each event than they'd receive for an ordinary race victory in Boston or New Jersey or Chicago. For Taylor the "must" victory could put him at the head of the table. Everything was set. The new track had been built on the north side of town, just a trip across the tracks and up the towpath from the neighborhood where Taylor grew up and his mother was buried.

His family had temporarily relocated to Chicago. Though Gilbert, nearing sixty, maintained a mailing address in Indianapolis, Taylor wrote down a Chicago location in his 1898 date book. A notation shows he visited him after the Indianapolis races and before his return to the East for the big match race with Jimmy Michael. In all likelihood, the family had moved to Chicago—Major's younger brother and two sisters included—to live with the eldest sibling, Lizzie, and her husband. When she was widowed a year later the family returned to Indianapolis. It's tempting to imagine Gilbert renewing his employment with the Southard family, now firmly ensconced on the North Side of the city, but there's no evidence of what he was doing for work. Whatever his job, Gilbert didn't make the short train trip to Indianapolis, as many racing fans did.

Saturday was the last official day of the meet. The final was to be held in the afternoon so that the spectators could celebrate the hometown lad's victory in the evening at Broad Ripple Park, where everyone was welcome to free roller-coaster rides, a band concert, and a cruise on the canal excursion steamer *Sunshine*.

The weather on August 12 was perfect, and Taylor said he felt like it would take a lasso to pull him back. Though the Kentuckian Owen Kimble had unexpectedly defeated him earlier in the week in a middle-distance event, Taylor's forte was the mile. As he banked into the turn before the final straightaway, he was leading McFarland and could see the finish post. Spectators urged him on, screaming to him to look out. Others were firing rounds of blank cartridges from their revolvers, filling the air with the sound of "musketry." McFarland, his powerful legs hammering, his eyes focused on the small of his opponent's back, crept even with Taylor down the homestretch and thrust his long torso (and the bicycle frame beneath it) forward to break the tape a fraction of a second ahead. The predictions that this would be a record-setting performance were correct: McFarland's time of 1:58 shaved two seconds off the mile record in a competition (or non-exhibition) event and broke the mythical two-minute barrier. Afterward, the cycling press was at a loss to explain the outcome: "It was a remarkable occurrence in cycle racing history that two riders not considered first class sprinters should prevent a colored man from becoming a national champion," an Indianapolis writer summed up. "In the eyes of those who draw the color-line, the defeats of 'Major' Taylor by Kimble and McFarland were more due to a sort of heroism than to any speed abilities they possessed."

McFarland had, as he loudly predicted, wrecked Taylor's homecoming; Munger's, too. Almost worse still, he had done so cleanly. "A New Star," read a national headline, "F. A. McFarland." The Californian's "great effort" dropped Taylor to third in the national standings, one place behind McFarland.

About the only consolation Taylor could take from the day was the absence of his father. A seat had been reserved for Gilbert Taylor, but he had decided not to come. Why the elder Taylor would refuse his son's request on the biggest day of his life is hard to explain, except that perhaps he had a hunch. Having lost his wife only a year earlier, and having lost his stake long before that, he was accustomed to living with defeat. He didn't need to chance his son's.

CHAPTER 8

Civil War

OCTOBER 1898
TRENTON, NEW JERSEY

Progress is born of agitation. It is agitation or stagnation.
— EUGENE V. DEBS

In LATE OCTOBER, JUST TWO months later, a confident and well-prepared McFarland presided at another venue, this one off the track and behind closed doors. The top racers in America, witnessed by a few trusted newspapermen, were voting on a matter that had been hinted at for weeks: a new league run by the riders.

For two years now, McFarland began, shouting down the cackling gathering in Trenton, New Jersey, they had had no voice in the running of their league, with neither a vote nor a representative to advocate on their behalf. "Amateurs have been allowed membership, prize fighters, football and baseball players have all been eligible," he said, "but the poor professional racing man who makes an honest living and participates in the cleanest athletic sport known to the world today has been frozen out. . . . It's time for a change."

The riders in the room stamped their feet, pumped fists, and chanted, "Down with tyranny, Down with the LAW." The ensuing vote was unanimous: the top riders, minus a few absentees, decided to divorce themselves from LAW and create a new entity that would allow the riders and track owners unprecedented liberties. The cap on race purses would be lifted, encouraging bidding wars among competing race officials. Riders would not be forced to go to any race, nor would they be fined, but rather they would go where they wanted, when they wanted. The Grand Circuit, as McFarland called it, might involve ten races in the nation's biggest race cities; everything else was up for grabs. In addition, the moratorium on Sunday racing would be lifted—riders would be free to do what they wished, based on their religion, but the new organization would not prevent races from taking place on the Sabbath.

When LAW chief Albert Mott suggested that the riders' union was merely a ragtag group of disgruntled track owners and racers, McFarland was ready. The American Racing Cyclist's Union (ARCU) already had thirty-seven of the top prize winners in their camp and had agreements with every major track owner in the South and west of the Mississippi. The division seemed to suggest a racial component. With a strong coalition of southern and western tracks, the focus of the circuit would shift away from the East, and, more ominously for Taylor, away from the places he was welcome.

LAW hadn't been a crusader for equal rights. In 1894 it had, at the behest of its southern membership, agreed to bar blacks from membership. The impact on Taylor was, however, largely nominal since the bylaw applied to overall membership, not racing. Individual track owners were free to do as they pleased, and for most, at least in the East, it hardly made sense to exclude Taylor since he was a racer spectators wished to see in action. He put people in the seats. Ironically, as an irritated McFarland pointed out in his opening remarks at Trenton, the exclusionary membership laws weren't limited to blacks but affected racers of all persuasions. To be lumped into a low-class, bottom-dwelling category with blacks had been a pet peeve of McFarland's all along.

With the historic Trenton vote McFarland showed himself to be the most powerful man in the sport. He had effectively divided and conquered, bringing down one of the strongest organizations in America. "Our success," he predicted, "will be looked upon as one of the grandest accomplishments in athletic sports."

Taylor was not present at the meeting, and within hours the breakaway riders' union and LAW's Mott were battling hard for his support. Taylor's position was ticklish. At the time of the debate, the 1898 race season was coming to a close and Taylor was within a few points of being atop the national standings. Though in most people's eyes he was just in front of a "southerner from Kentucky bent upon beating out a colored man," Taylor was the odds-on choice to become the new American champion. He had to understand the risk of putting his destiny in the hands of his sworn rivals, but he couldn't help himself. He was so close. It was like Munger and his peerless bicycle, or Brady and his Broadway ambition—he couldn't control a certain impulse that boiled inside him. He agreed to join the other pro riders in ARCU.

Almost immediately he realized he had been played. The penultimate race for the national title was going to be held on a Sunday, even though McFarland's group had promised it wouldn't do that. It was Taylor's first time to wrestle with his conscience, though it wouldn't be his last. Were he to race on Sunday, Taylor knew he'd hear whispers that he was a backslider, a sporting man of cheap blood posing as a man of faith.

He chose to skip the race and await the final event in Cape Girardeau, Missouri. Arrangements had been made for him to stay at the home of a black hotelkeeper. When he went to the hotel for dinner he was told he'd have to eat in the kitchen. Outraged, Taylor packed his bags and returned to Worcester, sacrificing for the second consecutive year his chance at the national title. "They told me that if I failed to ride in the races that afternoon they would see to it that I was barred forever from the racing tracks of the country," wrote Taylor of McFarland and the other riders who now controlled the biggest U.S. events. "I replied I was not interested in the future but was deeply concerned with the present."

For the next several months Taylor's professional racing career was in limbo; he reapplied to the League of American Wheelmen, which was to run a rival slate of events, but a scorned Mott insisted he first had to pay a $500 fine.

McFarland had won once more. He was not only the mile champion for 1898 but the leading money winner. He had defeated Taylor, perhaps even exposed his weakness for wishing his troubles away— why else would he ally with the same men who months earlier vowed to "do" him. As threatened, the McFarland-led group followed up with a certified letter to Taylor's Worcester address notifying him of his lifetime ban. In essence they had figured out a way to isolate Taylor and impose a color line without imposing a color line. "Majah is not certain of his future," the *Boston Globe* reported. "He realizes that success for the secessionists probably means the closing of his career upon the path." It was a brilliant flanking move, with all the earmarks of a McFarland-engineered setup—one that Taylor had blithely walked right into.

For the first two years of Taylor's career it was McFarland's presence that haunted him. Now it was his absence. He couldn't get to him. They rode on rival circuits for the next two years. When Taylor won the world championship in Montreal in 1899 he did so in a diluted field lacking all the top pros, including McFarland. His national title in the same year—finally the American championship he'd hungered for—was similarly tainted. Eight of the top ten riders in 1899 rode on the competing circuit, not the one Taylor raced on. His victories—all but the ones against the clock—felt hollow. In boxing the challengers for the heavyweight title would stalk the champion, torment and slander him, hoping to coerce a weak moment when the champ could take it no longer and capitulate to a fight. McFarland, however, was perfectly insulated: Taylor had walked out on them. He had done himself in.

* * *

WITH MCFARLAND DOMINATING the new professional league, Taylor began to take an accounting. He had endured much. He had been chased from a training camp in Georgia. He had his national championship stolen. After he won a ⅓-mile sprint race at Tioga wearing the number 13 in the thirteenth event of the day, a *Philadelphia Inquirer* writer wondered if he had black magic at his disposal and recently been "among old Virginia ancestors hunting up some of their voodoo remedies."

He had found the business of living in a white world exhausting. Being a recognized black celebrity was difficult, too. A chasm was widening between the nation's foremost black leaders, Booker T. Washington and W. E. B. Du Bois. The former advocated patience, hard work, and vocational education—paying one's dues to show the white man, compel him to recognize, that one was worthy. Du Bois saw black advancement in a different light. Colored-only staircases, ticket booths, bathrooms, and drinking fountains added up to less than a whole existence, Du Bois argued. The black man wasn't being treated as equal and wouldn't be until he demanded equal rights. A half manhood was unacceptable; a period of proving was a degradation. Time was a-wasting. The age was about speed; what better application than a speedy correction of historic, century-old wrongs?

Marshall Taylor, coming of age, followed the speeches and activities of both leaders. He felt the same conflicts as civil-rights-era athletes caught between the fiery, emotion-laden rhetoric of Malcolm X and the restrained pleas for nonviolence of Martin Luther King Jr. Taylor thought he embodied the Washington model—influence and progress through reasonable accommodation—but was beginning to understand Du Bois' impatience.

When Taylor entered the season he saw himself as an ambassador for Washington. He was working hard, honing his skills as

Washington's Tuskegee students did. He tried to turn the other cheek when the episode in Savannah occurred, and wanted to get along in Missouri when he was told to eat out back. But he was finding another part of himself unable to resist a response. *Two souls, two thoughts, two unreconciled strivings, two warring ideals in one dark body.* He read Du Bois' soon-to-be famous words over and over again and he began, what in retrospect would be a personal journey as difficult and as elusive as an American championship.

When he returned to Worcester in 1899 he sought wholeness. He reached out to two areas he knew he could trust: church and family.

HE HAD FOUND A REFUGE IN WORCESTER, his adopted hometown. When he had first arrived as a sixteen-year-old in 1895 he had been so green, so earnest. Munger had been training him, but he had also put him to work in his bicycle manufacturing factory.

Taylor's speed had shone there, too. Speaking of Taylor's initial stint as a teenage machinist in a massive, sweaty Middletown factory, a foreman noted Taylor always tried to see how fast he could do everything, and "he would always have the machinery geared to the highest mark and turn out nearly double the amount of work as his fellow workmen."

Initially, he and Munger had lived in the Hotel Kimball, in downtown Worcester. Still an amateur, Taylor had made an immediate impression in his first eastern race. On October 20, the *Worcester Spy* noted, "Munger's protégé, Major Taylor, captures the Time Prize with a record of 29 minutes and 15 seconds" in a 10-mile road race with strafing headwinds. "Taylor is not well known here but he has a reputation of being a very fast man and his work Saturday demonstrated this fact." The paper went on to explain that Munger had kept up his interest in Taylor after retiring, and "were it not for Munger the Major would never have come to the city."

The former steel plant where Taylor worked when he had first come to Worcester was three stories high and long as a freight train—the biggest structure Taylor had ever seen. The onrushing heat had come from the basement, where a massive blast furnace raged to extract steel from iron ore, shapely lightweight tubing from solid hunks. Great swarms of hopeful men peering into fires had stamped out molds. The faces were exotic to Taylor—the linear Armenians, the round Irish, the dour Finns and Swedes.

Worcester wasn't considered one of the East's best-endowed cities. There was no sculpted harbor to receive immigrants, no long, deepwater docks to field shipments of exotic goods and people. Landlocked and surrounded by low hills, everything that Worcester was it would have to make itself. By the latter part of the 19th century the progress was astounding. Rail lines linked Worcester to New York, Providence, and Boston. Electric trolleys coursed down Main Street and great rivers of telephone wire hovered above, sizzling with voice traffic.

Immigrants came to Worcester like never before: Swedes, Irish, French Canadians, and, most recent of all, the war-stricken Armenians. Turf lines were established, with the Irish clustered on Shrewsbury Street, the Swedes in Belmont Hill, and the French Canadians along Hamilton Street. Water and Providence Streets were heavily Jewish. Southern blacks were also arriving at Union Station, leaving the fields, drawn to the city's steam, heat, and power.

The cornerstone for the city's new courthouse had recently been laid and was a newsworthy enterprise. A stately edifice with white Greek Revival columns, it would symbolize the people's ambition and a certain reverence for American justice. The courthouse occupied the east corner of Lincoln Square, a favorite of shoppers and fashionable strollers. The downtown trains were integrated, and at White City, the amusement park on Lake Quinsigamond, the rides were open to all who dared.

When Major Taylor arrived at sixteen, he had been an immigrant,

maybe the immigrant. No doubt the signs on the walls of the factory
captured Taylor's attentive eyes. One exhorted:

> *He rang in a little sooner*
> *Than the fellows in this shop;*
> *And he stayed a little longer*
> *When the whistle ordered "stop,"*
> *He worked a little harder*
> *And he talked a little less;*
> *He seemed but little hurried*
> *And he showed but little stress,*
> *For every little movement*
> *His efficiency expressed.*
> *Thus his envelope grew just*
> *A little thicker than the rest*

He had been worried. Like a small boy who has gone off to
school with his name sewed into his coat, he dutifully filled out the
blanks in a "things to be remembered" column of a small personal
diary: the number of the case of his watch, the number of the works
and his bankbook. His weight was 150 pounds, he wrote, his hat size
7¼, shoes a 6, and waist 32 inches. In a separate piece of paper taped
within, he added: "My name is Major Taylor. I am from Worcester
MASS. In case of accident please notify my sister . . ."

"I am from Worcester MASS." It was as if, like his parents in
Louisville, he was a shadow presence, an anonymous figure whose
hardships, or even disappearance, might not draw the notice of a
single soul.

BLACKS HAD BEEN COMING TO WORCESTER since before the
Civil War. Unlike its bigger, more famous neighbors, New York and
Boston, the city had a track record of caring. The keystone example:

In 1854, the active abolitionist community not only refused to sur-
render a runaway slave to a U.S. marshal but threatened to string up
the slave-catcher for trespass of the city limits. For a brief time
Worcester made headlines as a city of hope, principle, and virtue.
When Taylor arrived and walked down the narrow downtown streets
he saw what he had been told he'd see. "There was no such race
prejudice . . . as I had experienced in Indianapolis," he wrote.

He had been admitted to the YMCA without objection and
encouraged to race wherever and whenever he wanted. The papers
said there were hundreds of blacks who owned and rode bikes, a fair
percentage in a minority population no more than a thousand. The
Albion Cycling Club had started a few months before his arrival:
"Colored Cycle Club Coming," announced the *Worcester Telegram*
headline. "Latest Fad Among the Dusky Denizens of Worcester-
town—One Hundred Twinkling Wheels Form in Bright Array—
Maids of Ebon Hue Will Likely Join It, Too."

Back then he had traveled extensively for Munger, moving
between what were two factories, one in Worcester and the other
seventy-five miles away in Middletown, Connecticut. They had sales
offices on Wall Street, and the factory site in Worcester was extensive,
some seven acres on the footprint of the former New England Steel
Works. The other factory in Connecticut was a "magnificent works
completely fitted with the most modern machinery." The Special was
built there.

At a New Year's Eve gala—only days before the unveiling of the
Birdie Special at the 1896 New York City trade show—they celebrated their breakthrough with Gatsby-like excess. Select gentlemen
arrived at the company headquarters in black tie, their women in silk
and pearls. They danced to the Wells Brothers Orchestra until 3:00 A.M.
At some time in the giddy post-midnight hour the music stopped and
the dancers stepped aside to watch the protégé Taylor unveil the
Munger "wheel." Wearing his sleek racing uniform, the teenager

mounted the bicycle and ascended a plank not much wider than his
tire until he was six feet above the floor and peering down on a sea of
ruddy faces. Across a platform he went, then down a flight of stairs
as the room erupted with toasts to the brilliant architect and his
"dark secret." Wrote an admiring society reporter, "The burned-to-
a-crisp tamale swept along like a swallow on the wing."

That first winter in Worcester, in 1896, Taylor had trained with
weights and Indian clubs; he jumped rope and used a rope-and-pulley
Whitely exerciser every night at his apartment. By pulling the lines
overhead with his back to the machine he strengthened his shoulders;
standing spread-eagled with arms fully extended to the side, he drew
the taut lines to a point in front of his body, contracting the muscular
latticework across his chest. Mostly he cycled up the hill at George
Street, a 500-foot stretch that reared up like a steel mills smokestack.
The hill was an anomalous bit of extreme topography in Worcester.
The word was nobody could make it up the hill. Taylor rode the hill
two, three, and four times a day, rode it as long and hard as he could
until he couldn't turn over his pedals and he couldn't see straight.
When the wheels stopped, he fell to the ground.

In the two years since his arrival he had drawn close to the community. He was one of Worcester's own according to the local
papers. After the tumultuous 1898 season he invited his seventeen-
year-old sister Gertrude to stay with him. He had seen little future for
her in returning to Indianapolis with the others. Their brother John
was busy as an apprentice hatter, and his father was aging and having
difficulty providing for both her and the youngest of the Taylors,
fifteen-year-old Eva. Like the old days he took care of her: Taylor
enrolled Gertrude in the Worcester high school and brought her to
church with him. On Sunday, January 1, 1899, she was his witness
when he was formally welcomed into the flock at the John Street
Baptist Church.

*   *   *

BEHIND THEM WAS A SMALL gathering, perhaps fifty, in the
rows of pine pews. A powerful shaft of sunlight streamed through the
trinity of high south-facing windows. There was nothing ornate in
the interior, no extras; the fact that the little congregation had a
building was a miracle. Taylor, dressed in a dark suit, nervously awaited
judgment. "I did not see any great sights," he told the congregation
of his awakening, "but there was an inward rejoicing."

The Reverend Hiram Conway, draped in a simple gray cloak,
raised his glistening hand from the baptismal well. Taylor, a famous
man of twenty, bowed his head and waited. He had come to this little
white clapboard church, Worcester's newest, to sanctify his awakening of a year ago but also to continue the hard work, to apply the
same kind of force of will he applied on the track and in the gym. He
had been denied membership when he applied a year earlier. Pastor
Conway and the deacons had concerns about a sporting man, even
one who was an Endeavorer. They met in private and asked him to
kindly return in a year, so they could sit back and watch in the
interim.

He had sought out, on the face of it, an unlikely fellowship. The
evangelicals in the pews were older southern Baptists, some former
slaves. There were other black churches in Worcester that were more
prestigious, but he chose the southern-style one, where they ate pudding
bread, rattled the joint with singing, clapping, and dancing, and were,
in the view of their buttoned-up northern kin, "hopelessly heathen."

Perhaps Taylor was merely drawn to another underdog. More
likely the inscrutable sensation, already well regarded for his public
self-restraint and passivity, had found a refuge. There was no shame
in cultural heritage, no self-loathing for a face too black or lips too
full. He breathed anew, laughed out loud, and sang to be heard. It
would've been hard to distinguish between the trickle of holy water

on his cheeks and a rivulet of tears. Each Sunday his guilty sins were wiped away and he embraced the skin God gave him.

"I am not a religious crank," he once told a reporter, explaining his refusal to ride on the Sabbath, "nor anything else excepting a man who has his own ideas as to right and wrong."

His autonomy, and his willingness to embrace it, seemed to blossom after his New Year's Day confirmation. During the winter he independently traveled from city to city, promoting the same chainless bicycle he made famous at his record camp in Philadelphia. What was once only whispered he now floated out loud: at his next record camp he would be paced by an all-black team he had recruited and trained. It was a radical step, made more radical by the interpretation it received. "The novel record camp is to come in the spring before the season opens up, and the mark Taylor will go after will be the mile in 1:30," reported the *Freeman*. "It seems that Taylor believes that black men properly trained are faster than white men."

It was an idea that, oddly enough, had some support in the scientific literature. Increasingly there was evidence that blacks were superior to whites in the athletic arenas where they were allowed to compete. Of course, this was troublesome, especially with ever more attention and Anglo-Saxon respect paid to the ennobling efforts of cyclists, runners, boxers, and those select few deities who personified the luminous Greek concept of *agon*. The French whirlwind Baron Pierre de Coubertin, who had dug through the ancient rubble to reintroduce the Olympics after a lapse of 1,000 years, had given *agon* as the reason for all the bother. Roughly defined, he described it as the primal compulsion to seek personal supremacy. It was a hallowed gift.

In the scientific scramble to explain the contributing racial factors an academic consensus was reached in which the Negro was granted a physiological leg up. The *Encyclopaedia Britannica* noted a few of the physiological advantages, describing "the abnormal length of the arm, which in the erect position sometimes reaches the kneepan, and which on an average exceeds that of the Caucasian by about two inches," and "the low instep, divergent and somewhat prehensile great toe, and heel projection backwards." As *Sport and the Color Line* editors Patrick Miller and David Wiggins point out, the mainstream culture began to qualify the meanings of excellence in sport. The Caucasian was, in effect, at a perpetual handicap. It was a kind of reverse intelligent design but poetic nonetheless and absolutely reeking of *agon*. The reason the Floyd McFarlands of the world managed to win as often as they did was, in this view, a tribute to superior intellect. The Negro was a physical beast, like the ape. A sporting victory was confirmation that the Caucasian was the higher species and God's graced one; every loss was comparatively insignificant. Taylor's self-selected team of black cyclists might well be faster and might well win, but so what, it proved nothing in the larger context. Physical endowment didn't truly enhance the Negro race but rather confirmed its hierarchal woefulness. In the then-well-respected world of phrenology, where scientists equated cranial size with intellect, a Negro was ranked inferior to every other human race.

Publicly Taylor took the scientific backpedaling in stride, not wanting to waste his breath or chance his career with a hard rebuttal. But privately Taylor continued striking out, searching, and educating himself more diligently than ever. He recorded in a daybook the purchase of a copy of *Andrews Manual of the Constitution*—and his scrapbooks were cluttered with newspaper stories about pioneering black combat battalions serving in Cuba's equatorial Torrid Zone. Young men like Taylor were overwhelmed by the deeds of their enlisted brothers, uplifted by the brave Ninth and Tenth Cavalry and the Twenty-fourth and Twenty-fifth Infantry—black regiments all— which were said to have served with more distinction than any other fighting force in the Spanish-American War. He clipped and saved an article about the crusading black activist Ida B. Wells-Barnett and her refusal to ride a service elevator at Chicago's luxury Palmer Hotel. The activists speaking out, the soldiers returning, the all-black pace team he was assembling, and the swaying church people who regularly surrounded him—they were all reminders that he was not alone.

He had built himself back up and then some.

CHAPTER 9

No Limits

An Englishman is a person who does things because they have
been done before. An American is a person who does things
because they haven't been done before.

— MARK TWAIN

AT SEASON'S END MCFARLAND would have strode aboard
a westbound train and felt the joy of being a king. On a lavish Pullman coach towed along the scenic Union Pacific line,
he unfurled his long body in the comfort of unequaled luxury. The
"palace on wheels" featured inlaid wood interiors, elegant chande-
liers, and a waitstaff that could be counted on for libations as well as
betting lines. Out the window he would have seen sights hurdling
toward him that only a few years earlier were the province of explor-
ers—the Holy Cross Wilderness in Colorado, the rushing Yellow-
stone River, and the soaring big walls at Yosemite. The Pullman car
was a beautiful place to celebrate one's elevated place in the world: it
was quick, cozy, and—maybe most comforting of all to a racer—
dazzlingly fast. The elapsed time on the run from Chicago to Los
Angeles was down to sixty hours.

It was a time when a nationally worshiped sportsman such as

McFarland or a baseball player such as Cy Young brought out the admiring bands. Brady explained the people's peculiar attraction to athletes in an anecdote about an excursion of his with James Corbett, the former heavyweight champ, and William McKinley, the next president of the United States. A giddy onlooker turned to him and said, "Is that really Jimmy Corbett?"

Less humorously, the whitest of the white athletes seemed to hold sway. Cap Anson, an Iowan, had single-handedly commandeered baseball and forced the color line. The Ku Klux Klan was in its ascendancy and mob justice ruled throughout Georgia and border states. More than one hundred black men were lynched in 1900 alone. The indifferent northerner was one thing, but the southern bigot had resurrected himself as the fateful intimidator, the person who believed himself to be smarter, bolder, and more American than anyone else. The acceptance level for the racial hierarchy of the U.S. citizenry was never higher.

McFarland's constituency of fans was huge, especially in his native California. He was one of the state's first superstar athletes (he had long since eclipsed Otto Ziegler), and he was a man who took care of his own. He had made sure that the new race circuit would have as its sanctioning body the California racing association, thus shifting the axis of power from East to West. When his train pulled into San Jose he would have been met by applauding hordes, bands in uniforms, politicos, and members of the Garden City cycling club, all parading back to the McFarland and Juth saloon he ran with his brother James on Lightston Street.

Amidst the adulation he didn't sense a single thing wrong. But the ground was shifting again, and this time it would throw even him. The sport's growth had flattened and people's interest was wandering. Taylor's heroics at Philadelphia had whetted the appetite for more speed-busting efforts—people wanted to know where the barrier lie. McFarland understood Taylor had caused a commotion, but he believed the old-style circuit was still the mainstream crowd's fascination. He saw the Kentucky Derby and its 30,000 on-lookers in the fringed grandstands of Churchill Downs and he mapped out the same trajectory for bicycle racing: big tracks, big gates, a windfall for the track owners and riders alike.

As the season got under way he began to see the error of his projections. The gates were down. Cynical spectators had begun to sense that the sport was tricked up. According to an admonishing *New York Herald*, "The public has been so disgusted with these tactics that it is now no uncommon occurrence for a bicycle race to be ridden amid the vociferous jeers of an onlooking and not too easily fooled crowd." There were too many split purses, too many instances where riders were not representing Coubertin's "primal compulsion to seek personal supremacy." Betting scandals erupted seemingly every other week. McFarland came to realize that the absence of Taylor had hurt them: he had been a guarantee for spectators that the races were true and fair. With him gone, there was no knowing if the results were real or doctored. By season's end McFarland finished atop the standings table and had been invited to the Paris World's Fair—both laudable accomplishments—but the sport was in disarray and nowhere near the "great success" he had predicted a year earlier.

They were being done in by a fickle public; as Brady recognized, it was freak contests the people enjoyed, and there was nothing more freakishly alluring than massive objects hurtling forward. On June 30, 1899, on a railroad track on Long Island, an event diverted the public's attention so completely that the race circuit run by McFarland and the one run by LAW were knocked into almost complete oblivion. In an increasingly illustrative age it was the ultimate expression of death-defying speed: a lone cyclist chasing a speeding, heat-throbbing locomotive down the track.

*   *   *

CHARLES MURPHY, A SEMIRETIRED Brooklyn racer, had dreamed of the stunt for years. He said the limitation to maximum speed wasn't so much the racer as the bike, its gearing, and the apparatus doing the pacing. It was physics. In the absence of wind resistance, as with a home trainer, unthinkable speeds were possible. On a big-geared stationary bike he claimed speeds as fast as 80 mph. A ninety-one-ton express train going 60 mph would produce an almost magical vacuum. "There is not a locomotive built which can get away from me," he pronounced. The Long Island Rail Road agent, a wheelman himself, found himself persuaded.

On June 30, the day of the trial, a one-mile stretch of track at Maywood, New York, was specially fitted with a ten-inch-wide plank inside the rails. At the rear of the locomotive-drawn coach, a hooded enclosure had been constructed to surround Murphy and shield him from slashing wind currents. On his sixth and final trial, Murphy appeared to be losing ground when suddenly he found strength. In the final quarter mile he was moving faster than the locomotive as he closed to within feet of its protective bumper. The last push, through what he described as a "maelstrom of swirling dust and hot cinders," had nothing to do with training; rather, he appealed to the Lord, and the Lord answered. "The acceleration was wonderfully rapid," he reported. He was clocked at 57⅘ seconds for the mile.

How he was able to do what he did entranced the public. The phenomenon of pacesetting wasn't altogether new, but high-speed trials were. There appeared to be a magical zone in the slipstream of a bulleting object, a place where the normal physical laws did not apply, where mere mortals became gods. Jockeys had noticed it first— that it required less effort to ride in the pack than to lead. The drag was the air resistance. The lead cyclist took the brunt of the air's friction, while the follower was spared. But there was more to it, a truth hidden in the way particles interact.

Later sports scientists would try to demystify the lovely effect of following pace. Air resistance, they proved, increased exponentially with speed. A solo rider going 50 kilometers per hour needed approximately 600 watts of power. If he chose to go 40, however, the power requirement halved. Thus, negating air resistance was the secret to humans producing bulleting speeds.

They'd also find that the nonstreamlined elements of a bicycle, such as the tubes and the person powering it, produced a turbulent air wake with a low pressure region. The larger the pressure difference between front and back, the greater the frictional drag. When following another rider or riders or a motorized pacing machine, a pocket of plush, almost molecularly somnambulant air was created in the area inches from the leader's rear wheel. The effect wasn't a suction force, as many suspected with Murphy's stunt, but the absence of a monstrous drag force. Murphy's anecdotal observations were proven out. Going 25 mph, a pace follower needed to produce 30 percent less power than the leader. As the leader's speed increased— be it man, beast, or machine—the power gap widened. In layman's terms, a slipstream was magical.

Charles "Mile a Minute" Murphy—who the day after his record ride became the most famous cyclist in the land—changed McFarland's, Taylor's, and everyone else's program. Heretofore Taylor and McFarland's speed records had reigned supreme, both in the books and in the popular imagination, but Murphy's exploits altered everything. The public wondered anew where the threshold lay. If plain Charlie Murphy could travel 60 mph, what could men acclaimed as the world's best sprinters do?

Immediately Munger redoubled his effort, with hopes of finding a perfect straightaway and a pacing vehicle both less contrived and less hazardous than Murphy's No. 74 locomotive. He had actually assisted the Murphy effort as a kind of technical advisor and trainer; he had figured the minute mile was possible and had trained Murphy to improve his pedal stroke, but even he was surprised by the quick success. Now he had to duplicate the feat, but safely. He wanted to show it was not a cartoonish novelty or some masterly trick of illusion, but real and reproducible.

As Murphy recounted to rapt audiences, the risk in riding 60 mph wasn't so much speeding up as slowing down. Murphy had nearly run out of planking when the train's hulking brakeman leaned off the end of the rattling coach, summoning a "marvelous show of strength" as he hoisted the cyclist from under the armpits and deposited him in the coach.

The mile-a-minute feat had almost happened too soon, like a lab experiment that is expected to derive a clue, not the eureka. Murphy had described an alternative universe with slashing currents and unpredictable stillness, each falling right next to one another depending on his position behind the locomotive. It was a little like being atop a giant curling wave; at one moment you were safely riding on top, stretched out, sun-warmed, at perfect balance. But the next moment you were in a black liquid tornado, at the mercy of an energy system that was violent, deadly, and infinite. Murphy braced himself against the rattling air turbulence, utterly unaware of where the eddy was and how to get there. Depending on how you looked at it, he'd either gotten lucky or been blessed. He felt he had let go and hurtled into the realm where the self ends and divine force takes hold. Ever after, Charles Murphy was a changed man. He embraced religion—or, rather, was embraced by it. He had, in effect, found a higher power; the shape and form was yet to be determined.

Taylor wondered about the place Murphy had been. A part of him craved it; another part of him wasn't sure. Murphy's quest had nearly killed him. Taylor chose to focus on a more temporal though barely less challenging course: to revive the sagging race circuit. He failed. In Peoria, a peak-condition Taylor won all the races but didn't receive his $500 in earnings when the promoter slipped town. His expenses for the meet were $150. Quipped Taylor, "It cost me $150 to lose $500." It was the same story later in Janesville, Wisconsin.

The public's attention had turned to the spurts and starts of mechanical innovation; racers such as McFarland and Taylor were forced along for the ride. Several engine-equipped pacers were tried and discarded. The most popular design was a tandem bicycle fitted with either a gasoline or steam-powered engine. In Chaplinesque displays the "motor bicycles" exploded, didn't start, lost power. At Manhattan Beach a year earlier a heralded French-made electric bike broke down after traveling 20 feet, throwing its riders and showering trackside spectators with searing battery fluid. Fans came to watch blinding speed, immense firepower, human and mechanical synchronicity . . . but instead saw mishaps and a rushing cavalry of mechanics. There were insufferably long delays. When the machines worked, the hissing steam and smoke obscured views. Without mufflers to deaden the rumble, the noise was deafening. "To a certain extent the contests have lost some of their picturesqueness," lamented a cycling columnist.

Munger, almost more than Taylor, was on the hot seat. The financial support for a dream racing bike was gone, but a motorized bicycle spurred new commercial interest. He commissioned the Newton, Massachusetts, twins Freelan and Francis Stanley to produce a high-powered steam motor. To Munger's mind, steam pace was the only alternative, since the single-cylinder engine, though slightly more reliable, wasn't nearly powerful enough yet. The fastest things in the world were propelled by steam—ships and trains. The formula for success on a bicycle track—as opposed to oceans and the open country of transcontinental trains—was far dicier. The Stanley brothers, quirky Renaissance men who had successfully driven a steam-powered carriage through the streets of Newton a few years earlier, estimated that 800 pounds of water was necessary to produce enough steam to propel two riders and a 75-pound steel frame some 45 mph over the required distance. Thus, the prototype was saddled with massive boiler tanks that looked like mini-barn silos. The man in front was charged with keeping the motor bicycle upright, while the rider in the rear had the equally unattractive task of operating the motor. Most believed, especially after seeing the inaugural trials at the Charles River velodrome, that it was asking rather much of a bicycle. All summer the steam engine was on again and off again, mostly the latter. Most of the models were equipped with a conventional pedal-driven drivetrain in the eventuality that the engine didn't work. The Stanley brothers, notoriously elusive due to their dalliances in writing, photography, and violin making, worked slowly.

In late July, a month after Murphy's accomplishment, Taylor traveled to Chicago, which had the fastest track in the country. If Munger wasn't feeling enough pressure, he was greeted with the news that Taylor's latest rival, an old McFarland teammate named Eddie McDuffee, had just reduced the mile mark in New Bedford, Massachusetts. He had used a similar but far more reliable steam-pacing machine to notch a time of 1:28. As the week wore on, the troubles mounted. Munger's pacing motor didn't appear capable of sustaining speed; the best it could do was for a quarter or half mile. Some days it didn't work at all. The boiler leaked, valves stuck, and high-pressure explosions threatened. On one occasion the boiler tipped over and swamped the board track. Munger, at a veritable loss to explain the engine, proposed they switch tracks, leaving the wind-protected Ravenswood track for the exposed concrete one at Garfield Park. The pacing machine might benefit from a track with fewer turns, Munger said.

GARFIELD PARK, WEST of the city, was the lagoon-bordered centerpiece of a William Jenney–designed parks system. Soon to become heroic for figuring out how to plant skyscrapers in the famously thin Chicago soil, Jenney did not shrink from risk taking. His bicycle track was yet another example. For a man who made his reputation building straight, upright things, Garfield Park was his respite. It was circular, not oval like other tracks, and longer than normal—a half mile from starting post to starting post. Unwittingly he had created a perfect pace-following track. There was, however, a problem. Politically speaking, Garfield Park was quintessential Chicago in the amount of corruption found there. Monies earned at the racetracks, concessions, and amusements found its way into the strangest places. Around the time of the record bid the park was widely considered the most graft-filled enterprise in the city. Taylor and Munger would've had to pay a high, near-bankrupting user's fee, a fact that only added to their urgency.

On August 3, Munger and Taylor were a week into the record camp with no records. At 6:30 P.M. only a relatively small crowd was on hand at the track. Most had left when the machine had broken down earlier in the afternoon; it was thought so likely to break down again that a triplet of human pacemakers circled the track with instructions to listen for the low drone that would signal a failing steam engine. Taylor's bicycle was said to weigh a wispy twenty-one pounds and had been fitted with a gargantuan 114-inch gear. Machine and man began their warm-up orbits together, each needing time to produce maximum speed. In Taylor's case the gear was so large it took several roundings of the half-mile track to build up to his customary high pedal cadence. In the engine's case Munger needed to apportion just the right amount of steam—too much too soon and the motor might not have enough left in the final quarter mile, too little and Taylor wouldn't get enough pace to set the record.

At the three-quarters-of-a-mile mark, Munger turned the yellow monster wide open. Taylor fell behind briefly, then accelerated as they crossed the "flying start" line and dozens of official and unofficial stopwatches clicked in unison. Within a few yards, Taylor had tucked in within a few inches of the rear wheel, Munger an arm's length from his protégé, coaxing him to hold the wheel. Each quarter was faster than the last as man and machine hit maximum pace. Munger called out the splits: 20⅝, 19 flat, and 20 seconds. "Now spurt," cried Munger, as they approached the final turn. They crossed the line together, Munger in his "perverse" machine and Taylor on his diamond-framed bicycle. The time was 1:22⅖, a new world record.

It was the culmination of a year's worth of work for Munger. His exploration of the terrain beyond human pace turned into a hot field. In the limelight of the track speed trials the public and the business community saw the potential for an engine-powered bicycle. Later that year, the makers of the Orient would offer the first motorized bicycle for consumer purchase. A year after that a race circuit would be started. Inadvertently he had helped begin the new age and end the one he loved so dearly.

For Billy Brady it was a triumph, too. He had been the first to suggest Taylor should pursue speed trials. At Manhattan Beach he had brought in the biggest single-day gate of the year, some 25,000 fans. He had recognized, as he always did, the paying public's hunger for records and its titillation with the death and mayhem of a run-amok motor. More surprisingly, he had seen in Taylor the right combination of assets to produce a superb pace follower. It wasn't for the faint of heart, and some men weren't cut out for it. As mild-mannered as Taylor was, he possessed a feistiness both respected and feared. Undoubtedly part of his self-possession had to with Munger, who was inches away, urging him on. But there was more. "He is one of the most daring men on the track," said a rival. "I would not take the chances he takes, under any circumstances."

As for Taylor, there was more than a hint of how he felt about his accomplishments. In a fussy little daybook that records everything for the year 1899, from his hosiery size to his expenses, Taylor left a page or two for his more memorable personal visits. One of them, in Chicago, was to a long-lost boyhood friend, Dan Southard. The reunion—especially on such an auspicious occasion—would have pleased both.

THREE HOURS AFTER his Chicago triumph, Taylor left for Montreal and his first world championships. When he won the world championship title for the mile a week later in Montreal it was a modest story as compared to the record-setting duels. He also won the half mile. In the absence of other racing stars like McFarland no one much seemed to care. He was the first black man to hold a major sports world title and nobody gave a damn. He held McFarland accountable.

For a time Taylor returned briefly to the beleaguered LAW circuit, but in November he got a call again from Sanger, who told him McDuffee was in Chicago attempting more records. He had already broken Taylor's mark in Brockton, using steam pace and an innovative windshield. Sanger told Taylor to go wherever he needed to go to match the marks. Taylor, in a bit of gamesmanship, decided to surprise McDuffee in Chicago. "Chicago will be scene of the greatest battle that has ever been fought for the mile, the blue ribbon record of the cycling path," wrote a Chicago columnist.

For a week the Garfield Park trials were daily, same cement track, each rider attached to his own hurtling big engine machine at speeds of between 45 and 55 mph. McDuffee had added windshields, long V-shaped pieces of metal that enclosed the rider in a mini-vacuum. Taylor declared it a contrivance but followed suit. Each said he'd keep racing until the other quit. On November 14, though yelling at Munger to give him more pace, Taylor raised the bar with a 1:19 mile. The time was typically imprecise. Two of the timekeepers recorded 1:19, while a third announced 1:22. When a survey of bystanders watches revealed times of either 1:18 or 1:19, the track officials declared the third timepiece faulty. "I could have gone faster if the motor had gone," said Taylor, "I did not find the slightest trouble clinging to it."

Two days later a defeated McDuffee left Chicago and announced his intention to retire from cycling and go into the automobile business.

MUNGER'S MACHINE WAS A FICKLE PIECE of machinery that acted like a wayward child. It seemed human in its perversity. Yet by the end of the trials, there was renewed hope in its dependability. According to the prevailing rumor, Taylor intended to challenge Murphy's mile-a-minute time. Munger and a team of a dozen men had fanned out around the country from New Jersey to Florida in search of the right stretch of roadway. Three miles of telephone wires had been acquired with the notion of constructing an electrical timing device that would be beyond reproach. "Give me the pick of track and day, and a little warmer than I had at Chicago and you will see me reel off a 1:10 mile, and make no mistake. I will do it on a regulation track too," said Taylor. "Such time on a good strip of road would be dead easy."

Everything seemed ready to go, but the effort was never mounted, and he never explained why. Whatever regret he had at forgoing the ultimate trial was tempered years later. Harry Elkes, a fearless pace specialist and regular rival of Taylor's, was traveling at nearly a mile a minute on the Charles River track in Cambridge, Massachusetts, when his tire burst. With 10,000 horror-struck witnesses looking on, he was killed instantly.

CHAPTER 10

Something at the End

1900

AMERICA

O God, be with us in our trouble. Teach the people who
control this city that we have immortal souls,
however black we may be.
—A MINISTER AFTER A RACE RIOT
IN THE TENDERLOIN NEIGHBORHOOD
OF NEW YORK CITY

STILL, THEY WERE BUILDING racetracks everywhere one
looked. It was like a civic necessity—an event of any stature
required a racetrack. At Indianapolis in 1898 the occasion had
been the national LAW convention. Architect Herbert Foltz, a wheelman whose design credits included the city's elegant YMCA building,
overlooked nothing. Miles of copper wire provided for fifty electric
arc lights for night racing, while the bleacher stands were a nonstan-
dard width for maximum comfort. Box seats were only five feet from
the track. There was piped-in water for hot and cold showers, eighty-
five rubbing boards, and a staff of hundreds. The quarter-mile track
itself was made of matched and dressed white pine boards that were
wire-brushed once against the grain and once with it, then dipped in
a wood preservative before being nailed down with the rough side of
the plank up. The two-minute tracks of old were already outdated.

The new, aggressive whaleback design accounted for swifter, more pace-friendly transitions.

The tracks were testimony to an age. They were put up to mark territory, to instill pride, to dwarf the settled landscape like church steeples. But increasingly they were half full or even nearly empty. The sport was on the wane, or at least the version of the sport that had been popular a few years ago, and the sheer drama of erecting a giant structure no longer promised an audience. People's attention roamed. In 1899 Stanley's Steamer went up the carriage road at Mount Washington, the highest peak in the Northeast, in a time of two hours. The endurance feats were the precursor to shorter, more dynamic forms of racing, just as they had been with bicycles. The motorized machines were gaining.

Opportunity increasingly seemed to be abroad. Horse racing was in the midst of a deep decline in the United States, with many future Hall of Fame jockeys fleeing for Europe and better paydays. "European racetracks seemed paved with gold," wrote Ed Hotaling in his book *Wink*. "It was the only major talent drain ever in American sports." There was a sense among bicycle racers that their time was perilously short and the money about to go away. Maybe it was time to jump.

Taylor felt it. He was world champion, the premier paced sprinter in the world, possessor of seven world records, and arguably the national champion, but he had little to show for it. Floyd McFarland felt it. He started the 1900 season training in Arkansas, hopeful that he could find a niche nobody had thought of. The handicap king knew his brand of racing was no longer in vogue. He vowed to remake himself as a middle-distance match racer or as a motor pace follower. He resuscitated Jimmy "Midget" Michael, bringing him back to New York for a series of duels. McFarland was Gulliver, Michael a Lilliputian. Just seeing the two of them together was entertaining. McFarland was plucking money where he could, but he couldn't escape the truth: he ruled a sport that was crashing in on itself. Once upon a time the game had seemed plenty robust enough to support Taylor and McFarland on their respective race circuits. Now, the two began to slowly gravitate back to each other, precipitated by economics but furthered by something more primal.

In the summer an offer came McFarland's way to race abroad. Initially he wasn't interested, but with the U.S. scene looking slack he and his San Jose sidekick, Orlando Stevens, and Detroit's Tom Cooper got on a steamer and headed to France for a series of championship events to coincide with the World's Fair in Paris. He was the first prominent American athlete to be brought to Europe in a decade. As a symbol of sorts—of both his own tenaciousness and the dominance of the American "breed"—he also shipped across his race circuit companion, a large pet bulldog named Bullie.

The Exposition Universelle de 1900 was many things to many people. Described as a "force of unequaled attraction," cycling occupied as large a space at the fair as any of the French interests: it was somehow telling that the amateur victors were rewarded with the country's other formidable passion, artwork. A brand-new stadium for 45,000 was erected at Vincennes called the Parc du Princes. A slate of events included all the popular disciplines, sprinting races, marathons, team pursuits, and middle-distance events. The sporting agenda at the World's Fair dwarfed the Olympic Games in Athens: a record 1,500 foreign athletes came to compete in Paris, compared to just eighty-one at the 1896 games. There was an anticipation bordering on insanity as race day neared and national fervor built.

McFarland led a U.S. racing team that was backed by Albert Pope's American Bicycle Company, a massive enterprise on its way to buying out more than fifty struggling U.S. bike manufacturers. Pope's desire to see McFarland and the others do well was evident: he would be in attendance in France, hoping to show American might and superiority. When it looked like McFarland wouldn't be able to compete because of some race circuit misbehavior back in the States, he quickly took care of what was at the time an astronomical $400 fine.

And McFarland didn't disappoint his patron. He whipped the French cracks, taking two of the most prominent events in September, a 25-mile paced race against their middle-distance star, Constant Huret, and the Grand Race of Nations, a three-man relay at a sprint distance of 1,500 meters. The Frenchman Edmond Jacquelin, a beloved national hero who was expected to dispatch the Americans, was winless in the major events when the final exposition-closing match race took place on October 21 at the Parc des Princes. A full crowd was in attendance and redemption the order of the day. As the two combatants approached the start line, McFarland began to gesticulate to the officials, obviously displeased with something. Within minutes the overflow crowd was told the American had refused to start, complaining of the sodden track conditions. A card was displayed announcing that Jacquelin would ride the course alone.

When the Frenchman's pacing tandem broke down, however, the time trial event was postponed. "The spectators placed the blame for their disappointment upon the visitor and nearly mobbed him," wrote the *New York Time*'s Paris correspondent. Thousands had stormed the track and looked to exact revenge. Seeing the feverish anti-American anger and fearing a deadly riot, the track manager, Henri Desgrange, expelled the Americans and all other foreign riders for the duration of the fair. When McFarland came ashore in the United States in November he said he had earned $3,000 for his trouble. He didn't really seem bothered. The hullabaloo was rather ordinary for him, even if it did happen at the single biggest, most prestigious international sporting competition in the modern era.

The event had left its mark on him, however. He had loved the bohemian carnival of Paris, the sensuous appetites, the illicit liaisons,

sultry Montmartre. It was live and let live. A pile of gambling-related
suicides in Nice and Monte Carlo—several of them American—
curtailed no one. The Moulin Rouge, the Café Américain, and the
Folics Bergère filled nightly despite sordid tales of lost souls. Increasingly innocent American women were said to be lured to the gaming
tables by bankrupt men of title. "The American colony is fairly hum-
ming with gossip about certain American society women whose revels at Monte Carlo would be considered scandalous at home," a U.S.
newspaper reported. McFarland drank it all in, wishing he could
bottle the place and bring it back to New York. They'd all be rich.
His appetite wasn't near sated.

His hosts asked him repeatedly about *le nègre:* what was he like,
would he come over and race? McFarland, sensing the direction
of things, began to consider a plan that was outrageous even by his
outsized standards: a partnership with Taylor. Why not? He could
put aside almost anything—in Taylor's case, a lifelong grudge—if the
result was a windfall. He really had no ironclad convictions about
right and wrong, as Taylor had put it, only what was profitable and
what was not. He was a capitalist, a good one.

Taylor, conversely, was not. The Paris Exposition organizers had
offered him $10,000 to compete in the same races as McFarland, but
he had said no.

ON THE HEELS OF HIS RECORD-BREAKING season, Taylor
had been the obvious choice to go to the World's Fair in Paris. An
emissary of the organizers had come to Worcester in the spring and
personally extended the offer. The catch was he had to race on Sunday, which even a hundred-plus years later remains the traditional
race day in Europe. There were several reasons to seriously consider
the offer, not the least of which was his frustration with U.S. racing.
In December the League of American Wheelmen had disallowed his
second batch of records at Chicago, saying the windshield was an

illegal aid. In January a weakened LAW dissolved altogether, abandoning the racing scene once and for all. Taylor, the one stalwart for the original league, was left high and dry. The McFarland-led stars league had no intention of reinstating him, not yet.

Meanwhile, Taylor's reputation had actually been blemished at the world championships in Montreal despite his spectacular and historic wins. Organizers had demanded he race the amateur mile champion, Tom Summergil, to determine the grand overall champion—a kind of match race itself between the villainous pro and the angelic amateur worlds—but Taylor had refused, saying he had no interest in doing so when there was no prize money offered. Several newspapers took the opportunity to skewer him. "Major Taylor refused to fulfill his obligations as a sportsman today," wrote a New York columnist. "He developed a grand streak of yellow."

Personally, he was distraught. His younger sister Gertrude, whom he'd brought to Worcester to live with him, was seriously ill. He'd delayed his record attempts when she was diagnosed with tuberculosis in the fall. Only nineteen and a third-year student at Worcester's high school, she'd been confined to bed rest in January. Taylor had spent the winter trying to nurse her back to health. He had gone to extraordinary lengths, including spending most of his race earnings to purchase a large, fancy house in a fashionable new development for her convalescence. He didn't want to admit her to a hospital. His notebook is full of notations about the expenses: the charges for insurance, furnishings, drapes. "She was delighted with her new home," wrote a newspaperman, "but was only able to leave her room once after she had entered."

The house purchase, meanwhile, had caused an ugly firestorm of controversy that put an edge on his relationship with Worcester. The two-story still stands today, though not as the brilliant showpiece and first-rate residence it was described as a century ago. Several of the "Worcester 400," those residents who owned homes in the "swell section" of the city, objected to a black man living in their upscale West End neighborhood. The chastised seller, who said he originally mistook Taylor for someone's coachman, offered to buy it back for twice what he had paid for the house but Taylor refused to back down. "I don't know why I haven't as much right to buy a place . . . as any man in town," he said, sounding exhausted.

Gertrude Taylor's condition worsened. On Sunday, April 20, she passed away at Taylor's 2 Hobson Avenue home. Taylor accompanied the body back to Indianapolis, where she was buried, like her mother, in Crown Hill Cemetery. The family once more reunited on the occasion of a death. Gilbert, Eva, and John were back living on the North Side, while Taylor's older sisters had also returned to Indianapolis. What had become of William Taylor, who had looked after Major Taylor during the Six-Day and the turbulent 1897 season, was unclear. Unlike their mother, Saphronia, whose obituary was eventful and complete, Gertrude was virtually unknown in Indianapolis, having lived part of her young life in Chicago and Worcester. The funeral was accordingly small. It was the second burial Taylor had arranged in three years, and he memorialized her by having a Worcester newspaper publish Eugene Field's poem with her death notice:

> *Out yonder in the moonlight, wherein*
> *God's Acre lies,*
> *Go angels walking to and fro, singing their*
> *Lullabies:*
> *Their radiant wings are folded and their*
> *Eyes are bended low,*
> *As they sing among the beds whereon the*
> *Flowers delight to grow:*
> *"Sleep, oh, sleep:*
> *The Shepherd guardeth His sheep:*
> *Fast speedeth the night away.*

Soon cometh the glorious day:
Sleep, weary ones, while ye may—
Sleep, oh, sleep!"

Amidst all this tumult the French offer hung like a biblical temptation. Throughout the spring there were rumors about his pending decision. Taylor had said yes, the newspapers reported, betraying his own principle never to race on Sunday. The articles ridiculed Taylor as just another sporting man, no better, no worse—or maybe worse, actually, because he had claimed to be better. He was a hypocrite. "Love of fame and a thirst for coin have conquered the religious scruples of Major Taylor," a columnist began.

The Sunday question wasn't just a personal quandary for Taylor; it was an ongoing, passion-filled national debate for workaday Christians throughout the country. The desecration of the Lord's Day was seen as the road to ruination, a brand of backsliding that disrespected all those who put their faith first. For Taylor, the consequences were dire: he himself wasn't merely a backslider, in the Baptist Church's view, but an example of a poor conversion, a Judas who brought disgrace upon himself and the church and people who spawned him.

There was no wiggle room, no provision for extenuating circumstances. Your soul was either saved or it wasn't. He felt the eyes of not just his mother and his sister but also his church upon him. How would his congregation at John Street react if he abandoned the Sunday dictate? Would they merely whisper among themselves, or, indignant, would they rescind his Worcester refuge?

Taylor's reported decision didn't make sense to Munger. Months earlier, at the Woodside Chicago track, Munger had almost had a row with Taylor over his uncompromising Sunday stand. He had been working on the pacing motorbike prior to the decisive last week. If the machine wasn't repaired, they'd have no chance at a record—or a payday, since Taylor's employer was commissioning him only in the event of a record. Taylor happened onto the workshop, looked at the half-disassembled motorbike, and asked Munger to stop his work. It was Sunday. The two argued, but Taylor threatened to quit the trials if Munger didn't stop working. Of course Munger's point was that Taylor, even when his best interests weren't in it, was committed to his principles. What, he wondered, had come over him?

As the spring progressed Taylor evidently experienced a change of heart and stoically decided to reject the European offer. There was more criticism, this time from the black community, including the Indianapolis-based *Freeman,* which suggested he was a fool and wondered why it was that the white man got the money but the Negro got religion. "We all want to go to Heaven I believe, but as we are here and will probably stay for a while yet, let us seek for some of both," the columnist urged. "Go to Europe Major and show the world that you are without a peer."

Taylor's conflicted sentiments ultimately came forth in an odd place, the letters-to-the-editor section of a small newspaper in northern New Hampshire. Taylor's response was to a letter writer who had congratulated him for his uncompromising faith. "Your letter brought much encouragement and just at the right time too; for sometimes it comes to me so forcibly that it seems as a mountain to overcome," he began.

> I need some money very bad just now and that only makes the temptation all the stronger. It isn't as though I had lots of money and could afford to say I don't need to race on Sunday, and I am sure if the general public knew my heart as God knows it, they would appreciate what I am doing even better than they do. I am laboring under the greatest temptation of my life, and I pray each day for God to give me more grace and more faith to stand up for what I know to be right. . . . I could do no different now if

I wished. I have no fear for the future for I feel that I will be taken care, although things seem very cloudy at present.

IN EARLY DECEMBER the sport's last best chance to regain the fans' trust was the Six-Day race at Madison Square Garden. It was the race that had launched Taylor's professional career, and to a large extent that of every professional rider in America. In 1900 it was seen as the hoped-for kickoff to a new revival in American racing. Unfortunately, social reformers and New York governor Theodore Roosevelt were gumming things up by threatening to prohibit the event unless their humanitarian concerns were addressed.

Billy Brady, hoping to save the sport, stepped in to suggest a compromise: Teams of two (thus sharing the inhumane misery) would ride the six days, this time with neither rider allowed to pedal more than twelve hours per day. The same rules and objective applied: to accumulate the most miles over a week of racing. With only a few days to spare, Governor Roosevelt signed a legislative bill, and the two-man compromise—which Brady later characterized as a desperate bid to "salvage something out of the wreck"—went ahead as planned.

In a twist that nobody anticipated, McFarland approached Taylor and asked him to be his racing partner. McFarland, financially secure after his Paris adventure, explained that he was looking at semiretirement as an active racer but wished to continue in the sport as a manager. He knew how bad Taylor wanted to race in Europe. Mac had been there, could walk him through the countries, the contacts, everything. He knew he could negotiate the best possible deal. He conceded that if Taylor was able to beat the fastest riders in the world, and McFarland said he thought Taylor could, then he could rightfully be called American and world champion. "He wants Taylor to cross with him early next season, and race in the spring," the

Worcester Telegram reported. "McFarland will devote himself to racing behind motor machines in middle distance racing."

The proposal was brilliantly seductive: sworn enemies bound together for the most hellish race on the planet, in the most flamboyant and lawless city in the world. It would be the greatest attraction the cycling world, and possibly the sporting world, had yet seen. McFarland's timing was perfect, mirroring an epic move in a hotly contested championship race. He had come out of nowhere with a jump off the high, steeply angled banking; he had slotted through a pocket with seemingly no gaps. McFarland had once again pounced when everybody least expected it.

Taylor was flabbergasted. It was like the late Governor George Wallace offering the lieutenant governorship to Martin Luther King Jr. in the 1960s. At first Taylor accepted—almost, it seemed, because he could think of nothing to say. It was a practical solution to both men's problems, which for the moment were money and the sport's declining popularity. Taylor hadn't had much elbow-to-elbow racing contact with McFarland in the last two years, and undoubtedly the latter dangled the prospect of reinstating Taylor for the 1901 U.S. racing season.

On November 22, two weeks before the race, Taylor walked away from the lucrative deal. He was diplomatic, saying his new bicycle sponsor, Iver Johnson, wished him to focus on sprint records and he couldn't very well do both. He probably also did some research and understood that McFarland had made his share of enemies in Europe, something that would adversely affect his ability to be his liason. But more than any of it, there was a sense of feeling dirty, of gross opportunism. He was different than McFarland and the others, wasn't he?

Not fond of being said no to, and even less fond of losing a career-closing payday, McFarland privately vowed a holy war. He and Harry Elkes, a lanky middle distance sprinter from the Buffalo area, entered as a pair instead. He wouldn't have Taylor as his drawing card, but McFarland figured he could still hawk the idea that two sprint-distance specialists were challenging the turf of the endurance warlords.

But there was more. To sweeten the racing bill, McFarland had helped bring a new element to the Six-Day—foreign teams. There was a tandem team from France, one from Switzerland, another from Canada. With national pride at stake, the event took on immense drama. Crowds poured into the Garden day after day. As a hedge against boredom, there would also be periodic sprint match races. The poor living-dead cyclists would be shooed down onto the inner apron while the speedsters orbited around them.

One of them, much to McFarland's discomfort, was Marshall Taylor. His opponent was Tom Cooper, the Detroit crack who had accompanied McFarland to Europe earlier in the year and had gamely trounced the French champ Jacquelin. If Taylor could beat Cooper, he would be, at least on paper, the equal of Jacquelin. Cooper also represented a personal score to settle for Taylor. He was considered a McFarland lieutenant, one of those who had kept Taylor barred from racing. For two years the openly racist Cooper had refused to meet him. Brady stepped in. Scheduled for the December 9 opening night, the pair met in a series of mile heats before 7,000 spectators with a $500 purse for the man who took two out of three.

The Garden track had been refurbished and steepened for faster times. In the box seats, which were literally squared-off sections with the grandstand throngs pressing behind them, were such luminaries as the actor Joseph Jefferson and the Union Pacific giant E. H. Harriman. The gamesmanship began the moment Taylor left his training quarters.

"Tawm has a fine assortment of brand-new tactics, fresh from Paris . . . and will proceed to hand your little darkey the most artistic trimming of his young life," drawled Cooper's manager, the irrepressible Tom Eck. A contemporary of Munger's who was a teammate in the Chicago high-wheel days, Eck had played an influential behind-the-scenes role in LAW's 1894 vote to impose the color line. "I have cautioned Tawm," he added, "that in the best interest of the sport and for the good of all concerned, not to beat the little darkey badly."

Taylor was determined not to be outsmarted. In the early part of the race he counted Cooper's pedal revolutions and compared them to his own. A sprinter at full gale might spin a midsized gear at 160 revolutions per minute. If they were going the same speed, a slower cadence meant Cooper was winding up a larger gear. Racers experimented with a variety of gearing arrangements based on the type of rider they were, tactics, and race format. In paced races behind motorbikes Taylor and others employed huge gears since once they pulled in behind the pacing machine the work they did was lessened by the draft effect. In a match sprint or handicap race their choices were more difficult since a bigger gear meant more power but also sizeable risk. Gear inches had been the standard in use since the high-wheel days and referred to the diameter of the wheel. One hundred gear inches was the workload equivalent of budging a story-high wheel. By knowing a rival's cadence and speed you could easily compute the gear he was using.

When Taylor figured out the size of Cooper's gear he almost immediately knew what race strategy to expect. Cooper monstrous cog—108 inches verses Taylor's 92—meant Cooper would try to get "the jump on me down the steepest part of the banking," where he could get his big gear turning over to keep him away. "I knew that once he got that big gear rolling it would be a very difficult task for me to beat him out at the finish line."

As forecast, Cooper began edging away from the pole so he could use the high banking to drop into top speed. At the same moment he began his gradual buildup, Taylor jumped, suddenly giving "him everything I had." Taylor was twelve lengths ahead with a lap and a half to go. Though later, in his autobiography, Taylor said that he'd originally intended to ease back and allow Cooper a dignified finish, instead he abruptly accelerated. Sounding slightly contrite, Taylor wrote later that this race was the first time he ever tried to humiliate an opponent and his manager. In the second heat, Taylor continued his generalship of the track, faking Cooper repeatedly with threatened jumps each time Cooper tried to rise up the banking. Fearful of a repeat performance, Cooper was forced to come back down and mark Taylor. Without the banking to work with, he was late in unwinding his big gear, and though Taylor stopped pedaling with a lap to go, thinking the race was over, he still won by half a bike length. "If ever a race was run for blood this was," Taylor confessed.

Cooper's career was effectively over. The disheartened champion would never be the same rider, retiring just a year later to claim a coal mining stake in Colorado. In a letter back to his friends, Cooper said he had a "good thing in his hole in the ground." It was as if a defeat to Taylor sucked a vital force from his rivals—what also happened to Michael and then the time-trialing demon McDuffee. He was knocking off one "unbeatable" after the other—first Cooper, next Europe, and last but not least McFarland.

WHILE TAYLOR AND COOPER were battling, the Six-Day race continued at full throttle. The pace was ferocious—some said suicidal. Unlike the Six-Days of old, the teams were able to keep pace with each other, thereby building (and some suspected manipulating) the suspense to the final cataclysmic day. Not that there weren't legitimate heroics. McFarland, new to the long-distance game, was singled out in particular, having overcome one concussive fall after another. In one accident on the next-to-last day several teams went down, with three foreign riders requiring emergency medical care. Half the fourteen-team starting field had had to quit. Defending champion Charley

Miller, the Chicago grocer who'd managed to get married en route to his victory in 1898, busted his collarbone. The whole field suffered from extreme exhaustion, cramping, and bronchial distress due to the suffocating levels of smoke and dust hovering above the track.

Meanwhile, the side intrigues mounted. Onlookers watched as the various race camps sent emissaries to the others, evidently discussing tactics and who knew what. There were strange uncustomary lapses where nobody was on the track, and mysterious potions transformed moribund riders into robust, sprint-primed condition.

At ten o'clock on Saturday three teams remained in contention. To some observers, including the race's creator, Brady, the event was already a farce. "It's just some hundred and forty-odd hours of stalling, interspersed by artificially staged sprints, and then a last hour of furious pedaling to make it look like something at the end," wrote Brady. "Those may be harsh words, but nobody has a better right to run a thing down than the fellow who invented it."

The McFarland-led U.S. team had a slight lead on a Canadian pair in the final lap, while the French were a lap down. There was no dynamic finish, the papers reporting that the teams were "evidently content with their positions." McFarland and Elkes crossed the tape victorious, having accumulated 2,628 miles. A flag-waving victory lap in front of 12,000 spectators should have been a triumphant moment for McFarland, the battle-weary victor.

But days later the scandal broke: the race had been fixed, with McFarland getting the help of the second-place Canadian team in return for a promised split of the first- and second-place prize money. Knowing that the Europeans Jean Gougoltz and César Simar were superior sprinters, he had persuaded the Canadians to block the foreigners to keep them from getting close. The Canadians had spoken out only after McFarland backed out on his promise to split the $2,500 in earnings.

But there was more. Reports leaked out of widespread doping

abuse—McFarland included—in the latter portions of the race. Moreover, the newly humane race had resulted in its first casualty, the Brooklyn rider Oscar Aronson. The twenty-five-year-old died at New York Hospital a day after his spill, with doctors citing as causes his spine-damaging crash and the Garden's foul, smoke-filled air, which led to pneumonia.

It was one of the biggest disasters in the history of American cycling; it didn't mark the end of the U.S. cycling circuit, but the league would never again regain its luster, that crucial Hellenic glow. Instead, the circuit races began to take on another form, with crowds clamoring for the only discipline they knew was real, the big, noisy, pace-following events against the clock. Not coincidentally, it was easily the most dangerous, life-risking thing you could legally pay to see.

CHAPTER 11

La Belle Epoque

PARIS 1901

Make a little fence of trust
Around today
Fill the space with loving work
And therein stay
Look not through the sheltering bars
Upon tomorrow
God will help thee bear what comes
Of joy or sorrow

— MARSHALL TAYLOR
(WRITTEN FOR DAISY MORRIS)

MARSHALL TAYLOR WAS THE LONE person keeping the heaving, scandal-torn sport out of the gutter. Jay Eaton and Orlando Stevens, both racers and members of the rider's executive board, had recently confessed to race fixing at the popular Vailsburg track in New Jersey. By contrast, the pious Taylor cruised, untouchable, above it all. Almost daily columnists wrote about his religious devotion and sportsmanship, and in a more general (though incredulous) sense that he was "very white for a colored person." He was so clean and the sport so dirty people speculated on his comeuppance, on the moment—the right amount of

159

money, the leggy, blond-haired flirt—that would make his righteous façade crumble. There were salacious rumors about him being married or keeping a woman somewhere in private. Was she white? A working girl? Kinky-haired?

"It's really surprising the number of people who seem bent on having me married," he told the *Worcester Telegram*. When he bought his marvelous house at 2 Hobson Avenue and spent a reported $1,000 on furnishing it, tongues went wagging once more.

Amused for the most part, Taylor sometimes played along. Once he leaked the Chicago address of his supposed mystery bride, sending a phony telegram to "Mrs. Major Taylor, Dearborne St., Chicago." Within twenty-four hours news stories appeared in the Worcester, Boston, and New York papers with the gist being, *Aha! It's true!* "Taylor a Benedict," screamed a headline. "Colored Cyclone Has Been Married a Year . . . Has Dusky Bride in Chicago." Then somebody knocked on the door at that address on Chicago's South Side. The occupant was Taylor's sister.

In truth Taylor *was* looking for companionship. He was twenty-three. He had a large, well-furnished home that he now occupied by himself. His kid sister was dead, and the rest of his family lived 1,000 miles away. If not chaste, Taylor was exhaustingly careful and scrupulous with his personal affairs. Given the concern his church application caused, he felt judging eyes upon him. Sometime in the early fall, however, within the respectable setting of a Worcester church social, he met a woman who would complete him. The speed with which it all happened was dazzling, but then romance was not immune to the law of the track. A rider could lie in wait for most of a race, but when the right opportunity presented itself he jumped. An impression sparked the ignition; the rest was mystery. What Taylor saw he never described; all he said was that he jumped. "It was love at first sight," he wrote in a letter years later.

Her name was Daisy Morris, and they met a few days after the

1900 season ended. It was October 11, 1900, a date recorded with a soaring flourish in his personal daybook. It was a Thursday, a fair but improving day in a week worth of nor'easters and sea-surging gales along the New England coast. The occasion was likely a mid-week Christian Endeavor social, a newfound staple of the young adult's social life. A magic lantern show was typically on the docket, the still, hand-colored images writ large with a primitive brass projector and a showman's fast hand so that the giddy illusion of cinematic motion rose in front of disbelieving eyes. Women and men sat on opposite sides of the aisle, sneaking looks toward members of the opposite sex in the smoky glow of refracted light. It's tempting to imagine images of a bicycle race before the assembly, but more likely it was the recently concluded Paris Exposition they saw and heard, the wizardry of the emcee encompassing not only a blizzard of light but the romantic Gallic accents, the melodramatic pitch and yaw of orchestral strings, the future.

Daisy was new to the city, the young ward of the Reverend L. H. Taylor (no relation). She was tall and light-skinned, with a refined, stately bearing that made her seem much older than her twenty-four years. She had a way about her that was beyond composed: it was as if the careening world slowed down in her presence to a manageable and civilized pace. Taylor would have wondered why a single woman had left her family and he would have known there was a story to her arrival in Worcester, just as there had been a story to his. Intrigued, he learned that she was boarding at the African Methodist Episcopal Church on Sever Street. Her interest in the Endeavorers pleased him; both were well acquainted with the idea that the success of their conversion—she had been saved, too—was dependent upon the company of like-minded servants who could administer "loving interest." The promise of the Endeavorers was that God would take care of them if they walked the right path, looked in the right places, joined in fraternal harmony with the right kind. Taylor had found comfort in his belief, an intimacy with the fellowship. Now his focus, like the beaming, aggrandized image on a magic lantern screen, was directed to one.

When the two met Taylor had just signed a contract with a well-known Boston vaudeville producer to perform a series of stationary bicycle races against none other than Charles "Mile a Minute" Murphy. The inaugural shows the following week would be in Worcester, with the two sporting celebrities mounting their stationary steeds under the sweltering spotlights at the Park Theater. Their wheels spun on rollers and were attached to a gigantic dial at the rear of the stage. The arrows representing each rider described their arc as they sped to the 5-mile virtual finish line. Their skin glistened with steamy sweat and the big audience "applauded until it was tired and cheered until it was hoarse," reported the papers.

He would've wanted her to be at one of his shows in Worcester. He was proud of his star turn and seemed to enjoy the experience, sharing the stage with Parisian chartreuses, black comedians, and acrobat families. He even recorded little quips and one-liners in his diary, as if they might assist him with someone he hoped to impress. "It matters not how hungry a horse may be," he scribbled. "He can't take a bite." The vaudeville races were lighthearted entertainment, for the most part—just like the breezy, church-sponsored magic lantern shows—but in the last Worcester performance, perhaps because Daisy was in the house, the competition grew so fierce en route to the virtual finish line that Taylor and Murphy's bicycles broke loose from their stands and both men, their chests heaving and mouths open gasping for air, crashed to the floor.

It was a few weeks later that Taylor backed out of the engagement at the Madison Square Garden Six-Day with McFarland. A reference to "D.M." is also noted in his notebook next to an additional train fare to New York. It turned into a holiday: he and Daisy had begun their furtive courtship.

Daisy Victoria Morris around the time of her wedding to Major Taylor in 1902. *Source: From the Collection of the Indiana State Museum and Historic Sites*

Daisy's fair complexion—years later Taylor would be accosted in San Francisco for escorting a white woman—had a mesmerizing effect on people, Taylor included. It was the time of the Blue Vein and Bon Ton Societies, exclusive social clubs that restricted membership to those with a mulatto birthright. In the case of the former, the litmus test was elegantly simple: If your skin displayed the blue of a vein at the wrist, you were admitted. Fancier churches were known to compare a new member's skin shade to a brown paper bag. In slavery days, a softer shade intimated a special relationship with the master and a set of privileges for her and her offspring others didn't have. There was no judgment attached to such circumstances, just a weary recognition that the shade of one's skin was a difference maker.

Daisy Morris' adult life had been launched a decade earlier on the east side of Hartford. The woman Taylor met in Worcester had already come a long way—in fact, as far as he had.

SHE WAS BORN IN 1876 in Hudson, New York, an idyllic vacation town situated on a long bend of the Hudson River. Hudson was popularly ticketed as a healthful, fresh air respite only a half hour's steamship ride from the squalor and pungent mess of Manhattan. At a glance the description appeared spot-on: Hudson was a lovely place with mountain views and charming boutique-filled streets sloping to the river. There was a private classical academy on a hill, a charming promenade overlook along the river, and a lavish Persian villa rising to fruition on the farm of painter Frederic Edwin Church. Church's oil works, like his *Sunset in Hudson,* softened the surrounding ridgelines with dramatic swells of divinely inspired light. The landscape, like the sweeping Catskill mountaintops to the west, was evidence of God's inspired creation.

But to those who made the passage more compulsively year after year there was a different, less wholesome attraction. It was called

Diamond Street, a flourishing red-light district with a century-old history of satisfying less sunny desires.

For her entire childhood, Diamond Street was Daisy Morris's home. She grew up in a small rented wood frame with her widowed grandmother Charlotte, several aunts and uncles, and her unwed mother, Mary. Charlotte was a domestic and her uncles Howard and Madison were steamboat waiters, but her mother's occupation was never recorded. In the year Daisy was born Hudson was rocked by a sensational double murder involving a prostitute, a gambler, and a mistress. This was the way of Hudson, and the only thing one can know for sure about Mary A. Morris was that she gave her daughter mulatto skin, the by-product of a white companion. He was from New York, though Daisy later told census takers he was English. She didn't appear to acquire her middle name until she left Hudson. The "V" stood for Victoria, the reigning queen of the British Empire.

Part of the family—there was a brother, Paul, ten years older than she—moved to Hartford in the late 1880s. They met the Reverend L. H. Taylor at his East Side "African" church, a refuge in the heart of the black slums near the river. When he moved to the AME church in Worcester, Daisy went with him. When Taylor heard the story of her flight he would be reminded of his own departure with Munger. Paul and Mary stayed behind. Paul was a candymaker, a grocer, and later a fireman. Mary was an utter mystery, even in death. After she died in Hartford on December 22, 1901, her body was brought back to Hudson and buried next to Charlotte's. The official death certificate said she was fifty-four and had died of pausis, a rarely used Victorian medical term sometimes associated with insanity. The death certificate erroneously said she was white.

To the gossip-mongering newsies in New York, Boston, Chicago, and elsewhere the possibilities would've been titillating: Who was Daisy's father, who was her mother? Had she been lost, now found?

Did the lady who scorched Taylor's heart yield all to him like a dam burst, the long lies and sordid stories pouring forth before eyes that maybe weren't as untroubled or pure as they seemed? But they didn't get the story. Whatever Taylor knew or didn't know about Daisy was somewhat immaterial the moment he wrote, "Daisy V. Morris, Oct. 11, 1900." The past didn't matter. It was love at first sight.

ON MARCH 5, 1901, Taylor boarded the stately ocean liner *Kaiser Wilhelm der Grosse* in New York, bound for Europe. A deal had finally been consummated to bring *le nègre* to Paris and other European capitals for a two-month circuit of races against the leading foreign cracks. "I reckon six days in the week will be enough for them to find out what I can do," he swaggered, alluding to his success in negotiating a no-Sunday-race rule.

From the moment he left until the day he returned he deluged Daisy with postcards. Like the big dial at the Park Theater, she could follow his progress from a bewildering number of postmarks. First was a card showing a park in Berlin, then cottages from Belgium, villas in Italy, castles in Bavaria, and dozens of innocuous street scenes. What he sent was eclectic and somewhat random-seeming—unlike his unerring style on the track, he was a little unsure of this courtship territory—but the urgency and volume made it plain she was on his mind constantly. The pictures formed a visual stereoscope of where he was, and typically he posted one the moment his train pulled into a new city. Part of the reason they said so little (and sometimes nothing at all) was because he supplemented them with letters. Unfortunately, the letters either did not survive or Daisy put them somewhere where they have never been found. A few envelopes that contained those letters have survived and give a hint of how indomitable she and they felt. From Hartford, an exuberant Daisy addressed her Paris-bound letter "Major Taylor, World's Greatest Cyclist."

After a rough couple of early races as he worked up his fitness—

LA VIE AU GRAND AIR

ABONNEMENTS	10 Mars 1901. — N° 130	PUBLICITÉ

Taylor was pictured on the front page of the French sporting broadsheet *La Vie Au Grand Air* when he announced he'd race in Paris in the spring of 1901. *Source:* La Vie Au Grand Air

"I am mortal like anyone else," he reminded an interviewer, "when I can't ride I become slower"—Taylor found his form. In the twenty-four races he entered in France, Belgium, Holland, Switzerland, and Germany he won eighteen times. He defeated the fair-haired Louis

Grogna in Brussels, Willy Arend in Berlin, the Danish champ Thor
Ellegaard, Momo of Italy, and the Londoner Gasgoyne. He'd make
jumps off the banking one day, along the pole the next. He dropped
on the finish line like a pouncing cat, bent low and hard to the top
tube of his flashing bike as though there were a greased hinge at his
trim waist. The European racers favored a more upright and rigid
position. The difference seemed important: Taylor appeared to be
born to a bicycle, the others merely chained to it.

His training method, or apparent lack thereof, added to his
larger-than-life aura. He didn't seem to do much in his workout ses-
sions. It was deflating for the spectators who expected to be enlightened, or at least entertained in the way that modern baseball park
crowds are when a legendary slugger swats ball after ball out of the
park in batting practice. While others would steam around the track
endlessly until it was all they could do to drag themselves to their
dressing quarters, Taylor sped around a few times and then proceeded to his rubdown. It wasn't always the same, but, in essence,
Taylor pioneered a less-is-more philosophy, one that sports scientists
would later prove out was ideally suited to the one thing that mattered to him: speed.

Unlike a Tour de France cyclist, he wasn't attempting to be fast
over a prolonged period of time; rather, he needed to be explosive in
a chosen moment. Elite athletes abided by the law that more was better, which in almost every other discipline it was, but speed was the
exception. The harmonious law of conservation of energy—an equal
amount in for an equal amount out—didn't really apply. Because the
efforts he needed to prepare for were enormous and far more damag-
ing to muscle cells, recovery was the critical component.

Taylor's understanding of how you nurtured speed, how it couldn't
be stubbornly commanded forward or rushed to fruition, was the par-
adox in his life. Everything else he did was doctrinaire—his scriptural
attentiveness, his tiresome maxims for success—but when it came to

speed he was intuitive. Nobody taught then what he seemed to simply feel or divine. Speed was hard to live with because it required immense discipline and patience, and because it wasn't really about moving fast. Sprinting was a combination of speed and strength. Throughout his career he trained his upper body with the persistence of a boxer. Taylor understood—though neither he nor Munger had anything but anecdotal experience to go on—that the kind of man he was, fussy, disciplined, and preternaturally calm at moments when you'd least expect it, was the kind of man speed thrived in.

"Large crowds await his appearance at his hotel each morning with an inquiry as to his manner of spending the night," recapped the American papers about Taylor's journey across Europe. The Continent had seen American sporting heroes before and hadn't always responded with such frenzy. When Billy Brady took the fighter Corbett to Europe there had been a flat reaction; the boxing game was low, and though Corbett was different, there was a separation between the joy of watching what boxers did and the admiration for whom they were. "The English were tough," recalled Brady, who lost a bundle attempting to stage a boxing theatrical production on Drury Lane.

But cycling was different and so was Taylor. Spectators loved his long walks from the training quarters in his full-length hooded warm-up robes. He looked like a biblical figure, some thought; no, said others, there was something about the languorous sensual walk, the hands deep in the pockets, and the calm nod of acknowledgment that made him distinctly modern. He had something that intimated he was both accustomed to and faintly bored by the adulation.

French fans couldn't get enough: they ignored their countrymen and talked about his training, his clothes, and the food he ate. They asked if he was married or thought about being married. They didn't know about Daisy. He was the first American sports celebrity. Men of science wrote things like "Major Taylor réalise un admirable modèle de sculpture humaine: c'est un bronze vivant"—Major Taylor is an impressive model of human sculpture: a living bronze.

With neck, arm, and calf similar in size and chiseled definition, he was an image of the idealized Greek statues European archaeologists had recently excavated from the arid ground at the base of Mount Olympus. Amidst the infatuation with Greek classicism and the athletic human form, Taylor appeared before the French like the exalted Discobolus or Doryphorus sprung to life.

He was a sensation, and back in the States, Floyd McFarland could only sit back and boil. He had been there first, just as he had turned pro first. He had gone and conquered. But Taylor, always Taylor, stole the show. "The man is remarkable," applauded a Paris-based writer. "Unlike the fox in the fable, his song is as beautiful as his plumage."

THE TABLE HAD BEEN SET FOR Taylor's arrival in a way he couldn't have imagined. Some six months earlier the Paris Exposition had riveted the nation and for that matter the world. There had been much more at work than simply an impressive slate of cycling races. The Left Bank of the Seine seemed in danger of crumbling beneath the weight of voluminous exhibits, architectural wonders, and culture. The exposition trumped America's 1893 version on a number of fronts, but more than anything it provided the forum that Frederick Douglass had been denied at the Chicago World Fair. At the Paris Exposition, the enraptured public got what was then the most complete look at the progress and power of the American Negro ever presented.

The leading conceptual architect of the exhibit was W. E. B. Du Bois, who attended to the project so scrupulously that he virtually ran out of money in the days before he was to ship out, forcing the esteemed Atlanta professor to bunk in common steerage. He had assembled hundreds of poignant documentary photographs and other materials that black men such as himself had pieced together to tell the story. As he pointed out: "We have thus, it may be seen, an honest, straightforward exhibit of a small nation of people, picturing their life and development without apology or gloss, and above all made by themselves." He wasn't free to do exactly as he pleased. To receive U.S. government grant money the exhibit couldn't be overtly political. There wasn't talk about recent race riots in the United States or the headline-making mob lynching, immolation, and dismemberment of a Georgia laborer named Sam Hose. Still, the artful Du Bois managed to get his point across just the same.

The average Parisian strolled into the gleaming white Palace of Social Economy and found a treasure trove of visual and expository proof of the American Negro's advancement. This wasn't the fierce and savage Dahomean warriors glaring down at them or Aunt Jemima flipping pancakes but long lists of literary works by black American authors such as Frederick Douglass' *Life and Times,* John Sampson's *Temperament and Phrenology of the Negro Race,* and Booker T. Washington's *Future of the American Negro;* it was photos of callused black farmers, studious, high-collared piano teachers, till-watching hotelkeepers, and praiseful Baptist church congregations. It was professional charts depicting sharp spikes in literacy, in population growth, in urban professions. It was the revered poet Paul Laurence Dunbar and his "A Negro Love Song":

> *Seen my lady home las' night,*
> *Jump back, honey, jump back.*
> *Hel' huh han' an' sque'z it tight,*
> *Jump back, honey, jump back.*
> *Hyeahd huh sigh a little sigh,*
> *Seen a light gleam f'om huh eye,*
> *An' a smile go flittin' by —*
> *Jump back, honey, jump back.*

Frances Benjamin Johnston's portraits and her expositional pictures of Virginia's Hampton Normal and Agricultural Institute won the top prize awarded at the fair. Du Bois won a gold medal for driving the project. He discovered later that he had done such a fine job of showcasing the black people in America that many visitors came away with the erroneous idea that the "Negro problem in America," such as it was, had been solved.

For anyone who spent any time visiting the exhibit it would have been abundantly clear that American blacks were strong, industrious, and on the rise. They had a new place in the French heart—just not a face yet. In April 1901 the face arrived. It was, of course, Major Taylor.

As the Paris Exposition intimated, the French claimed a special connection with black people in America. Taylor himself had talked of moving to France as early as 1897, only a year into his career. The French had their colonialist warts, but they maintained a beaconlike glow, propelled among the educated black elite to the forefront of enlightened nations because of their intellectual heritage. First Rousseau and then Tocqueville had set the tone, creating the indelible image of a true north. "In Paris . . . no one regards me curiously," wrote the painter Henry Ossawa Tanner, who left Pittsburgh for the Left Bank in 1891. "I am simply 'M. Tanner, an American artist.' Nobody knows nor cares what was the complexion of my forebears. I live and work on terms of absolute social equality."

Tanner was just one of many 19th-century artists, entertainers, and intellectuals who had found a refuge in Paris. Taylor followed in the rich tradition of Douglass and Du Bois, and even the black jockey Ike Murphy. He enjoyed the attention, particularly the Parisian nonchalance when it came to his skin color. It wasn't that the French were color-blind or racially so progressive, but they weren't overly preoccupied, either. Talent simply superseded racial bias.

There was also something undeniably impressive and exciting about the accomplished black man. A day before Taylor's match race with French world champion Edmond Jacquelin, a risqué pictorial appeared in the French newspapers showing the hypermuscular Taylor in scanty briefs with the covetous camera lens fixing on his body—his taut quadriceps, broad shoulders, and pan-flat stomach. It would've made American viewers shade their eyes and blush. Taylor took it in stride. It was Paris.

Those images were captured during an even more revealing session in which several French scientists took lab measurements, exploring *le nègre* for a map to his gift. Inspecting athletes was increasingly in vogue, and scientists didn't limit themselves to black men. In fact, the renowned Harvard scientist Dr. Dudley A. Sargent had already applied tape measure and calipers to the musculature of vaudevillian strongmen Louis Cyr and Eugen Sandow. Cyr, Sargent soberly reported, had bulbous calves the size of an adolescent's waist. The exam treatment in Taylor's case was even more extensive. "Several medical experts," a French newspaper reported, "measured him in all directions, examined, and X-rayed him." The doctors in Bordeaux, the article continued, reached the same conclusions as prominent doctors in the United States, who had already scrutinized him "inside and out."

What the French scientists found was a "masterpiece of human anatomy . . . it is difficult to imagine a human being endowed with a more perfect balance of strength, flexibility, and elegance. His skeleton is surrounded by strong muscles . . . his joints are surprisingly thin; lean, light, built with harmonious lines." The writer added that appearances can be deceiving and that muscles don't define an athletic result, quality does. "Major Taylor has content and form. He has quality," the author concluded.

The momentum from his continental victories and the glowing scientific report seemed to put poor Jacquelin at an unrecoverable disadvantage. Unlike McFarland, who'd practically been run out of

The international showdown on May 16, 1901, between Taylor and the reigning European champion, Edmond Jacquelin. *Source:* La Vie Illustree

Paris on a rail, Taylor's popularity grew each week. By the time his May 16 championship match with Jacquelin arrived—the slate of European races had been arranged like a giant undercard—all of Paris seemed to be in a tizzy.

Bookies said privately it was like finding money to receive bets on Jacquelin. Harry K. Thaw, the "Prince of Pittsburgh," turned a few heads by wagering $20,000 on the American (the equivalent of more than $250,000 in 2006 currency). A speed-obsessed Harvard dropout named William K. Vanderbilt Jr., added his own $3,000. As the start time neared, the atmosphere at the Parc des Princes track in Paris was electric. Though prices had doubled for admission, some 30,000 spectators stormed the gates on the unusually chilly and gray night. Jacquelin wore a bicolor jersey, smirking with surprising confidence as he followed Taylor to the start line. Taylor donned an African robe, a stunning affirmation of his comfort in his surroundings. He had never worn anything hinting at his cultural heritage in the United States; in fact, the only thing that he'd made a point of doing was wearing the number 13, a number he routinely took to requesting because early in his career the "unlucky" number had been forced on him. The robed entry was a visual spectacle the French artists adored.

The distance was a kilometer and the racers began slowly, each trying to force the other to take the early lead. What was derisively called "loafing" in the States was described as craftiness in Europe; it was easier to respond than initiate in a sprint race, and almost always the advantage lay with the racer who could mark the opponent in front of him. The rider who was forced to the front had to constantly look over his shoulder, anxiously waiting for the jump.

With 300 yards to go and Taylor sitting in superb marking position, Jacquelin made his jump and in shockingly easy fashion rode away. Taylor looked frozen. In the second heat Taylor took a different tact and led on the final straightaway but lost by a bike's length. Jacquelin's screaming French followers, stunned but ecstatic, threw the racer on their shoulders and paraded around the track singing "La Marseillaise." As for Taylor, it was the harshest loss of his career. The *Cycling Gazette* ran a photograph of what they called the "supremely unhappy nigger" as he walked back to the locker room alone and defeated.

The Americans in attendance were thunderstruck. The loss would be especially hard on the tempestuous Thaw, as he never liked losing. Five years later, having evidently lost his actress wife, Evelyn Nesbit, he tracked her paramour, Stanford White, to the rooftop of Madison Square Garden, where he shot the famous architect three times in the face.

IN THE STATESIDE ANALYSIS OF Taylor's defeat, many said the bitter cold had been a contributing factor, but they also blamed Taylor for playing Jacquelin's game. Taylor should have forced the issue, steered clear of "loafing," and adopted the American style by "riding a bicycle from start to finish so fast that the other man could not keep up." The French were renowned as steely tacticians, the track sophisticates to the American brawns. Taylor had needed to overwhelm the Frenchman with his God-given gift. Afterward a circumspect Taylor paid Jacquelin his due but privately seethed. In the final heat the Frenchman had shown him up by raising his fingers to his nose as he accelerated by. Jacquelin probably meant no serious offense; he thought of himself as an entertainer and would often play the house for laughs. Taylor, however, considered the gesture an affront, and subconsciously let it fester in his tender belly until he had formed the prescriptive agent critical to all great sporting endeavors—rage.

The importance he gave the race is reflected in one of his scrapbooks. French-language clippings, pages of business cards, and decorative border drawings done years later by Daisy have as their centerpiece an almost sequential string of race-day photographs. The images begin with Jacquelin at the track posing for formal portraiture. He wears a long black frock and stands with his chest jutting forward, hands nested behind his back as if he were listening to a string quartet or awaiting his own coronation. Other grainy photos show the warm-up, the start, and, finally, the mass hysteria at the end. Men in dark suits and bowlers can be seen streaming across the infield in full stride, desperate to lend a hand in lifting up the victorious Jacquelin. If Taylor thumbed through the images quickly he could've felt the immediacy and emotion of watching his own defeat in moving pictures. He didn't want to forget how it felt to lose what was then the biggest race of his life.

Perhaps, too, he culled his anger from a more exacting translation of the article written about his Bordeaux medical testing. Tacked onto the end of the story as a kind of addendum, the investigators explained to readers that the Negro was the beneficiary of an invaluable disposition for physical effort. "The black man, who by nature is little inclined to intellectual work, is well disposed towards material work," they wrote. "His brain inferiority is compensated by a considerable superiority of the senses . . . hence, perhaps, the Negro's passion for shiny objects."

LESS THAN TWO WEEKS LATER the two met again. Taylor wore tight-fitting dark shorts, a long-sleeved white shirt, and a silk American flag wrapping his waist like a sash. Jacquelin emerged from the dressing room in his lucky bicolor jersey. It was expected that Taylor would push the pace. Instead he did the opposite. Having gotten a stiff shove out of the starting blocks and the unwanted lead position, Taylor slowed down and coaxed Jacquelin to draw even. Instead Jacquelin responded in kind, his eyes fixed on his rival's lower back. Stubbornly, Taylor refused to give in. He stopped on the track, standing

Taylor and Jacquelin racing in Paris at the Parc des Princes velodrome. *Source:* La
Vie Au Grand Air

on his pedals but not turning them so the bike stayed upright but
moved not an inch. A less patient rider might have exploded with a
burst of acceleration, unable to withstand the temptation of seeing
the fastest man in the world at a dead stop. But Jacquelin merely
stopped, too, balanced upon his bike on the lower apron of the track
like a circus performer on the high wire.

The crowd leaned in, entranced. Certain Taylor had run out of
tricks, they instead watched in disbelief as the American rode backward until he was abreast of the Frenchman. Jacquelin could do
nothing but accept the front-runner's position. In the finish line
sprint, Taylor bolted around him easily to win.

Twenty minutes later, before the start of the second heat, Taylor
kept up the gamesmanship. This time, prior to the gun, he threw out
his hand in an apparent gesture of may-the-best-man-win magna-

nimity. In actuality—and evidently Jacquelin understood it—Taylor was suggesting the best man had already won, and he was simply thanking him for the chivalrous gesture of a rematch. Taylor handed the official race photographer a new Kodak camera and asked him to take a shot of Jacquelin and himself for his scrapbook.

Taylor won easily, taking his small silk American flag from his waistband to wave above his head during his joyous victory lap. The band struck up "The Stars and Stripes Forever." Paris seemed to swoon as one. A French newspaperman noted that it had discovered that Taylor's mother was from the tribal African nation of Dahomey and his father from Senegal, and as these were now French colonies, the reporter suggested, it was within reason to claim Taylor as one of their own.

Unlike McFarland, Taylor's return next season was eagerly awaited. Privately, Taylor began to make plans of his own. The next time he came to the City of Light, he would not be alone. Daisy Victoria Morris would see for herself what exactly he was talking about.

CHAPTER 12

Twoness

LABOR DAY, 1901
MADISON SQUARE GARDEN
NEW YORK

I have none o' yer bawling, praying, singing niggers
on my place . . . I'm your church now.
— SIMON LEGREE IN HARRIET BEECHER
STOWE'S *Uncle Tom's Cabin*

WHEN THE NARRATOR in the novel *Ragtime* observed that turn-of-the-century entertainment involved "great swarms of people," he might've looked no further than Labor Day, 1901, when the New York metropolitan area was aquiver with the pageantry of the human spectacle. At Coney Island the temperance firebrand Carry Nation denounced the New York state government as a lot of "beer-besmeared, nicotine-faced, beaked-nosed devils." In other parts of the city Tammany speechmakers rallied working men and women at Union Square, Washington Square Park, and across the river in Newark, wooing the masses with—what else?—Mrs. Nation's villainous draughts.

The sporting program was simply endless, with streetcars and avenues full of families and straw-hatted gamblers alike heading to the ball fields, riversides, horse tracks, and cycling venues. The financially struggling summerlong pro race circuit was a shell of its former self, but you wouldn't have known that on Labor Day. At the Vailsburg velodrome in Newark, a championship slate of races included the likes of Frank Kramer, Willie Fenn, and the recently returned European superstar Taylor. In some cases the expectation of grand sporting entertainment dulled the senses. At Rockaway Beach, a fancy swimmer named George Belcher drowned in full sight of hundreds when the onlookers mistook his seizure and his daughter's frenzied screaming for a part of the dramatic performance.

But of all the riotous activities vying for the human eye, one would later stand out above all others. It was the New Jersey state championship bicycle race at the Highland Park track in New Brunswick. The overflow Labor Day crowd, which was estimated at 2,000 went far beyond the family and friends of sixteen-year-olds racing the mile handicap. They had come to see a special exhibition, a five-mile "automobile match race." There had never been such a thing on U.S. soil.

The two drivers, Louis de Franklin Munger and William J. McDade, were neighbors. There is no information on what they raced, though Munger probably drove one of the Stanley brothers' high-performing "locomobiles." In a scenario that perfectly described his recent good fortune, Munger finished without a crash and won in a time of 14 minutes and 59 seconds.

Munger wasn't really back in racing, but he did want to publicize his newest product, the pneumatic automobile tire. He had a new company, the New Brunswick–based Munger Vehicle Tire Company, and a new passion, automobiles. Unlike anything in his unlucky past history—it was his third company in four years—his timing was perfect. The nation was turning to the automobile with the enthusiasm and the hysteria with which it had embraced the bicycle a decade before. Races were popping off on urban tracks, Florida sand, and

Back on home soil Taylor matches up with Iver Lawson and Willie Fenn.
McFarland is pushing off Lawson. *Source: U.S. Bicycle Hall of Fame*

mountain roads in New Hampshire. In little more than a year,
Munger's company had found a prominent and healthy niche.

He left others to dicker with perfecting the motor, while he had
become, in the parlance of the time, a man of rubber. Munger was no
longer functioning as Taylor's trainer—in Europe, Taylor had successfully shown himself capable of charting his own training course—
but the pair remained close. As record-breaking speeds became
increasingly reliant on crucial technological improvements, Munger
shifted roles, becoming Taylor's key collaborator in developing top-
performing gear. From Taylor on, the mastery of technical matters
would be a hallmark of great racing champions. In the early 1980s
the multiple Tour de France winner Greg LeMond would show up
each year in France with a gear innovation the others didn't have
and immediately came to fear. In 1987 it was aero bars, a reengi-

neered ultralightweight handlebar that allowed the racer a more consistent streamlined position. The next year it was a wind-tunnel-
tested time trial helmet. A decade later Lance Armstrong would wait
on his next superbike and assorted gadgets, calling the collection
"the shit that would kill them." The best, most righteous equipment
was important psychologically, too, giving the racers confidence that
they possessed an edge in all ways. The rest of the field was always
trying to catch up—at least it felt that way. Munger's tinkering and
his links to the most brilliant engineers in America ensured Taylor's
superiority in his own mind—and, just as importantly, in the mind
of others.

Originally Munger jumped into the rubber field in an effort to
better control the forces at work in Taylor's future record attempts.
The pacing engines were increasingly reliable, but also bigger and
attached to more cumbersome, heavy-duty tandem machines. At the
small coliseum tracks, such as Madison Square Garden, the large
motor tandems, moving at ferocious speeds, put increasing pressure
on the tires supporting them. Almost all the accidents were caused
by bursting tires. "The heavy tandems with the heavy men aboard
cause too much pressure on the tires, when said tires are used on a
small track," complained the *Globe*'s cycling writer. "Naturally to
hold a machine up on a small track, said track has to be banked at
least 45 degrees and when this machine is whizzing around a high-
banked track the speed forces the tandem hard against the board
surface, and the pressure on the rubber is enormous, and as the
machine slips continually, the rubber is worn, or, in cycling parlance,
'burned off.'"

Munger's efforts hadn't quite solved the safety crisis of motor
pacing, but he did produce a light, durable, and easily changed tire—
a near perfect automobile tire. It was the most fortunate idea that
had ever come into his fertile head, and investors immediately rushed

in. He was suddenly and unexpectedly flush with money. The papers described him as wealthy and found his stature significant enough to report on a robbery at his home on Bayard Street. The crime sounded like a case of Munger's past and present meeting: the intruder had declared himself to the family maid as an old friend and, though the Mungers were out, had convincingly helped himself to lunch, wine, and Birdie's best cigars.

Success was everywhere Taylor looked. Billy Brady continued to represent Taylor and prop up the racing game (he had a scheme to bring Jacquelin to America and to develop a city-against-city team racing league), but he had made his theatrical breakthrough and found not only a new fortune but critical acceptance. Brady had gone completely against type to produce Harriet Beecher Stowe's serious, socially conscientious *Uncle Tom's Cabin,* the wrenching story of slavery in antebellum America. He seemed the least likely man to touch the pulse of the story, but he had found himself surprisingly moved when he reread the epic. Perhaps his relationship with Taylor—whose family had been chased North like the book's ill-fated heroine, Eliza—predisposed him to buy the rights and mortgage most everything he owned to get the production to Broadway. Or perhaps, as his lifelong relationships with underdogs such as Taylor, Jim Corbett, and later the black explorer Matthew Henson suggested, he wasn't quite the soulless, greed-driven businessman he sold himself to be.

On the evening of the opening, Brady steeled himself for a haughty critical execution. But the papers failed him. The audience that crowded the Academy Theater from top to bottom was attractively mixed, began the *Times* brightly; Brady's "splendid scenic production" had brought out society swells, the elderly, and theater regulars. The reviews were uniformly ecstatic. Later in the year, *Way Down East,* a sweet tale of betrayal and redemption, overcame a disastrous Broadway opening to become a blockbuster hit on the road.

Taylor had appeared to arrive as well. He had burnished America's reputation abroad and was coming off one of the most successful sporting seasons in history. In 1901, he would earn well over $20,000 in appearance fees, race earnings, record bonuses, and bicycle sponsorships. Cy Young, a top wage earner in professional baseball, made $2,500. Taylor was a good businessman who knew how to manage his affairs. After saying as a young man that he would never race anything but a Munger bicycle, he signed contracts to ride a Comet, a Sanger, an Orient, and an Iver Johnson. Munger understood. It was business, and there was no income to be earned from being blindly loyal to an out-of-production bicycle.

He lived well in his house on Hobson Avenue, wore fine, custommade suits when he went on the road, and employed servants to cook and clean for him. He was one of the home-owning "Worcester 400," and though his fortune was accumulated in the "cheap" world of sporting endeavor, it was universally accepted as honorable. His reputation, among whites, blacks, and foreigners, was spotless. Every immigrant in America saw him as a streak of hope, one of the downtrodden who'd beaten the system. In a small Texas town Jack Johnson, the future black heavyweight champion of the world, said he was thinking of the famous Taylor when he took up bicycle racing for the first time. It was a vintage Johnson exaggeration, since the two were actually the same age, but it didn't negate the fact that Johnson and others like him revered the news-making cyclist. He may have seemed older to Johnson because he'd already been through so much and been written about for so long.

With Taylor's plaudits abroad and Munger and Brady's successes at home, there was a sense that the problems with rival riders such as McFarland would sort themselves out. There was also the expectation that the warm embrace Taylor had received in Europe would be duplicated in the United States. Neither came to pass.

In the span of a few weeks late in the 1901 season, he found things worse than ever. At the Vanderbilt Hotel in Syracuse a racist clerk, who evidently didn't recognize the famous international cyclist, had him forcibly removed from the lobby, screaming, "Get out or I'll kick you out." At stops in Springfield and Worcester in Massachusetts and in Providence, Rhode Island, Taylor got into altercations with rival riders who, he said, had banded together to defeat him.

Floyd McFarland had redoubled his efforts at sabotage. Still smarting from Taylor's refusal to ride with him in New York or be managed by him in Europe, "McFarland declared that I would never again be champion of America," Taylor wrote.

McFarland had successfully regrouped after the mess in New York, returning afterward to San Jose, where he successfully promoted and raced in several off-season bicycle meets. With a field of popular leading riders and an eclectic range of races involving motors and men, he brought in upward of 2,000 fans. His brother James, a popular man-about-town in San Jose, helped make the arrangements and drum up the publicity. The pair had practically guaranteed the gate by choosing a day in the week when entertainment was almost impossible to come by—a Sunday. During his California racing season Floyd refueled, relaxing in the company of friends and family. His father, Thomas, continued to auction off everything from blue-blooded cattle to 800-acre farms; his brother Robert was a clerk in the constable's office, and his other brother, a Stanford professor, breezed in for society events from time to time. But Floyd was the star. By the time he returned East he was racing, and the manager and promoter guiding the career of Frank Kramer, the newest whiz kid racer. Kramer's young pinwheeling legs and McFarland's Machiavellian brilliance seemed to make an unbeatable combination. Kramer won the national sprinting championship in 1901 and appeared likely to do so again in 1902.

With the sport controlled by McFarland, a dismayed Taylor said he had no choice but to retire. A month after he left Europe he did so. He also sued the hotel where he'd been kicked out. He was losing patience. "His recent trip where he was praised by men and women not of his own color has completely spoiled him," hissed a New York columnist.

For the first time the black newspapers raced to his defense. Because Taylor refused to let others make "a nigger of him he is forced to retire," an editorial railed. "That's right Major retire: You've got money, now live easy. These fellows are jealous of your honors and prejudiced to your color."

The public's opinion of Taylor began to split upon racial lines. Sympathizers and critics came and went with the unfolding of the day's cycling column. In the early years Taylor had been an unknown in the black community but found plenty of white admirers who saw in his fair play and churchgoing habits a sporting figure to root for. His skin color was less of a factor for everyday spectators, who in some ways saw it as the sort of underdog trait they could identify with. In immigrant America, who wasn't oppressed and exploited?

In American cities there was an almost visible partition, a feeling of great separation, with a few doing the orchestrating and everyone else being orchestrated. But at some indistinct point, Taylor had lost prestige in the white community just as he gained it in the black community. The posters in the Tenderloin pool halls of a triumphant Taylor, the ring of friendships with Booker T. Washington and influential publishers like the *Freeman*'s Charles Knox—he was theirs now.

TAYLOR DID TAKE BACK HIS retirement threat, but he never seemed to recover his composure. In fact, he became uncharacteristically erratic in his behavior as the East Coast racing season drew to a close. It wasn't merely that he lost races he normally would've won; it was the way he lost them. For the first time he appeared to be complacent, to not have his heart in it. Even the normally sympathetic Boston newspapers ran less than laudatory headlines. "Colored Man Loses Heart Early in Five-Mile Race," the *Globe* reported in late September, describing his defeat in Baltimore against a newcomer named Archie McEachern.

In other races, again for the first time, Taylor's sportsmanship was called into question. In a match race against Kramer, Taylor was said to obstruct his opponent by veering into Kramer's line. The ploy escaped the eyes of the race referee but not the hissing crowd. At the Charles River Park in Cambridge, Taylor seemed to snap altogether, a rather innocuous-appearing if unfortunate collision prompting him to explode in fury. He disgustedly flung his wheel into the middle of the track and confronted the rival rider en route to the training room. Taylor, a trained boxer, had raised his fists and cornered his opponent when a police officer stepped in and forced him to step away.

Taylor's self-control was a hallmark and part of his aura. He had always stood out, and not just because of his stony calmness in the face of racial abuse. He had deadened himself to it somehow, desensitized the sting, processing only hollow words and nothing more. But the physical sport itself was abusive, physical, and testosterone-laden. Racers were compulsively primal for days on end, heat after heat. Their vocabulary was peppered with predatory phraseology— "attacks" and "jumps" and "chases." When a rival collapsed in a panting, muscle-deadened heap and sat up dispirited, he was said to have had his legs broken. The tension built for days, sometimes weeks. There were measured paces, agreed-upon dictates, and finally the raised starter's gun. It began as a gentlemanly duel and ended as a bare-knuckle fistfight. Lance Armstrong once said that every time he exploded past a rival he felt an adrenaline surge, a pleasing bloodlust, as if he'd just landed a knockout punch. It didn't happen often in long-distance races, but on the tracks it happened heat after heat.

To avoid the ignominy of a loss, a racer would do most anything. In avenging a wrong, he could not help himself. The retaliation almost always took place in the frenzied, blood-boiling postrace moments. The temporary forms of insanity took the form of a round-house swing or a chokehold or a torrent of profanity. In a Washington, D.C., race McFarland felt a teammate had fouled him, and before he could stop himself he blindsided the Swede with a right cross. Even in modern times, almost a century after McFarland's punch, a track race at the Lehigh Velodrome that ended with a crash was followed by a barroom-style brawl involving racers, coaches, and referees. Taylor had always been the exception, containing the may-hem, perhaps saving it somehow, storing it like the molecular fuel embedded in muscle. He had done so famously and without fail until now.

The object of his worst tantrum was a twenty-year-old Swede named Iver Lawson, Floyd McFarland's newest protégé. Lawson had only recently come to the United States from a tour of Australia, where his explosive sprint had drawn generous comparisons to Tay-lor. In their first meeting he had beaten Taylor in the half mile. He was the last of three brothers to emigrate from Sweden, the family having already earned an iron-man reputation in cycling circles. At the 1899 Six-Day race in San Francisco his brother John had proven so irrationally incapable of stopping despite life-threatening injuries that the crowd had had to interfere to prevent him from doing him-self in. Iver himself would nearly die in the fall of 1901 when typhoid fever kept him shuttered for weeks and left him a skeletal 100 pounds, but by the spring he was racing in Europe. The Lawsons, depending on your perspective, were either warriors or madmen. Their collective nickname was the "Terrible Swedes." Taylor had rea-son to believe his latest rival, who was said to be wanted for the race circuit in Europe, might be the toughest yet.

As distressing as Lawson's emergence was, it wasn't the only reason for Taylor's troubled state of mind. That could be traced back to
an event at Madison Square Garden a month earlier, the evening
punctuation mark on the daylong Labor Day sporting extravaganza.
It was a pairing put together at the last moment, perhaps by Mc-
Farland, who was sensing a bit of weakness in his old adversary.
Interestingly, he didn't put any of his new charges forward for the
main event; rather, it was he himself. He was riding selectively now,
still training and trying to maintain his fighting trim, but racing only
when the purse and the foe were suitably attractive.

It was Taylor and McFarland's first match race in two years.
Madison Square Garden was once more filled with spectators, and
the heavy-duty tandem machines with their big motors roared
around the track well before the two combatants entered. It was
almost impossible to believe that the noisy machines could hold the
track—they were like SUVs on a roller derby short track. The drivers
had 520 feet to work with on each lap, four severe turns, and only a
scrap of straightaway.

Taylor was arguably at his peak while McFarland was stumbling
in his attempts to regain his old form. A July crash on the same
Garden track had crushed his cheekbone. In a 20-mile motor-paced
match race a week earlier against the comeback-driven Jimmy
Michael he had finished a mile and a half in arrears—strong evidence, a *Globe* reporter wrote, "that the Californian was not in
the same class with the top notchers." The distances at the Garden
were one and two miles—pure sprinting arrangements that were better suited to Taylor's abilities than McFarland's.

But from the sound of the gun it was clear Taylor wasn't comfortable. He exhibited none of the customary swagger despite an audience that appeared to be pulling for him. He was tentative, taking
soft, uncharacteristic lines, dangling a little farther out from the tan-

dem's rear wheel than he needed to. He wasn't getting all the draft
he could because he either couldn't or wouldn't close the gap. Mc-
Farland was fearless, holding tight to his tandem in and out of the
turns, inches from the burning rubber that might expose the inner
tube and explode without warning.

McFarland won going away, taking the first race by ten yards and
the second by a humiliating fifty.

A disconsolate Taylor would look at himself in the mirror after
the race and wonder how it had happened. His physique was as
ribbed with muscle as it always had been. He was still drawn to those
two seconds where his power found ultimate form, still displaying his
magic in races against other opponents, but never did it emerge
against McFarland. Perhaps Munger had advised him to take it easy,
that he had yet to solve the problems of bursting tires and fiery explosions and that for this meeting it was better to be safe than sorry. Or
perhaps he had merely been at a loss without the comfort of Munger
aboard the tandem, coaxing him through the twisting turns. He was
elsewhere, excitedly talking to reporters about the car he had raced, a
moment in the sun for the old warrior.

Taylor couldn't make the pieces fit neatly, however; there was
something more to the day than his issues. It was as if McFarland had
an antidote, a voodoo spell to rob him of what he possessed. Quality
was a mystery—he agreed with the French journalist's observation
that it wasn't something you could see, touch, or even feel. It was elusive at best, fleeting at worst. There was no statistical way to explain
his domination by the one man he wanted to defeat more than any
other. McFarland simply had his number. The gods inexplicably
smiled on him.

TAYLOR COULDN'T WAIT TO GET AWAY AND return to Europe,
the place where he had found he was "thought something of." He

planned to bring Daisy with him. Their fine Christian courtship had
been going on for what must have seemed like an interminable duration; even though he'd known he loved her the moment he set eyes on
her, he was compelled to adhere to the strict practices of the day. (By
contrast, Floyd McFarland would, a few years later, famously meet
Mildred Jolly in the latter stages of a Garden Six-Day, propose, and
marry her in less than twenty-four hours. Their hasty postrace ceremony at the Little Church Around the Corner "broke all previous
records as far as marital affairs of cyclists are concerned," noted the
San Jose Mercury News). During the months of endless good-byes as
he was about to board a train, he had to be content with "that hand
clasp, those endearing glances." Only the engaged were permitted the
intimacy of a sterile good-bye kiss. The all-aboard of the conductor
and the whistle of the engine were nearly madness-inducing, wrote
an Endeavorer from the same time period, also enduring a hellish test
of self-restraint. "I think if I had been a Tarzan I would have pulled
that train back. But such are the ways of life for a young man, so I
pulled myself together and started all over again."

Taylor was a pragmatist; he understood the problems of America
and the black man in it, and he recognized that one of his problems
was Daisy. In Paris a few years earlier the painter Henry O. Tanner
had married a Frenchwoman and there was barely a blip. But in the
United States, the separation of classes was nearly as important as the
separation of races. Taylor, as America's first citizen of color, needed
a partner of equal weight, of regalness. It was an obligation, Taylor
understood.

Daisy Morris remained his secret, her story untold. When they
finally married on March 21, 1902 (six months after his season-
ending defeat to McFarland), it was away from the press in Ansonia,
Connecticut, at the home of the Reverend L. H. Taylor, who was the
newly installed pastor in the mill town. "Major Taylor Married,"
read the headline in the *Ansonia Evening Sentinel*. "He Takes Miss

A marriage portrait of Major and Daisy prior to their 1902–1903 around-the-world honeymoon. *Source: From the Collection of the Indiana State Museum and Historic Sites*

Daisy V. Morris for Better or for Worse . . . Worldwide Known
Cyclist to Journey to Paris with His Bride."

But just days after they married Taylor thought better of it and
went to Europe for his return engagement alone, conveniently escap-
ing the deluge of inquiries about just who she was and if they might
talk to her. By the time everybody knew of the marriage Taylor was
aboard a passenger ship to Europe and Daisy was back home in Connecticut. The story lost steam.

A few months later the *Colored American Magazine,* a periodical
financed by Booker T. Washington and run by a former Indianapolis
Freeman editor, was given the exclusive. "Ever since the announce-
ment of Major Taylor's marriage," the writer narrated, "the curious
public have been more than anxious to see or even read of the lady
who won the heart of a man who has never been beaten in a match
race until Cupid arranged a race of hearts' affections which resulted
in his losing his first match race, and yet winning the dearest and best
prize of all in his racing career—Miss Daisy Victoria Morris." With
the cooperation of Taylor and Daisy they printed a modern-day fairy
tale. He was a glamorous superstar, she a woman of refinement
and education. Daisy was a graduate of the Hudson Academy and
the "best all around girl athlete" in an unnamed college. In Hartford she had been an ardent worker in the Amphion Social Club and
the Ladies' Auxiliary of the Sumner Club. "Mrs. Taylor is a most
beautiful woman, an ideal hostess, a charming and brilliant conver-
sationalist," the exclusive continued.

For the remainder of Taylor's career her story stayed as they
had presented it, finding its way into books, movies, and the genealo-
gies of modern ancestors. The screenwriter for the Taylor biopic portrayed Daisy's father as a doting white gentleman farmer who
couldn't stand to see his daughter marry a black man, remembering
the pain he and his wife had endured in their own mixed-race mar-

riage. The father was played by the distinguished American actor Robert Vaughn.

But the original story—the one printed in *Colored American*—was never true. She was not privately educated at the Hudson Academy; it had closed before she was of school age. In Hartford, as in Worcester, she was a servant, not a black debutante. Nor was there any evidence that her father was ever known to her. The wedding certificate she filled out in Ansonia listed Charles Morris as her father, but in fact he was her eldest uncle.

A hundred years later Daisy and Major Taylor's two great-granddaughters, one of whom lived in Washington, the other in Boston, found the story captivating but also, they said, not terribly surprising. All families have secrets, necessary to the times they lived through—a grandfather whose Native American ancestry was closeted, a great-uncle with an uncertain sexuality.

The more Karen Brown Donovan, the D.C. descendant, thought about the scenario, the more she said she saw the story as doing anything but diminishing the Taylor legacy. The episode aggrandized him all the more in her eyes by making him more fully human. Knowing his principles and his desire to fulfill the Christian ideal, he would not have lightly taken the step of fabricating his wife's past. Theirs was a brilliant deception, necessary for the era in which they lived, both for reasons of class and for reasons of love. As Taylor said, and this was always true, it was love at first sight. The rest merely had to be taken care of. The story, in fact, was so flawlessly embellished that it would reasonably seem the product of another hand, perhaps Billy Brady's. You could almost hear the violins in full stir, an orchestral mimicry to the tape-breaking finish.

However the arrangement was made, Daisy's meteoric rise to the top tier of society was every bit as thrilling and courageous as her new husband's. Neither needed be alone anymore. "I have every confidence in you Dearie," he wrote, "we have nothing to fear."

* * *

THE BRADY-NEGOTIATED CONTRACT to race in Europe was for a whopping $5,000 in addition to whatever prize money he earned. He was almost as dominant as on the first tour, winning every high-profile man-to-man match race in addition to forty other races. His letters and postcards back to Daisy were more evocative and far more numerous. Postcards alone—not counting letters and telegrams—now came sometimes twice a day. "Wish you were here," he wrote from Berlin, Napoli, Liège, and a dozen other cities. From Bavaria he offered "just a little huggy."

He was an athlete in his absolute prime, at a point, at least in Europe, where he had little doubt about his physical and mental abilities. He was single-handedly credited with bringing back the European race scene from the dead. What he was unsure of was being away; he felt more fully human and vulnerable than he could ever recall. He dreamed of Daisy and of home every night, he said. He worried about the distance between them. A full six years later, after they had a child together, the same worries possessed him. In 1908, and no doubt in 1901 and all the years in between, Major Taylor wrote Daisy Morris some of the most moving love letters a man has ever written.

In the throes of a six-month separation, Taylor wrote about the perfumed allure of Paris but reminded Daisy "that I have one Granny and she is all in this world to me and best of all I don't mind telling her." He wrote about a hotel where they had stayed once and the red bedspread they admired, and the picture of her he placed on it. "I can look at you the last thing at night and the first thing in the morning, isn't that beautiful? Is there any wonder I dream of you every night?"

She had added a new dimension to his enigmatic team, a person whose interest was neither entertainment nor track performance but simply him. "Paris is a beautiful place," he wrote, "but believe me when I say it has no charms for I have one [Daisy] . . . Do you remember the little kiss I used to give you and you would give me just before I would go to the race track to train? Well, how do I miss it."

As the 1902 season concluded it occurred to Taylor that there were two things missing in all his European victories. One was Daisy; the other was McFarland.

CHAPTER 13

Steal Away

Nobody thought about racism except black people.

— MAX MORATH

FUNERALS WERE AN INCREASING OCCURRENCE within the cycling fraternity. Prominent racing men, in dark suits and solemn looks, gathered before open caskets in Brooklyn, Atlantic City, and elsewhere to comfort loved ones and pay their respects. Invariably the man killed in a race would be said to be a "gamer" and have been thinking about quitting the sport on the exact day he died.

No popular sport had ever experienced such a streak of carnage. It had begun the previous Labor Day with Johnny Nelson, a young, curly-haired Swede who had gone much of the season undefeated. A tire on his pacing machine burst; Nelson slid out and was pinned under his machine when another motor tandem drove over him. The pin-wheeling steel pedals—the earliest motorbikes came with pedals in case the engine failed—savagely ripped through his leg like a rotating cleaver. Doctors amputated above the knee when gangrene set in, but within a week he was dead, memorialized by three score of his cycling associates as a star in the making who had been taken before his time.

The account of his last ride was almost as disturbing as the crash itself. He had started the race, which was held at Madison Square Garden, still in bandages from another pacing accident two weeks earlier. Right up until the gun, the twenty-one-year-old had pleaded with organizers to let him postpone the event because of his unhealed injuries and the haunted feeling his number was up.

Nelson's death prompted the usual calls for reform. The motor pacing tandems were too large and powerful for aggressive track venues such as Madison Square Garden, where the miniaturized 1/10-mile circuit was far smaller and more treacherous than the average outdoor track. The weak point in the pacing machines continued to be the tires, which were unable to withstand frictional forces and overheated on the hard, unyielding tracks. Others machines suffered from neglect: as the property of tracks, which were increasingly insolvent, the poorly maintained machines were often ticking time bombs. Young racers such as Nelson dreamed of making enough money to purchase their own pacing machines, which they could maintain and be sure of. He wasn't the only one to be maimed or killed before he got a chance.

In May 1902, with Taylor back in Europe, it got worse. The Canadian Archie McEachern, who was on a record-setting tear of his own, was closely following a pace machine in an attempt to break Taylor's mile record at Atlantic City when the chain snapped and the contraption suddenly lost power. Unable to react quickly enough, McEachern collided with the fast-decelerating machine and "shot up in the air like a rocket." A sharp projecting board broke his landing but severed his jugular. Blood poured forth like the fountain at Rockefeller Center. McEachern, twenty, died within hours.

Every professional sprint cyclist seemed to be playing a gamble against either death, disfigurement, or permanent disability: just a little more time, just a little more money, then easy street. Taylor was no exception. Pace-following record runs had had a revival and were the best payday to be found. Taylor was waiting on a big 10-horsepower motor pacing machine for a record-making camp in the summer of 1902 when he decided to join the national circuit races and renew his quest for a national championship.

His decision was difficult to fathom. The previous summer he'd said he was going to quit racing in the United States, and while in Europe he hinted at the possibility of complete retirement. But every year he stayed on, won money, saw new parts of the world, and saved a little more. His nest egg was considerable. He was still the number one gate attraction.

In some ways it seemed that Taylor, who unlike most other racers didn't wager on races, was playing the riskiest game of all. In cycling those who didn't know when to quit, who didn't attend to their hunches, paid the ultimate price. The only cyclist who had played the game without serious injury as long as Taylor was McFarland. And of late McFarland had gone down, too. A scary motor pacing mishap at Madison Square Garden a year earlier had ripped his face open and left him unconscious for minutes.

The impetus to keep racing may have been Daisy's influence, at least in part. They had yet to have a honeymoon, and since their marriage in March they had spent almost no time together. She hadn't seen him race. In July, Taylor made arrangements to compete in New Haven, Connecticut, a veritable stone's throw from Ansonia, where they were wed. Because of a scheduling snafu Taylor, who'd made no prior arrangements, was required to spend the night in the city, but when they went looking for a bed, Taylor and Daisy found themselves refused admission at several hotels. The one establishment that finally accepted them wouldn't serve them breakfast in the morning.

On Broad Street in Newark a week earlier—his first race back from Europe—he had been treated virtually the same way. "Taylor rapped with his knife but the restaurant people were deaf to his summons," the *Boston Globe* reported. "They did not decline to serve the cyclist; they simply did not go near enough to give him a chance to deliver an order for food."

Taylor fulfilled his contractual obligations and finished second overall—concluding his season with a win in September—but he announced shortly thereafter that he had had enough.

"Man to man, I have Kramer and all the other cyclists beat to a certainty," Taylor told reporters. "With an even break, and I say it without boasting, there is no rider in the world who can defeat me in a match race. Of the hundred or more two-man contests in which I have been engaged I lost only two. But I realize I have little chance the way things are running. Not only do I suffer in the races, but I am unable to get proper food in many of the cities in which I train."

Taylor promised he was serious this time. He even turned down a $5,000 offer to race in Australia and Europe and abandoned the project to produce a bigger, better, and safer pace machine. He knew the cost of pace following; he'd been at the Garden when Nelson crashed. Nobody could tempt him to return. The *Daily Northwestern* was one of many newspapers to say good riddance, insisting that he had exaggerated his persecution and that "much sympathy is wasted on the Worcester sprinter."

In late November, only days after saying he had "enough to support himself the rest of his days," he abruptly changed his mind again. On November 21 he and his wife rushed aboard a transcontinental train to catch the last Sydney-bound steamer out of San Francisco. He later wrote that he had always wanted to follow in the footsteps of his hero Arthur Zimmerman, who had raced in Australia in 1895—the first American to do so—but a day prior to departure he sounded anything but enthusiastic. The $2,000 promised him would pay for travel expenses, but he'd have to win to make the trip profitable. It was hardly a sure windfall, especially in his fatigued and questionably motivated state. The person he evidently couldn't say no to was Daisy. "I would've retired," he said later, "but I wanted to give my wife a trip around the world."

He was going to Australia, the newest and ultimately the last gold-rush destination for the sport. It would be the beginning of a road odyssey as arduous as any in sports history. Over the next eighteen months he would travel nonstop, racing exclusively beyond the borders of the United States. He would cross the country multiple times en route to San Francisco and make two separate ocean voyages to Australia; he would cross the Pacific, Atlantic, and Indian Oceans as he transited between the capitals of Australia and spring racing in Europe. He was like an itinerant preacher, utilizing trains, ships, and bicycles instead of the horseback of old. It would've occurred to him that the sport, or more succinctly the promise of a fair fight, was taking him to the farthest ends of the earth. Unlike France, which he had been attracted to all his adult life, Australia was a mystery, a frontier continent with strange creatures such as kangaroos and wallabies.

The pace he was running at—he was already coming off back-to-back seasons in Europe and the United States—concerned his friends. There were the stresses of transoceanic travel, of being newly married, and of being a national figure. Six months earlier, as he prepared to board his ship for a second invasion of Europe, Booker T. Washington and dozens of schoolchildren had seen him off at the dock. The eyes of all negritude were drawn to his exploits, said Washington. He had a stage, and he should use it. (And yet even with Washington's attempt at coronation, it seemed telling that in the day's papers the list of notable passengers didn't mention Taylor but did list George W. Vanderbilt II, a gambling compatriot of Harry Thaw's who was then distinguishing himself by largely depleting his fortune.)

When they left New York's train station Taylor and Daisy were dressed like the first couple they were. He was clipped and conservative in a smoothly knotted tie, high-collared white shirt, and dark, fitted sport coat. She was elegant in a white tailored shirtwaist and a slim piano man's tie. A narrow skirt funneled to her waist, and a large boater-style hat would have suggested the Gibson girl of popular magazines.

Though tired, Taylor felt, for the first time, as though there was an added purpose to his travels. He was racing, but he was also determined to show his wife a world where he and they were appreciated. He seemed to be searching as much as he was racing, looking for a perfect homeland.

The Negro problem had firmly divided Du Bois' "small nation"— his phrase in his introduction to the Paris exhibit of 1900—into two small nations. At the same time Taylor and Daisy were rumbling across country in a well-outfitted, lace-curtained Pullman coach, Du Bois was putting the final touches on a book of essays that would bring the split into the open. *The Souls of Black Folk* would make people, black people, take sides like never before.

The streamlined Central Pacific passenger train went as fast as 60 mph, whizzing across the Plains states and around the snowy mountain peaks in the Sierra. Taylor, his gaze alternating between his wife and the rich landscape passing his cabin window, had always been Booker T. Washington's poster boy for the "new Negro": hardworking, firm but reasonable with the white man, religious, and, well, white as any white man. But more problematically, Du Bois claimed him, too. He had struggled with the place of his allegiance almost his entire adult life. As Du Bois edited the *Souls of Black Folk* manuscript in Georgia, it was as if the sociologist was on that train with Taylor empathetically peering down. When he famously wrote about "twoness" there was no more prominent example in American life than Major Taylor.

After the Egyptian and Indian, the Greek and Roman, the Teuton and Mongolian, the Negro is a sort of seventh son, born with a veil, and gifted with second-sight in this American world,—a world which yields him no true self-consciousness, but only lets him see himself through the revelation of the other world. It is a peculiar sensation, this double-consciousness, this sense of always looking at one's self through the eyes of others, of measuring one's soul by the tape of a world that looks on in amused contempt and pity. One ever feels his twoness,—an American, a Negro; two warring souls, two thoughts, two unreconciled strivings; two warring ideals in one dark body, whose dogged strength alone keeps it from being torn asunder.

To go fast, to rush away, to let the frozen landscape blur into unrecognizable form seemed a blessing with so much unsettled. The train made fine time across the country, arriving in San Francisco in less than a week. A day later, on November 27, the Taylors' steamer, RMS *Ventura,* sailed.

Leaning on the top deck railing and watching the dock lines slip from their pilings, Daisy was radiant. She was relieved to have their relationship out in the open; they would be okay now. As a little girl in Hudson, New York, she grew up with ships; the steamers from the city brought the rummy, lust-filled tide of humanity to her doorstep each weekend. The lovely opportunity to be departing aboard a fine vessel wasn't wasted on her.

She had never been anywhere except a gritty patch of territory in the heart of the industrial Northeast. Their lives had been con-strained by the times, their background, their church. But now they were truly free—*she* was truly free. The grand excursion wouldn't stop just at Australian cities but would take them to all the European capitals, Paris included. Her motives weren't impure; her intent wasn't reckless indulgence but an education—the education she wished she had, the education she'd said she had. When she returned to New York City twelve months hence she'd be exactly the kind of Victorian woman the magazine, *Colored American*, said she was.

As the pilot boat led them into the deep water of San Francisco harbor, Taylor learned something about the "land of kangaroos" the tour promoters had failed to tell him. A year earlier, on December 23, 1901, the country had passed apartheid-like legislation restricting nonwhite immigration. It was called the "White Australia" policy, and among the objectionable races in what was once a multiracial Australia were Tahitians, Indians, Ceylonese, Chinese, Japanese, West Indians, Africans, and American Negroes. A triumphant member of the parliamentary majority cheered: "We are guarding the last part of the world in which the higher races can live and increase freely for the benefit of higher civilization."

Taylor's brave new world awaited. He had 15,000 nautical miles to wonder if he'd be welcomed or chased away.

CHAPTER 14

Australia

1903
NEW SOUTH WALES

Taylor is a full blooded Negro, about medium stature, heavily but cleanly built, and his whole physique is that of a man who has judiciously trained till in sporting parlance he is all wire.
—*Sydney Mail,* JANUARY 7, 1903

WHEN CAPTAIN JAMES COOK, on a daunting, shoaly odyssey not unlike Taylor's, reached the eastern coast of Australia in 1770 he noted the rocky prominences known as the Heads at the entrance to Sydney harbor and logged something about a probable safe anchorage within, but he was homeward bound and in too much of a rush to investigate. Though the harbor would be discovered a few decades later and exploited with the gold strikes in the mid-19th century, Cook's haste was typical. Australia was still an unknown, nobody much bothering to stop long enough to figure the place out. Those who stayed only did so because they had to—they were convicts, the original settlers. The only ones who willingly adopted the landscape, the native Aborigines, were shunned. The situation into which Taylor sailed could not have been more confusing.

As RMS *Ventura,* a gleaming new steamship, parted the deep waters between the Heads, Taylor and Daisy rushed to the deck to see what the commotion was about. Hundreds of boats—pilot steamers, sailboats, dories—had converged on the outer harbor, having received advance word on the morning of the twenty-second of Taylor's arrival. "It brought tears to my eyes," wrote Taylor, who more dramatically than ever before felt the acceptance and excitement associated with being an American champion. When he was handed a pair of binoculars, Taylor could see that the shoreline near the steamship terminal was mobbed with what appeared to be thousands of people. White people.

Chants and cheers rose up, foghorns blared, and bands played. With exquisite timing, a VIP launch came alongside and unloaded assorted welcoming dignitaries, including the promoter who had orchestrated Taylor's visit. In the weeks leading up to this moment, he had salted the daily papers with stories that projected Taylor as a dusky cross between Hercules and Solomon. It wasn't merely a sporting man coming to shore, another robber baron to slink away with the island continent's seemingly inexhaustible riches, but a man of moral force, steely resolve, and physical wonder. He would speak from the pulpit and blaze across the Sydney night sky. In the ongoing Victorian struggle between saints and sinners, between laws that forbade daylight swimming but allowed prostitution and gambling, he was something sensible for everybody. His coming conferred an importance to South Australia. People came out and stared toward the Heads as though the mythic Cook and his trusty *Endeavour* had returned, only this time with the intention of stopping.

Hugh McIntosh, Taylor's champion, had produced one of the greatest opening acts in sports history. It was telling that almost everyone's first impression of Taylor was that he was smaller than expected—they'd anticipated a giant. McIntosh himself was a force of nature, a man whose nose for money had brought him to outback silver mines and Sydney alleyways. His most recent enterprise, selling meat pies, had made him a fortune. Like countless others before him, the whiff of a big killing had brought him to cycling. He would later become known for importing world championship events to Australia, including two of the biggest heavyweight title fights ever. "Stop, Johnson!" McIntosh would scream in the bout between Jack Johnson and Tommy Burns, for which he was also the referee. But his start was in pies, cycling, and Major Taylor. When the two met, Taylor's glance lingered, trying to come to terms with a pair of boyish blue eyes and a broad nose that appeared to have been busted.

In McIntosh, Taylor would eventually see an awful lot of Billy Brady—the orphan upbringing, the winning smile, and the ability to never hear no as a final answer. It was as if Brady had shipped out a mirror copy of himself, with only the name, place, and accent different. McIntosh loved to tell dinner companions that he was born on a night when a murderous gale fell upon his beloved Sydney. Most thought it was a fib, but in fact McIntosh wasn't exaggerating. On the eve of his birth in 1876 the Dandenong Gale sank ships and blew homes into a boiling Tasmanian sea. In the relatively kind waters of the southern Pacific, it was the storm of the century. Whether he outright claimed it or not, the implication was clear: he gave the historic tempest a human form—and over the next several decades it seemed to prove out. Wonderful and perfectly awful things would happen in McIntosh's wake.

IN AN OLD MAJOR TAYLOR SCRAPBOOK is Daisy's complimentary grandstand entrance ticket to the Cycling Carnival at the Sydney Cricket Ground. The ladies' pavilion was on the turn, but the grandstand seats were on the finish line. A record crowd of 30,000 was on hand. The date was Saturday, January 3, 1903, only ten days after they had arrived. After workouts Wednesday and Friday, Taylor was already on his short sprinting form and blasting by others as if standing still, the papers reported. Several thousand came just to watch his training. "Mrs. Taylor, wife of the world's champion, Major Taylor, devotes all her attention to her husband, assisting him very materially in his training," a Sydney writer added. (Munger had always told Taylor that wherever he was and whomever he trained with, Munger would always be his coach. But when you get married, he added, your wife is your coach. He was right again.)

The paper happily contrasted the pairing: Taylor had a hardness in his dark features and the "blackest of black hair, telling an unmistakable tale," but Daisy was a dusky belle and an "admirable foil." Her blue veins, the writer might have added, were a boon to the family bloodline.

Taylor won the international quarter-mile championship, dispatching the young Aussie champion Don Walker. On the Sunday after his first race he preached at the Wesley church on Regent Street, a first for Taylor (and no doubt encouraged by McIntosh). He implored the young men in the long pews not to desecrate the Sabbath by going to the theater or the track. He related a story from his long ocean voyage in which he and a Catholic priest had a series of conversations about the resiliency of their faiths. "I am Baptist," Taylor recalled telling the priest in their first conversation. "'Oh well,' he remarked, 'I think you've got a chance.' Yes sir I said, I think I have got a chance, and a very good chance too."

The *New South Wales Baptist,* a newspaper that with stubborn Victorian restraint had previously ignored the discussion of all popular sports on its pages, devoted no less than five column inches in large type to an interview with Taylor. "He has been preaching to the sports world a silent but eloquent sermon of example," the paper noted. All of Australia seemed aglow in Taylor's white light.

As earnest as he was, there was another side of Taylor the Aussies seemed to fancy. He was both cocky and faithful to those who paid

Taylor, pictured here in Australia, arrived in Sydney to one of the greatest receptions ever accorded a foreign athlete. *Source: From the Collection of the Indiana State Museum and Historic Sites*

to see him. He was an individual who was refreshingly comfortable in his own skin—something that couldn't always be said for Sydneyites, whose lifestyles, propriety, and Headland-sized chip on their collective shoulder seemed fatally borrowed from Australia's colonizer, England. Asked to explain his nickname, he said, "It was Major to 30,000 people when I defeated their favorite Jacquelin in Paris and it is Major to the lift boy in my Sydney hotel." But he also said the good people of Sydney needn't take his word for it. They would see what he meant, and they could expect him to ride himself blind. He owed them that.

Two days later, in a half-mile handicap race, Taylor had his machine "moving as Victorians have never seen a bicycle traveling before." He seemed to fly. The track lacked speed—its surface was asphalt and the layout more circular than oval—but nobody except the racers seemed to notice. It was an evening session, the track gaily lit up with acetylene lanterns and the grandstand flooded with incandescent light. In the featured final heat Taylor had seemed lost in the back of the pack when he suddenly bolted to the highest portion of the track, overtaking rider after rider as he hugged the rail. With a final, otherworldly burst he made up a three-length deficit in the final straight to nip the Italian Boldi at the post. "He is really the marvel that the Continental and the American press proclaimed him to be," a Sydney article began.

By the conclusion of the two-week carnival in Sydney the impossible seemed to have happened—McIntosh's hype had proven accurate. Taylor was a tactical master and braver than anyone when it came to slotting through a jumble of watchful riders with elbows spread. But most wondrous of all was his jump. His bursts of speed—his ability, as one writer described it, to sprint out of a sprint—was what customers paid their hard-earned shillings for. In other words, he had a top gear and then, when necessary, he had another one atop that. It was like the pitching ace whose fastball is clocked at 96 mph all season long only to hit 100 mph when the bases are full in the ninth and the pennant is on the line.

Each race the Aussie fans stood and watched Taylor, hoping to dissect the mechanisms that he deployed to explode up the track and vanquish all those around him. Eyewitnesses abounded; descriptions filled Australian papers from Melbourne to Adelaide. They related the way he hovered over the saddle before the pounce, the way his eyes flitted about, both seeing everything and giving away nothing. They swore his front wheel seemed to rear up at the moment he made his move—it was like every ounce of his being flowed into the bicycle's drive train and jolted the inanimate steel to life. Their imagery encompassed stallions and leopards. In the end they gave up—he simply had something, some magical combination of instinct and physiology, that fermented to perfection in the hot South Wales sun. "I was watching him closely and was all ready for him, but Taylor was gone like a flash of gunpowder," recalled the Aussie champ Walker on their first encounter. His power was limitless, available anytime he wished and in whatever amounts he chose to dispense.

One newspaperman hoped to disabuse his readers of the Taylor-as-deity theory, noting that form or fitness was an elusive thing, that he might have started too hard too fast to impress the big Sydney crowds, and that his form would likely tail off by tour's end. In fact, Taylor had barely trained for his opening races because he and Daisy had gone sightseeing for several days after their arrival in Sydney. His form was only beginning to show. In his future races throughout February and March in Melbourne, Adelaide, and then back again in Sydney, he merely got stronger. In one handicap race he began a single-lap dash 80 yards behind the limit racer and still won with relative ease. Most, including Taylor, came to the conclusion that he had actually improved himself as a racer while competing in Australia, adding experience and know-how in the one form of racing he'd proven vulnerable at, handicap racing.

Race day at the legendary Sydney Cricket Grounds during Taylor's first visit. *Source: From the Collection of the Indiana State Museum and Historic Sites*

He finished with twenty-two wins and four second places in twenty-six starts, and when his prize winnings were added to his appearance fees he had amassed a total of £2,000. Almost scandalously, it was the equivalent of what an average Australian worker could expect to make over the course of twelve years on the job.

"Australia is essentially a land of muscle against brains, with all the advantage on the side of muscle, so far as profit is concerned," wrote a correspondent for the *New York Times,* explaining Taylor's financial successes. Before Taylor had gone prospecting down under, an American racer named William Martin had preceded him. He had left Australia wealthy, not on his prize winnings but because he'd bet on himself against a heavily favored field and won £10,000. The implication was that the poor pitiable Aussies couldn't help themselves.

It was an article that naturally got Floyd McFarland's attention. In the coming months he would begin a correspondence with Hugh McIntosh, outlining an even better and more lucrative scenario, one where the competition might be a bit more colorful and certainly more intense. One can fairly imagine the film playing in McIntosh's head. On the heels of his immense success with the Taylor tour he was now introducing himself as Hugh "Huge Deal" McIntosh. The scene he imagined was the biggest deal of all: Taylor versus McFarland, white versus black, East versus West, an ancient rivalry settled.

THE TRIP TO EUROPE took the Taylors a full month. They made a stop in India where locals presented him with an ebony cane. He stayed on the Continent for four months, traveling all over Europe en route to fifty-seven appearances. He finished first twenty-eight times and second twenty-one times. He did well, warming to the challenges after he'd had a few weeks to train after the long sea voyage. While Daisy stayed put at an apartment in Paris, he defeated the English crack sprinter Sid Jenkins at London, his first appearance there. A postcard he dispatched Daisy showed Kensington Palace. "Where the Queen was born!" he exclaimed. For two months he was incessantly on the go, racing, training, and keeping up his usual prodigious correspondence. He begged her not to sleep too much and wished her good luck with her new musical studies. He teased her, competing for her attention. Beneath a comic image of an airborne gentleman with umbrella lifted, he wrote, "He's got Santos Dumont beat a mile." The slightly jealous reference was to Alberto Santos-Dumont, a dashing Brazilian heartthrob who in 1901 flew a dirigible-like craft between the Parc de Saint Cloud and the Eiffel Tower. Another post-card showed a buxom, pouting *frau* lying suggestively on a four-poster bed. "Auch Nicht Schlecht," the caption read—"not bad either." The circumspect Taylor seemed unbound, or at least he hoped to appear so—every bit as carnal and attuned to the sexual landscape as the next randy Parisian.

It wasn't until September, when he finally returned to Paris at season's end to race an old foe, Thor Ellegaard, that he and Daisy reunited. She had spent the summer at the Right Bank hotel of Madame Marthe Denis on Boulevard Malesherbes. Paris, the City of Light, sprawled out before her balcony view. The Sorbonne and the opera house were down the street, as were an array of exclusive shopping avenues. To her north was the blinking, rouge-red temptress, Montmartre.

They did not, as some might suppose, hold back. Taylor's note-book recorded something more than dipping a toe in the white-hot Seine. There were late-night visits to the Casino de Paris, the Folies Bergère, the Olympia, the de la Café Place Blanche, the Américain Café, the Bal Tabarin, and the notorious Moulin Rouge. They embraced the whiplash of lights, the whirl of sequined divas, cancan girls, and sword swallowers. There was no one watching in Paris, nobody telling. In the morning, they would've walked through the palatial Louvre and the Jardin des Tuileries, a mannered garden as fastidiously arranged as the rest of Paris was not.

Whatever ugly memories survived Daisy's Hudson childhood seemed to vanish in the opulence and freedom of Paris. She drew, read, and performed, turning into the woman that previously she'd only wished she could be. All those who later met her would remember her as a lady with unmatched elegance and refinement. She was as determined to excel in her own way as Taylor was in his. They both, in the racing parlance, had found their form.

Celebrated in Paris for his singing, boxing, and all-around showmanship, Taylor is shown here at the Hotel Malesherbes. *Source:* La Vie Au Grand Air

TAYLOR'S FINAL RACE TOOK PLACE at the Parc des Princes in Paris. Ellegaard was the Danish racer who had recently triumphed at the July World Championships in Copenhagen. Taylor hadn't competed in the race because it took place on Sunday. In fact, every world championship since his victory in Montreal in 1899 had taken place on Sunday, which explained why Taylor never won again. Instead, Taylor would wait for the winner, then challenge him to a match race. In 1901 he had beaten the newly crowned world champion Jacquelin. A year earlier Taylor had downed Ellegaard right after the latter had won his first title in Rome.

Ellegaard, a twenty-six-year old from Odense, had had an even better season in 1903, dominating everyone in Europe, including Jacquelin. Both Taylor and Ellegaard were determined to finish off their season, and in Taylor's case his career, in fine fashion.

On August 27, Taylor won the first heat, overtaking the Dane with a burst in the last 50 yards. In the second heat Ellegaard took the inside position at the bell and went all out in the last lap, winning by a wheel's length. Taylor took the third heat, overtaking Ellegaard early in the bell lap and never letting him get close. "The Major won looking round with a face well wreathed in smiles," a reporter described.

It was a tremendous accomplishment, a highlight of course, but perhaps not *the* highlight. Weeks earlier, Taylor and Woody Hedspath, a black rider from South Africa, had been matched against Sue and Bourette, the leading tandem team in Europe. Three distances were contested—the 1,000-meter tandem, the 1,200-meter scratch, and a pursuit race. Taylor and Hedspath won the first two, but in the pursuit, in which the two trailing riders must chase down the leaders, Sue and Bourette were victorious. Because the pursuit was the featured race and was weighted more heavily, the points score was equal at the end of the night. The tiebreaker was a 330-yard sprint with a flying start; the best time would win. It was an occasion that brought out the best in Taylor. In a distance he had never before raced, he won easily, setting a world record of 18 seconds. The event, considered a stunt, was never reported in the States.

When he returned to the United States he possessed a sense that he really was finished. The U.S. and European racing games were flat.

The Canada Cycle and Motor Company (CCM), which had sponsored Taylor's trip to Australia, was about to drastically reduce its manufacture of bicycles and go into skate making. In Australia, a new season of racing seemed doubtful—with no local gate attractions even Taylor's appeal was diminished. The Aussies couldn't match the best U.S. sprinters.

Everywhere there was evidence the racing men had lost their appeal. Baseball had been dubbed "America's pastime," and in the fall of 1903 the newly organized major leagues would hold the first game of the first World Series at the Huntington Avenue baseball grounds in Boston. Basketball seeded itself in Springfield, Massachusetts, and found a home in hundreds of newly built YMCA gymnasiums. At New Haven, the Harvard-Yale football game drew 50,000 fans, turning minds to the notion of a pro variation. The golden era of spectator sports was about to dawn, eclipsing the one that had led them all, cycling.

For sheer thrills, flight had taken hold. At Kill Devil Hills in North Carolina, the Wright brothers had flown like a bird. The duration was just twelve seconds, but that would change. As if all that wasn't enough, the last of the dashing speed merchants, Harry Elkes, was gone. It was the last straw. Like Taylor, he was one of Billy Brady's favorite Manhattan Beach headliners. He had been following pace, traveling at the near incomprehensible speed of a mile a minute on a board track in Cambridge, Massachusetts, when a tire burst. Though the pacesetters now wore protective headgear and full leather suits, the poor pace followers, unable to afford the drag of leathers and bulky caps, were as exposed as ever. In yet another fiery immolation, Elkes died instantly. There was another funeral and another gathering of haggard wheelmen, this time in Buffalo, Elkes's hometown. Taylor would have noticed there were less of them than he remembered.

It was time. The sheer volume of goods he and Daisy had shipped back to Worcester reinforced the notion he really was retired. Among the items were a kangaroo, a poodle, cockatoos, parrots, and a French automobile. For two months Taylor kept as busy as he could in Worcester, enjoying his newfound creature comforts. He was stopped for speeding a few times and warned with a wink. He showed off his kangaroo for a time, but it only survived until the first New England frost.

Sometime before Thanksgiving the activity around Hobson Avenue suddenly stopped. With the suddenness of a wind gust he was gone. On November 13 the Worcester papers reported that Taylor was en route to Australia. Major and Daisy, along with Gilbert Taylor, who had been living with his son and daughter-in-law for at least a year, had left on the 10:12 train for New York. Gilbert would get off in Indianapolis, where he would reunite with his other children, while Major and Daisy would continue on to San Francisco and a November 17 berth on the *Samoa*. It would have been "passing up too good a thing," Taylor explained, outlining McIntosh's latest offer.

A few days later another item noted what was arguably the bigger inducement to retrace his steps to the ends of the earth. "Taylor will go into training [in Australia]," the article said. "And will meet his ancient enemy, McFarland."

CHAPTER 15

February Fires

WINTER 1903
PACIFIC OCEAN

Haven't you people got eyes?
— MAJOR TAYLOR, RESPONDING TO AN
AUSTRALIAN WRITER WHO ASKED IF THE
DECLINE OF CYCLE RACING WAS IMMINENT

EN ROUTE TO SYDNEY the captain of Taylor's steamer announced that the Iroquois Theater in Chicago, the age's new "fireproof" jewel, had become engulfed in flames and toxic fumes, with 600 dying in minutes. Many of the Iroquois' patrons had not seemed afraid when the fire started, Taylor would read later, some confidently sitting in their seats awaiting a sprinkler system that failed to work. A notable exception was Taylor's friend Billy Brady, who was at the theater on December 30, 1903, and bravely helped to free the mass of frenzied men, women, and children piled up at the lone exit door. "Nobody could have realized quite how quickly the worst would happen," Brady wrote in his memoirs. "Inside it was a reverberating figure eight of fire from stage to screen."

As his ship coursed along without consequence, Taylor reflected on the grand reception to come and how blissfully at ease he had felt at the Sydney Cricket Ground, one the grandest racetracks in the world. Many of the races were held at night with all the lights turned off in the giant stadium except those directly over the track. The riders were like comets bending a perfect orbit, the fierce hot light unbroken. It was a phenomenon to see such a thing; last year he had seemed to win every time, and they'd called the spectacle the "Major Taylor Carnival." Taylor expected his "electric Eden" to burn brighter than ever.

Taylor didn't seem to fully realize this tour would be radically different from all the others. He might not have assumed all would go smoothly, but, like the poor Iroquois patrons, he didn't fully comprehend the danger, either.

TAYLOR BEGAN HIS "very last campaign" in New Zealand. It had been a last-minute addition to his already jam-packed schedule. The crossing had been unusually stormy, with both Daisy and Taylor battling seasickness for much of the monthlong voyage. When they came ashore Taylor was royally greeted, then dispatched to the racetrack twenty-four hours later. He performed spottily during his week in New Zealand—no mystery, given the hard voyage and his overall lack of fall training back in Worcester. By contrast, McFarland seemed to be growing more dominant by the minute. He beat Taylor to Australia by several weeks and cleaned up in a series of tune-up races in the western territories. He was in the best form of his life, he happily told all those who asked. By getting to Australia early, McFarland had also enlisted the aid of several Aussie veterans. In return for keeping Taylor off the winner's podium, he promised them a generous portion of the winnings.

McFarland had come to Australia at a time when the sport seemed to be getting more corrupt by the moment. Many Australian pros were still smarting from the whipping they'd received from Taylor a year earlier. Taylor had pocketed the winner-take-all cash purse from the stakes races and impoverished the local cracks to the point where they were desperate for a payday. Suspicious happenings began to occur. Strong riders suddenly began to perform poorly, slumping into season-long lows. Bookies noticed spikes in successful side betting, with certain racers almost uncanny in their ability to choose the victor.

Of course, the game was rotten. The slumping riders were "riding dead" on purpose, showing poorly, so that when the rich season-ending wheel races came around, the ones created for the foreign stars in January and February, they'd be wrongly assessed as needing the biggest handicap. They were sandbagging. Other riders found the cash to buy competing riders for a predetermined result, then make side bets on the already known outcome. "The whole system was overdone," lamented an Aussie trainer, Curly Grivell.

When the Taylors arrived in Sydney on New Year's Eve, McFarland was waiting. So was Iver Lawson, whom Taylor may not have expected. Lawson was coming off a sensational U.S. season in which he'd beaten Kramer repeatedly. In McFarland and Lawson, the "Terrible Swede," McIntosh had imported the ultimate powerhouse duo. The former was described as "a gritty man, a war horse who can race for a mile and then have something in reserve for a finishing burst." The promoter had ordered the whole bloody spectacle lock, stock, and barrel. It was an American war he wanted this time, not a coronation.

There was a different tone around the streets of Sydney this time, perhaps the result of McFarland's poisonous presence. Many of the newspapers were plainly bored with Taylor's elevated moral standing, slighting him with rude cartoons and nicknames like "Holy Wheelist." One cartoonist drew him with savage features, while another showed a falsely pious Taylor looking heavenward with a wheel spinning halo-like above his head. Ominously, there was talk (spurred by his winnings the previous year) of enforcing the whites-only policy against Taylor as a "colored alien and immigrant under contract."

Taylor didn't think Lawson by himself was a threat, but together with McFarland they had both the finishing kick and the staying power. In the trio's first match on January 8, McFarland won but was jeered by the crowd, which detected collusion. It would be a consistent pattern throughout January and into early February: Taylor losing to the McFarland-Lawson combination. Several races had already been tainted, including a 5-mile handicap where McFarland and others forced Taylor off the track and into the grassy infield.

Still, the Sydney public couldn't get enough of the serial rivalry and nightly filled every inch of the Grand Old Ground, from the ladies' pavilion at the head of the homestretch to the smokers' pavilion on the final 40-degree banked turn. At night the crowds swelled to 20,000, with the theatrically inclined McIntosh tinkering with his staging to underscore the drama. What he finally arrived at was a stadium packaged in equal amounts of shadow and light, as if to mirror the primal forces at work, as if to remind the good people of Sydney of the holy and the demonic. The Sydney spectators, cast in utter darkness, howled bloody hell each night. Only the track itself was lit, a ring of fire in which a dark man singularly pedaled while his white rivals blended seamlessly into the torrent of parabolic light.

It was all merely a teaser, however. January had only been a warm-up for a highly anticipated series of match races between Taylor, Lawson, and McFarland. Because they were pure one-on-one contests with no possibility for team tactics, the promoters could rightly claim the victor as being the strongest cyclist in the world. Lawson had beaten Kramer, the American champion; Taylor had bested the Europeans. Three world championship events were scheduled during the month of February at Melbourne's Exhibition Oval, with the first meeting being between Lawson and Taylor on February 6.

GILBERT TAYLOR, WHO HAD FINALLY COME to know his adult son during his year-plus stay in Worcester, had encouraged the race with McFarland so that the championship could be settled once and for all. Taylor had fought in the Civil War to earn his freedom and had fled his native Louisville after the war to ensure it. A clear victory had never been his, nor in some ways had it been his son's. Gilbert had never been able to summon the mind-set of Christian forgiveness. He wished for his son to impose a resounding defeat. It was as he had said years earlier, when he had finally consented to watch his son race in Indianapolis in 1900: he was glad he had won but wished he had done so by a margin that his rivals would never recover from. "Why don't you beat those white boys out further at the finish line?" he'd complained. "I expected to see you leave them so far behind that you could get dressed and come out and see the rest of them fight it out for second, and third money." It was one of the only times Taylor's father saw him race.

His son had chalked up the sentiment to his father's ignorance. He had never experienced the sporting arena. Perhaps there was a time as a boy in Kentucky that Gilbert had imagined himself a champion jockey, an Ike Murphy with a thousand victories, a lavish home, and servants of his own. Gilbert Taylor knew horses and understood how to care for them and what a fine, racing thoroughbred looked like.

But times had changed and he'd moved on. In Indiana, his farm failed and he tucked into the shadow life, from which there was no escape: a coachman, a laborer, a widower. The last official mention of him was in the 1900 census, where, at sixty-one, he was still working as a day laborer. He was not religious like his wife and hadn't said much when his son left with a white man to pursue a fool's dream. It's not hard to imagine he was embarrassed by the circumstances.

He had watched his son race once and had expected miracles— he hadn't cared to educate himself to know much better. Yet Marshall had drawn his father back to him. They had been separated throughout adulthood, but he wanted his father to see what he had— the house on Hobson Avenue, the friends who waved to him from every corner. They walked together in Worcester, took the trolley to the lake, enjoyed the theater on a Saturday night. Taylor paid tribute to his father in the best possible way—with his company. Undoubtedly the mystery surrounding Daisy's absent white father made Taylor all the more convinced that this was what he wanted to do. He had a father; he just hadn't found time to know him.

Taylor understood that black men of his father's slave generation had dreamed of a proud defining moment, something to encapsulate why they had been through what they had, why they had fought, and why they had lived. Thirty-eight thousand black servicemen were killed in action during the Civil War. The nearly quarter million who enlisted (despite being paid half the monthly wage of their white counterparts) had arguably made the difference between a Union victory and defeat. Gilbert Taylor was looking for a moment beyond Juneteenth when celebrations were organized in the black communities to commemorate the ending of slavery in the United States, a moment beyond when President Theodore Roosevelt made headlines simply by inviting to dinner the black leader Booker T. Washington. It was perhaps an unfair expectation of his son, who after all was human, to produce such a moment.

But in 1904, in Australia of all places, this moment was coming. Future generations would remember precisely where they were when Joe Louis pounded Max Schmeling, or when Jackie Robinson took his first big-league at-bat. Gilbert Taylor didn't want to be in Worcester when his son's moment occurred. It would mean everything to be in Indianapolis—where he and his family had struggled, where his son had been banned from the Capital City track—when he received the news that his son had thumped Floyd McFarland. He would be among old friends from the U.S. Colored Troops, who together could savor the moment. His son had provided the race schedule and the promise he would send immediate word via telegram. Through a series of fraying deepwater cables and linked relays between Sydney and European capitals, a single word would flash into the telegram office on Market Street: *victory*. Hours later the details would be relayed to New York and New Brunswick, where two men, Billy Brady and Louis Munger, waited. Neither had a taste for overseas travel—more specifically, the slow, rolling ships that then transported people to faraway places. They would wait at home, wait and worry.

For Gilbert Taylor, however, the news never came. That same winter, as his son and McFarland approached a grandly decisive event, he was struck and killed by a speeding train car. His son's telegrams would go unretrieved, the splendid gatherings undone.

An insert in Taylor's earliest diary had read: "In case of emergency please contact . . ." He had carried it so somebody would know he'd been there, so he wouldn't vanish like all those a generation ago for whom no record was kept. But his father actually did vanish, his place of death and burial as unrecorded as his place of birth, marriage, and war service. His remains did not find their way to Crown Hill, like those of his wife and daughter, nor are they listed as resting in Marion County or anywhere else in Indiana. There is no known official mention of his death, no obituary or death notice in the newspapers where his surviving children then resided— Indianapolis, Chicago, Worcester.

Of all the funerals Major Taylor had attended in the decade—his mother's, his sister's, and those of countless colleagues—the one that meant most he missed. Everybody did. When and how he received the news he never mentioned. It might have struck him, as he ever so quietly eased into his warm-up laps at the Sydney Cricket Ground or Adelaide Oval or Melbourne's stadium, that the finality of death, a father's death, occurred with the greatest speed of all.

THE NOTION OF A DEFINING BIG-CITY, bright-lights title match, a championship extravaganza, was a page from Brady's book. In spite of the social restrictions of the Victorian amateur age, it was inevitable, like the premodern boneshaker en route to the whippet-like 14-pound racing frame. The golden age of professional sport had dawned—the World Series and the Tour de France had their inaugural editions in 1903; soon to follow were the Indianapolis 500 and others. The amateur ideal of Pierre de Coubertin—well-rounded, gentlemanly individuals in the divine quest for personal excellence—had been shoved off into one corner, while the main attraction was the unapologetic merging of entertainment and athletics. Money, fame, and drama were driving forces. A true pro championship necessarily became more than just another meeting among top-notchers; it became an emotional narrative of young and old, of failed and found, of black and white.

The Taylor-McFarland showdown—aided by a flame-throwing press and the pair's deep and well-known mutual dislike—was a first packaging of an international sporting classic. The spectacle elements were a work in progress, but McIntosh had the right instincts. He would realize the sumptuous potential of the form a few years later when (using the Taylor series as a blueprint) he brought over the black challenger Jack Johnson to fight the white heavyweight champion Tommy Burns. In that event he would play a perfect hand, building the championship encounter with spin and savoir faire. He'd coordinate the timing adroitly, making sure the bout coincided with the arrival of a ready-made audience, the thousands of U.S. sailors who pulled into Sydney harbor with the Great White Fleet days before the title fight. As if a mentoring Billy Brady were whispering in his ear, telling him this was the big one, that there was no limit to what could be said or done, McIntosh would go to town. At his behest Johnson would do speed demonstrations at his hotel base camp, where he'd catch a released wallaby, a rabbit, and a greased pig. It was Bradyesque theater, and McIntosh would live Brady's number one rule: "always go after the champion." Fans would start lining up at the ticket office window at 2:30 A.M. the day of the fight.

The irony was that the pioneering promotion that Brady dreamed of his whole life, the one combining story line, sports, and gobs of money, would occur under somebody else's watch: a black-versus-white title fight in a country described as "the world's last remaining white outpost." Brady could only watch from afar and wish he had ticketed himself to Australia first.

As if stirred by the stormy arrival of the American combatants, the normally perfect midsummer Victoria weather began to go to pot. Sleety rain and bitter gales—"fires in February!" exclaimed a columnist of the harsh front that parked itself over Melbourne throughout the month—postponed the first championship race between Taylor and Lawson for two days. On Monday the eighth, with conditions not much improving, organizers decided they could hold off the paying public no longer. Lawson stayed huddled in his training quarters right up until the start, limbering up next to a blazing woodstove. Taylor roared around the track behind a pacesetter, hoping to fight the cold with his own rising body heat. In the wait for Lawson, many in the crowd wondered if he was getting cold feet without McFarland to assist him in the race.

Lawson did show up and raced well, but Taylor won the best of three heats two straight. Taylor's performance was especially impressive given his well-known dislike of cold-weather racing. "Those two jumps, one on the outside and on the inside, fairly appealed to the crowd," a reporter wrote of the first heat. "Hats, handkerchiefs, programmes, wooden legs, or whatever came handy were waved in the air . . . as genuine as the sun's rays [the match racing] whetted the appetite for more."

With the Lawson match out of the way, the upcoming contest between Taylor and McFarland began to consume the public's focus. McFarland was lean but all muscle, wrote a Melbourne track reporter. He didn't smoke, which he said was bad for racers, but he wasn't quite a teetotaler. His engine roared at such a furious rate, he explained, that he was forced to eat almost constantly: porridge and chops in the morning, roast beef and milk pudding at midday, and roast beef and chops, or both, at the dinner hour.

Two days later Taylor and McFarland met for their race of truth on the same track. Though Taylor claimed the overall advantage in head-to-head meetings, McFarland had the lead in big wins (most notably Indianapolis and New York). The larger the purse, the more unbeatable McFarland was. The hype prior to the race touched on everything—the records, the dislike, and the litany of charges and countercharges spanning three continents and a decade of racing. "Skill, stamina, and condition is the only combination known to me," McFarland sniffed. "Major Taylor is not invincible, even at his own specialty—match riding." Illustrations showed an implacable McFarland sitting up on his bicycle with only an index finger tracing his handlebars. It was the posture of a racer on a victory lap. By contrast, Taylor appeared with an anxiety-ridden face, his body bowed over his bicycle and his hands clenched to the bars as though he was pedaling for all he was worth. He was chasing.

By the 8:00 P.M. race time, the Melbourne fans were in a frenzy. Prime grandstand seats had gone up a shilling in price. In the gamblers' minds, Taylor was the prohibitive favorite owing to his easy dispatch of Lawson, but other trackside gurus weren't so sure. They believed McFarland would set an all-out, desperately hard pace. He couldn't match Taylor's jump, but McFarland might be able to drain him so thoroughly in the lead-up to the finishing straight that Taylor would be left without any kick.

But McFarland did nothing of the sort. The two sparred, each loafing in the early part of the race in an effort to get the other to take the lead. McFarland won the opening heat by a length. The slowdown tactic seemed to catch Taylor off guard—at the climactic point in the second heat McFarland won over the crowd by grabbing onto a light post at the top of the track to watch his quivering rival's

balancing feat. McFarland knew Taylor's gift: he was easily the superior bike handler and could, if need be, stop dead on the track for
upward of thirty seconds. By spoofing his adversary, he seemed to
take away the advantage. The grandstand erupted with laughter,
patrons nudging one another to spot the wide grin on McFarland's
fresh, whiskerless face. Under the glare of a 2,000-candlepower
lamp, his star quality was unmistakable. The referee was forced to
call a restart.

In the rerun of the second heat, McFarland did what everyone
had expected him to do in the first place. He pushed the pace from
the start, and as the pair came roaring down the backstretch with
only fifteen lengths to go, it appeared he had his underdog victory.
Nobody could recall a rival catching McFarland from behind. But in
what a Sydney judge called the most extraordinary last kick he had
ever seen, Taylor exploded, responding as if Munger was before him,
urging him on with his booming, "Now spurt, now!" It was the
dream jump, his pedal cocked and loaded at the one o'clock position,
then propelled forward and downward in a neuromuscular blip, a
perfect transfer from mind to body, from unrealized wish to absolute
will. The force on the pedals wasn't constant but imperceptibly
and efficiently parsed so that the stroke wasn't one mashing bio-
mechanical moment but peculiarly orchestral, one revolution com-
prising moments of power and moments of conservation, meted out
in micro-adjusted applications of force. At either end of the stroke
the torque increased, but in between there was smoothness, lightness
even, a constant feathering to stimulate power but preserve economy.
He couldn't lift as much weight as McFarland, nor could he torque
the pedal as hard. There was no plausible reason for the jump's effec-
tiveness. It was the conundrum of speed: those who want it can't
always have it. There was something in the way that his energy
poured through his bike into the track. A century later scientists

would recognize the phenomenon, reduce it to a fraction of a second with digitized high-speed video, and still not be able to capture it.

Witnesses swore he was going twice McFarland's speed. As they came over the line the taller McFarland appeared to edge Taylor out, but their wheels crossed dead even. "Both crossed the mark simultaneously," a judge explained. "We only judge by the wheels, nothing else." The crowd, however, could not be appeased. Hoping to put the judges into the deepest difficulty possible, McFarland stormed out of the building in outrage, saying he'd won fair and square and had no intent to participate in a race-off. Though the crowd came close to rioting, the decision stood: McFarland had to return.

But he refused. Privately Taylor was furious. He expressed his feelings in a poem he never made public but kept in a scrapbook: "Haul down the poster. I can't race tonight, / I'll keep my money, it looks better white, / The Black Cloud may hit me, so just out of spite, / Oh! Haul down that notice. I can't race tonight."

It would take a week of negotiations until McFarland—threatened with being banned from racing in Australia and abroad—finally agreed to rerun the race. "I am confident of repeating my performance," he said beforehand, "and thereby staggering the 'Wise Guys' who freely asserted that in taking on the Major, I was biting off considerably more than I could chew. Unreservedly I here announce that I will win, and win decisively and cleanly . . . I want you to understand that I am fully alive to the fact that I am going up tonight against the toughest proposition of my whole cycling career."

This time the date was February 13. The first race featured Taylor versus Lawson, the second Taylor versus McFarland. In the most vengeful and bitter rivalry in sport, promoter McIntosh had seemingly teased out the battle perfectly, bringing it all down to one delicious night of near-biblical confrontation. Well over 20,000 fans poured into the stadium, which was now accommodated with better turnstiles to avoid the crush that had occurred before the last match race. In the first paced one-mile heat Taylor whipped Lawson by two lengths. In the second an angered Lawson (or a subservient one; some rumors had McFarland, who'd bet heavily on Lawson, ordering him to "chop" Taylor if he was losing) cut across Taylor's path in the midst of his jump. Of course, it was any racer's most vulnerable moment.

Both men fell heavily, but Taylor had had no time to prepare. The crowd erupted—thrilled, agitated, a little seduced—but the uproar coursing out of the grandstand seemed to accentuate the terrifying stillness on the track. Taylor, who left a fifteen-foot skid mark of blood, bone, and black tire tread, didn't move. His skull was split like a heaved melon. Later Taylor couldn't remember whether he'd heard the voices screaming, "Major's down! Major's down!" or simply been told about them later.

Watching from one of the farthest points from the track, deep within the grandstand, Daisy was thinking of a song: *I is a high born culled lady,* goes the "Bicycle Darkie Song." *Jes' hear dem wedding bells* . . . She felt a kick in her round belly. Daisy looked down, felt her fingers untangle from a tight clench. Everybody was screaming, and she felt she might faint. *I is a high born culled lady* . . . She felt a kick.

CHAPTER 16

The Last Best Race

FEBRUARY 27, 1904
ADELAIDE, AUSTRALIA

The colored man is the leftovers. Now, what's the colored
man gonna do with himself? That's what we waiting
to find out. But first we gotta know we the leftovers.
— TOLEDO, FROM
AUGUST WILSON'S *Ma Rainey's Black Bottom*

MARSHALL TAYLOR WAS ON HIS BACK in a Melbourne hospital ward, weighted with deep, agonizing bruises that kept him from sleep. The discoloration was impossible to see against his tar-black skin, but it was there. The twitchy race promoters, in their straw boaters and white funnel-collared dress shirts, had arrived in the morning. The distance they'd traveled through the night, though considerable, was nothing compared to the distance the rivalry had traveled. Taylor and McFarland were some 15,000 miles from where it had started.

Taylor nodded in response to the appeals of the businessmen clustered in a semicircle around his bed, but he was thinking about Daisy. She never should've come to Australia. They were on the far side of the world again, a long sea journey and hard overland travel between them and their new home together in Worcester, Massachusetts. She was carrying their first child, nearing term. Long after

Sydney was born, Daisy would stay with her daughter—through Sydney's divorce and a series of jobs—all the way until Daisy died in 1965. Daisy stayed with her and stood by her for forty years, as though she never lost the fear of losing her.

Taylor felt cold, his muscles fleshy. He was not an overly vain man, but there was a striking vitality to his torso, especially the legs. From the time he decided to race professionally he single-mindedly improved his body, boxing and lifting weights and doing countless calisthenics in the Y each winter until he had made his shoulders broad and his chest deep. He ran, jumped rope, and drank nothing stronger than milk. Nobody trained as hard or took better care of himself. The Parisian magazine pictorial had displayed his musculature with the raw fascination and sensual joy of Michelangelo's *David:* naked quadriceps and hamstrings in close-up, beamy and taut as a champion thorough-bred's, tapering to the knee, billowing like a gale-filled spinnaker at the calf. His ankle was well rounded, the Achilles tendon a softer contrasting shade. "The form of a marquise," the papers marveled, "you can all see the silhouette of light and the harmonious strength in his body of bronze living in the supple body."

His exhaustive preparations and saintly habits had seemed to form a bulletproof shield. Amid his vice-ridden, gutter-dwelling sport he somehow had never been seriously hurt. He was a marvel, like Harry Houdini, the era's other great escape artist—nobody knew how he did it.

But now the harmony was gone. The muscles had softened. He had never been hurt, not like this. He asked his wife to leave his room, to go rest herself. Her belly was full and perfect; his accident was not an omen, he told himself, but the doubt wouldn't go away.

HE WAS BEDRIDDEN in Melbourne for a fortnight. Having stitched up his skull, doctors hovered incessantly, discussing new therapies for speeding his recovery. Wires came from all points, including the States, where the race circuit organization, now known as the National Cycling Association, implored Taylor to get to Adelaide for the all-important rematch with McFarland. The sport needed an answer, a clear-cut victor.

The doctors initially held out hope he might meet his schedule for a conclusive championship race with McFarland and Lawson on February 27 in Adelaide, but several days into the recuperation they decided he would have to scratch. It would be at least three more weeks until Taylor could sit in his saddle. His injuries were more serious than they first appeared. Weak from so much racing and unending intercontinental travel, his immune system was responding poorly. He might've had a broken collarbone from his violent tumble, and his hundreds of lacerations were ripe for infection. The techniques for making an accurate prognosis were primitive.

It's easy to imagine that Daisy refused to leave his side, helping change bandages and reading him current news stories about the great canal to be built in Panama and Teddy Roosevelt's successful campaign swing west. And there was something else. In southwest Africa the Herero people, an ancient tribe of black farmers, had mounted a rebellion against their German colonizers. Their victories were numerous at first, but the Germans brought in reinforcements and pursued a scorched-earth strategy of "eradication." Within months the Herero were cornered and forced to retreat beyond their tribal homelands into the severe outlying desert. The only watering holes had been poisoned, supply lines cut off, and fencing raised to prevent escape. The captive Hereros dug water holes fifty feet deep to no avail. The men slit the throats of cattle to drink the blood, suckled the breasts of new mothers, cut open the bellies of the dead to drink the liquid from their stomachs. Infants withered and died in days. In April 1904 thousands of black men, women, and children were dying of thirst and starvation while their white opponents coolly recorded "the death rattles of the dying and the insane screams of fury." It was the first genocide of the 20th century, and only the beginning.

ON FRIDAY NIGHT the Adelaide promoters, McIntosh included, made a last-ditch effort, arriving in person in Taylor's hospital room. Undoubtedly they alerted him to the quotes plastered throughout the morning's newspaper. McFarland insisted Taylor, not Lawson, had caused the crash: "Taylor reached out his hand and pushed Lawson up the bank so that he could get through on the pole. Then he struck his pedal on the bank and dropped . . . he was beaten. If any other rider had done what Taylor did he would have to go under for a year." McFarland also said that Taylor's no-show in their evening match—injury or no injury—forfeited the championship to him. A stipulation in their contract, on account of McFarland's walkout, had stated that if either of the men didn't show up for the final, the other would win automatically. He said he understood Taylor had been roughed up but questioned how "game the nigger was."

That evening Taylor abruptly changed his mind. He rose from his hospital cot, took a carriage to the rail station, and against his doctors' and wife's objections hopped aboard the all-night Central Pacific for the 500-mile passage to Adelaide. Sometime in the early morning he passed within only a few miles of Peter Jackson's hometown of Sydney. Jackson had been the greatest fighter never to get a title shot. He was too good, and the contemporaries who refused to meet him in the ring, such as John L. Sullivan, knew it. Like Taylor, he was smart and deserving. But he had died not knowing if he would've won, and even his magnificent Brisbane tomb, which was inscribed with the words "This was a man," didn't make up for what he never had: a championship.

Upon arriving in Adelaide Saturday morning, Taylor went straight to the track and prepared for the evening races. News of his appearance, forwarded by wire, had circulated in an instant. Promoters scurried to run the ads and prime the gate. Lackluster ticket sales reversed course and the electric wire sparked to life at the bottom of oceans. Readers in New York, Paris, and London woke to the news of Taylor's midnight ride. Could Taylor actually be planning to race? reporters asked McFarland when they heard of Taylor's abrupt hospital departure. "It's almost impossible," McFarland said. "All the skin is off his thigh and he can't sit on his saddle. He may come over, but what is the use?"

When Taylor walked into the oval, even with only a few hours' advance notice, there were 20,000 people packing the grandstand, a cresting sea of dark suits and derby hats bearing down on a white picket fence track border. For every hundred men there was no more than a single lady, each attired in a long dress and a broad-brimmed, frilly chapeau. Normally Daisy would've sat in the shade of the classically carved, arched grandstand, out of the brutal southern Australia sun but still dying another death. Instead she stayed behind in Melbourne, saying she wasn't up to the travel but meaning she resented her husband's inability to turn away from the fans, the promoters, his rival.

During his convalescence he had gained five pounds. Still, she imagined a weakened man, pushed and prodded and outflanked to a blindingly well-lit place where he couldn't escape, a white picket fence everywhere he looked. Another black man in the desert.

TAYLOR HADN'T BEEN ABLE to get on his bike when he arrived. Behind the stadium they'd begun the process by stripping away the thick bandages that padded his right leg, arm, and hip. The abrasions had begun to scab, but the new skin restricted his range of motion. He couldn't complete a pedal stroke. They'd need to reopen the wounds, cutting the fresh skin to free the bound limbs. Blood oozed out all over again. Taylor mounted the bicycle, and with his trainer

slowly rolling his bike a fraction of a revolution forward and backward, more tissue was sliced away to allow his legs to trace the arc.
Blood watered the grass beneath his feet. A half revolution, three-
quarters . . . finally Taylor completed one full pedal stroke. He was
cleaned up with cotton swabs and rolled out into the stadium. The
thunderous applause that greeted his warm-up laps was a drug. The
Aussies weren't color-blind and they didn't like blacks much more
than the next person, but Taylor wasn't viewed as black. He was a
survivor. So were they.

In a Hollywood telling, Birdie Munger would've been there at the
track, hollering out splits, pleading with his charge like an ancestral
Burgess Meredith. But Munger was never much for crossing oceans—
he never went to Europe, much less Australia, nor could he have
afforded the trip. Every cent of his was tied up in a Supreme Court
case involving his tire invention and the biggest, most powerful rubber
company in the world. He was in a David vs. Goliath fight of his own.

He also knew he had already given everything he had to Taylor,
who was twenty-five now, not fifteen. Munger didn't need to be there
watching over him, and he wasn't. But there is reason to speculate he
wasn't entirely absent, either. It has never been clear what bike Taylor
rode in Australia and probably never will be. The frame never made
it home with him, vanishing in the aftermath of the race. He probably had an Orient or an Iver Johnson, old sponsorships of his, but
maybe not. It's pleasing to imagine that Taylor, resurrecting himself
in the biggest race of his life, had brought with him the bicycle he
once said he'd never race without—the Birdie Special.

The other racers had been watching him. McFarland and his
cohorts knew Taylor meant to win, not merely show up to put people
in the seats, and a plan was hatched to "pocket" Taylor, meaning
that several of the lesser riders would surround him just prior to the
homestretch sprint and prevent him from finding a free lane to chase

down the bolting McFarland. There was nothing new about such a plan, only the circumstances. One of the potential conspirators quietly walked away, disgusted. Bill MacDonald had seen Taylor in his bandages, seen him bleed out back, seen him pull his pedal around, grimacing all the while. He told Taylor of the plan and offered to be an ally. Taylor at first was too proud; he declined assistance, saying he would fight his own battles. But then he called the young Aussie back. "Go to the last lap at top speed," he said, "and be sure to hold the black line (the pole) all the way. Take no notice of me [but] I will be on the lookout for you."

There was nothing unscrupulous about the arrangement, but the fact that there was an arrangement at all lessened the pain a little more. One against eight was better than one against nine. MacDonald was, of course, white.

At the gun the ten riders in the final heat bolted for the inside position. It was at the race's start and end that the crashes usually occurred, and though Taylor was content to stay out of trouble and be conservative, he found himself well back after the first lap. In lesser races the field had been known to dawdle, content to reserve their effort for the bell lap. But on this day, much to the crowd's satisfaction, the pace was torrid. Taylor rightly guessed the first order of business would be to test him to see if he was fit enough to stay with the group. The leaders dashed around the track in excess of 30 mph, legs spinning furiously, backs flattened to prevent wind drag, and bodies canting precariously as they banked into the turns mere inches apart. The lap splits were dangerously fast: 30 seconds, 29, 28 . . .

Along the grandstand a long rope was pulled and a high-pitched bell made the old structure tremble. One lap to go. Taylor was shadowing the pacesetter when MacDonald came out of nowhere to grab the lead pole position. The move threw McFarland's carefully scripted race into chaos. He and several of his cronies rushed to cover the move, which they did skillfully. Suddenly Taylor found himself pocketed coming into the penultimate turn, no daylight anywhere to be found. McFarland, smelling victory, made his move, launching to the outside of MacDonald and setting up for his homestretch kick. Taylor did the only thing he could do: he sliced inside MacDonald along the pole. He had committed his wheel to a hair-thin edge of track, knowing that the slightest miscue would send him careening into the infield. The Aussie MacDonald saw him coming and seemed to inhale just enough to make way.

McFarland seemed to have been launched from a slingshot out of the final turn as he stretched his six-foot-four-inch frame to full extension for the sprint to the tape. With his powerful stroke and massive tree-trunk-sized legs, he felt sure he had victory in hand. The crowd was well aware he almost never relinquished a straightaway lead. But Taylor kept coming. With a hundred yards to go, Taylor pulled even. With fifty left, he had gained a bike length. McFarland's face showed nothing, but his legs were screaming. He raised his head just enough to see Taylor cross the tape, back ramrod straight and arms raised to the heavens.

The crowd let out a convulsive roar of approval, the likes of which Taylor had never heard before. The marching band played "The Stars and Stripes Forever" as he circled the track on his victory lap. Out of the corner of his eye he saw a raging McFarland screaming at the other racers, the officials, and even the fans.

Momentarily the wires would sizzle stateside, telling of the miracle race, of the holy ascension, of something that neither science nor common sense could explain. Billy Brady would want to tell the story to the world, fantasizing about a darkened theater, a muscular, odds-against hero on a wide screen, and streaming artificial light spilling everywhere. The film era was about to be born.

In New Brunswick, Birdie Munger would look at the automobile

The new parents Major and Daisy with daughter Sydney. *Source: From the Collection of the Indiana State Museum and Historic Sites*

tire he was perfecting and know that nothing would replace the feeling of powering a bike faster than the man next to you. His former competitor Henry Ford—wishing a little harder, perhaps—would personally pilot a 1904 Ford Model B to a new land speed record of 91 mph. The Wright brothers, knowing that anything was possible, returned to Kitty Hawk and this time piloted their *Flyer II* to a five-minute-plus flight. And Teddy Roosevelt, a dedicated fan of Taylor's, would tackle the campaign trail reinvigorated, promising "fair play and a square deal for every American man and woman."

A bouquet of red roses was placed atop Major Taylor's handlebars as a warm trickle of blood leaked from one of his wounds. Perhaps he thought of Daisy and wondered how he'd ever describe this to her, or of the dead and dying on the gruesomely still African desert. Or maybe he flashed back four years ago to his white neighbors in Worcester who'd objected to a black man buying a home on Hobson Avenue.

Over two months later, on May 11, the Taylors' daughter was born in a hospital in Sydney. Mother and child were healthy. Taylor, too, was also healed. It was time to go home.

Back home things were changing, like a warped wheel that's been trued. The landscape looked different. The black explorer Matthew Henson was on his way to the North Pole with Robert Peary, where he'd match the admiral step for step en route to the top of the world. Suddenly all black brothers and sisters seemed to be on the move, to Chicago, New York, Detroit, even Los Angeles. A great migration, a great surge in optimism, was under way. It was not a coincidence that Taylor's rise coincided with theirs. The sown seed had sprouted.

In Worcester, historians a hundred years later would puzzle over a small but influential black community that had planted itself on the city's exclusive West Side. Where had they come from and why? Taylor's home at 2 Hobson Avenue, bought in his swift and quietly determined way, had led the movement, of course, the first black-owned house in a neighborhood he'd supposedly had no business in.

When Taylor returned home on the weekend of July 4, a *Worcester Telegram* reporter futilely tried to get Taylor to talk about his racing prospects. "That's certainly my greatest prize I ever won in my life," he said, directing the reporter's attention to his months-old daughter, Sydney. "I think I'll stay home and take care of her now. I don't care much whether I ever do any more racing."

CHAPTER 17

Home

WHEN THE AMERICAN CYCLISTS SAILED from Sydney harbor in 1904 there was no boat flotilla and no gala farewell. It was as if the Yankees had sacked the place, a piratical invasion that had sucked away all color and promise and left in its wake a scene of numbing desolation. Public dismay could be measured by the increasingly empty racetrack grandstands and the venomous diatribes that took up hundreds of column inches in the Melbourne, Adelaide, and Sydney papers. Hugh McIntosh, ably sensing the wind shift, moved on to the next big thing. He wrote his first letter to the heavyweight contender Jack Johnson in 1908, laying out his vision of a grand title extravaganza to coincide with the much-anticipated arrival of Roosevelt's Great White Fleet. He, like Brady, understood there were no new stories, just a recasting of grand old ones. It was McFarland versus Taylor, black versus white, all over again.

In truth, the other cities weren't nearly as affronted as good and true Victorian Sydney, but poor Sydney had endured the worst the sport had to offer. In March its vaunted Sydney 1000, the richest single-day event in the history of cycling with a winner's purse of

$5,000, suffered the major scandal everyone knew was coming. Seven of the eleven starters were suspended when it was discovered they'd fixed the results. McFarland received a yearlong ban for his role as ringleader. McFarland and Taylor's meeting at Adelaide would be the last undisputed match of the season and the most meaningful battle of their lives. If there was any question amidst the confusion of rival race series and a widely dispersed band of top professional racers, Adelaide settled it: Taylor was the consensus world champion and the American champion.

After a brief visit to Europe, Taylor finally returned to Worcester. He seemed hopeful he could compete in the 1904 world championships in London—it was the first world championships since Montreal not to be run on Sunday—but he found himself physically exhausted. A self-proclaimed "wretched sailor," Taylor had traveled incessantly for the past three years, crisscrossing oceans and continents. As the money became tighter he'd made more concessions to race promoters, racing more often and in more places. Often on the day after he got off a boat he was scheduled to race. At each venue, no matter the circumstances, Taylor was expected to show his magic. If he didn't, he was ripped. He often pleaded for patience. "I know some people have a notion that a race track is kept aboard ship for me and that as soon as I land at a place I can race right away," he told a reporter in New Zealand, "but I'm only human."

The racing and travel finally caught up to him. Despite his rousing triumph over McFarland, the psychological strain took its full toll. He had dug phenomenally deep, perhaps too deep. He had so much to look forward to with his young family, but an ugly incident in the States shortly after he and Daisy arrived in San Francisco unbalanced him. As he and Daisy innocuously strolled down the street, a passerby took angry exception to Taylor's obvious affection for what the man believed was a white woman. Though Taylor acknowledged the episode in his autobiography, he didn't detail his uncontained fury, nor the humiliation in having the encounter happen while he was showing his country to a visitor from Australia, the racer Don Walker. Because Taylor was physically and mentally worn out, the moment took on lasting significance. He had no forgiveness left in him. When an earthquake buried the Bay Area two years later he recalled almost despairingly how he couldn't summon the strength (as so much of the rest of the country did) to help the victims out with a contribution.

What Taylor later described as a nervous breakdown in the summer of 1904 would coincide with both the end of his championship odyssey, his uncertainty about the future, and the still-fresh death of Gilbert Taylor. For several months he and Daisy and their newborn, Sydney, were recluses, burrowed into their home on Hobson Avenue to keep the rest of the world away.

Though he would be lured back to some campaigns in Europe, he never seriously raced again in the United States. In the fast-changing atmosphere of early twentieth-century America, he vanished from public consciousness in an astoundingly short time. He had saved much of his earnings, but none of his investments succeeded. When he attempted to attend college at Worcester Polytechnic Institute, he was unaccountably rejected for admission.

An incident in New Zealand, at the height of his celebrity, would come back to him on those days when he would knock on doors and look at blank faces. A popular former champ named Tom Busst had called on Taylor at his Christchurch hotel. Taylor not only didn't recognize the name but gave the impression he didn't much care. "Bully for you," Taylor remarked at Busst's assertion that he had once been champion of the world. Busst didn't stick around. "But don't forget," he warned when he left Taylor's doorway, "in a few years' time if anyone mentions the name of Major Taylor, another will say, 'Taylor—Taylor—who the hell's Major Taylor?' " By the second decade of the 20th century Busst's warning had proved true. Taylor, the biggest sporting celebrity at the dawn of the new century, had been forgotten.

He wasn't the only one to be forgotten. Almost everyone in the sport was. Munger, a pioneer, died of a heart attack in 1929 at the Hotel Dauphin in New York City. A tidy obituary mentioned his work on the demountable rim but nothing about his cross-country trip in 1886, his record runs in Boston, or his protégé Taylor. He left a wife, a stepson, and a storage shed of immaculate racing bikes. Besides his work with Taylor, a legacy came in the form of the Australian Superbike, a successful multimillion-dollar effort in the late 1990s to refashion the tubular steel frame and produce the lightest, fastest, most friction-free track bicycle ever created. It was formed from a carbon fiber composite and sliced through the onrushing air like a blade. In its wake fell dozens of world records.

FLOYD McFARLAND, who had attempted to resurrect the sport as a promoter, died well before the others. He was at the Newark Velodrome, superintending the place, when an enraged client plunged a screwdriver into his skull. They had been heatedly arguing over the placement of the vendors' signs when the disagreement turned violent. Few people knew he was a giant of racing when they saw his obituary. His reputation as a charming businessman had trumped his notoriety as a bullying competitor. His funeral on April 21, 1915, was one of the largest in New Jersey history. "Mac was a villain," an obituary writer began, "but a very likeable one."

The evolution of McFarland's dear hometown of San Jose might have made him turn over in his grave. The "Speed City" and the state university he and his family lived beside would become a top destination for the world's foremost track sprinters, many of them African American. Harry Edwards, a brilliant runner and a would-be civil rights leader, helped organize the school's African American student

The promoter and New Jersey velodrome manager Floyd McFarland not long before he was killed. *Source: Library of Congress, Prints & Photographs Division*

athletes into a powerful force for change. Two of his charges, Tommie Smith and John Carlos, both San Jose State students, famously raised their gloved fists skyward on the medal podium at the 1968 Summer Olympics in Mexico City. Were McFarland to return to his San Jose today, he would find a recently dedicated statue of the pair a mere stone's throw from the old homestead.

THE HEARTTHROB SPORT of track racing would never be the same. It peaked in the mid-1890s, had a modest resurgence through the 1920s, then disappeared. The Grand Circuit never returned, nor did the swarming Coney Island stadium crowds. The vast array of velodromes receded back into the earth, either crumbling completely into ruin or taken over by something else. In Cambridge, the Necco candy factory stands on the site of the old Charles River track. Brady's Manhattan Beach track was long ago bulldozed and replaced with a resort. As early as 1906 there were the "where-are-they-now" columns popping up in the newspapers. "Arthur Zimmerman owns a hotel at Manasquan, NJ," wrote Puddin McDaniel. "Willie Windle is a revivalist; Owen Kimble is in the cigar business at Terre Haute; Charlie Murphy is a motor cop in New York; Eddie Bald drives a racing car in summer and is an actor in winter; Otto Maya is 'resting' at Erie, Pennsylvania."

The sport enjoys brief moments of notoriety every four years when the Olympics come around and curious kids see the banked tracks and pack of sleek flyers tearing around, but the professional variation couldn't compete with next-generation speed merchants such as race car drivers and motorcycle daredevils. The popular interest in professional cycling resides with road racing and almost exclusively, as far as America goes, the Tour de France. Lance Armstrong, who was ushered into the U.S. Bicycling Hall of Fame the same year that Taylor was, in 1996, compiled a record seven straight victories, garnering great popular acclaim at home and more often than not heated controversy abroad. Deserved or not, his position in the swirl of finger-pointing accusations smacked of the old days and the fiery McFarland. Armstrong inspired a new class of bright and talented American racers, and with them the old-timers saw hope that the sport would shine once more—a hundred-year renaissance, perhaps. But distractions and scandal were always around the corner. The sport was plagued. In 2006, U.S. professional cycling hit a new low when the American Tour de France winner, Floyd Landis, the son of devout Lancaster County, Pennsylvania, Mennonites, was charged with doping. The sport, so close to something special, had crashed and burned once more.

*   *   *

BILLY BRADY DIDN'T DIE, but became William A. Brady, the
New York bon vivant, author, film pioneer, and producer of countless Broadway musicals. It was shortly after the 1904 World's Fair in
St. Louis that he, like Taylor, had had his day in the sun. He and his
fellow investors had spirited away a piece of marshland on Coney
Island and constructed, in addition to the world's biggest roller
coaster and merry-go-round, a massive gladiatorial sports stadium. It
was not for cycling but for the next best thing: war. The stadium
hosted a Brady-produced reenactment of the Boer War starring
actual British and Boer veterans newly imported from the bloody
African veldt. The hit show ran all summer long and made him enough
money to buy his way back into the serious theatrical world with *Street
Scene,* a coming-of-age melodrama with a Horatio Alger–like story
line oddly similar to his own. In time nobody remembered his Boer
"reality show," nor that he had also produced Six-Day races, the inaugural high-stakes match race, and the $1,000 dare that launched the
"Worcester Whirlwind" and sank the Welsh rarebit Jimmy Michael.

Without Brady nobody seemed left to tell the story.

Taylor died a few years after Munger, a string of business failures
behind him. The financial pressure put a tremendous strain on his
marriage with Daisy. At the time of his death—June 21, 1932—they
were separated. His last job had been peddling his autobiography in
Chicago. His Cook County death certificate listed him as married but
his wife was unknown. He had been living at 3763 South Wabash,
but he had left nothing in the way of possessions with the exception
of dozens of books by the same title, *The Fastest Bicycle Rider in the
World.* Evidently without means, and tragically not unlike his father,
Gilbert, he was buried in an unmarked grave.

In writing about another black client of his, the polar explorer
Matthew Henson, Brady wondered why so little had been made of

his accomplishments within the minority community. It seemed unfair that the boxer Joe Louis, a wonderful fighter but an inarticulate man, should get so much notoriety while talented, versatile, and courageous pioneers such as Henson and Taylor were comparatively ignored. Henson's Brady-promoted lecture tour, like Taylor's book, never found an audience. "He lives in Brooklyn now, holding down some obscure Federal job," wrote Brady, "which is all he ever got out of being a negro who had outdone all white men but one in the three-hundred-year race for the Pole."

By the late 1930s the only one left to champion Taylor was Daisy. She had moved first to New York and then to Pittsburgh to be with her now grown daughter, Sydney. Whatever the breach had been with her husband, it wasn't enough to erase the grandeur of their best years. She kept his scrapbooks, letters, trophies, and memorabilia. In the late 1940s, a decade and a half after he died, someone finally came calling—they called themselves the Bicycle Racing Stars of the 19th Century.

ON MAY 23, 1948, A PAIR OF BURLY men in gray overalls set out in the predawn hours for a small unmarked plot at the Mount Glenwood Cemetery in Chicago. The process of reopening the earth was never pleasant, but the grave was shallow and the ground tender from the lengthening days and an uncommonly sunny spring. It had been sixteen years since the man was heaped into this hole, and the diggers couldn't imagine what had happened between then and now that would prompt somebody to rearrange what was done. The expense was formidable.

Thump—the edge of the shovel head finally struck a hard pine top board. A little less carefully than perhaps they should—they had no idea who the deceased was—they scraped and scooped around the sides and finally eased the surprisingly light wooden casket from its resting place in the dark cool pit. The sun was up, poised like an incandescent wheel ready to roll across Lake Michigan. The men hurried along to inform the others. Even at this early hour people were waiting.

Unfortunately, it's impossible to know everyone who traveled to southwest Chicago to attend Taylor's belated memorial service. Old rivals such as Frank Kramer and Iver Lawson were still alive. Tom Hay, the ex-racer who gave Taylor his first job at the Hay and Willits bicycle shop, arrived from Indianapolis. There were all told a hundred people in the Memorial Garden of the Good Shepherd. After all the funerals Taylor had been to, and after all those his racing brethren had endured, it must have seemed natural to be gathering on a spring afternoon in the tree-shaded confines of a burial ground. The brightening turf beneath their feet felt soft and warm, their steps well placed so as not to trample daffodils. A soft easterly breeze repeatedly skidded across the expanse of Lake Michigan. A few of the attendees remembered the days a half century ago when the cyclists followed the roaring pacing machines at nearby Garfield Park.

Everybody nodded and clasped hands, feeling the life breath of their troubled and tortured fraternity draw them forward. They had once been the fastest men alive—a sacrifice that only those present probably understood. None of the greats thought Taylor would've minded the short jump that took his casket from the pauper's side of the cemetery to the more prominent eastern side; he'd always enjoyed being noticed. Whether it was their intention or not, the day of the service was a Sunday.

It being Chicago, there may have been a relative in attendance from Taylor's family, but if there was, the presence wasn't recorded. Sydney Taylor might have been abroad—she served as a social worker during World War II—but wherever she was, she never forgave herself for missing the memorial and losing track of her father in his dying days. "It was hard for her to talk about," remembers her granddaughter Karen, "really hard."

Several eulogies were given. He had set seven world records and won the world championship in 1899 and the national championship in 1900. His victories in Europe had brought him to the attention of the world. There were allusions to the complex and heroic battle he had fought on behalf of the oppressed black man. The pressures he endured nobody could really know. That day in the *Chicago Defender,* Taylor's pioneering descendant Jackie Robinson found himself under fire from prominent black activists for departing the Negro Leagues in favor of his experiment with the Dodgers' Branch Rickey. "I charge Jackie Robinson with being ungrateful and more likely stupid," said Effa Manley, the owner of the Newark Eagles.

Taylor had seemed to understand he was living in a time and place where his example meant more than his testimony. Some read his reluctance to be politically vocal as a weakness, as ungrateful. Taylor wrestled with his role, never certain he could be as unequivocal in his denunciations of white America as others wished him to be. He had suffered through the most racially charged era in U.S. history, but he had also benefited from a few extraordinary individuals who happened to be white. The autobiography in which he wrote of the "monster prejudice" he also dedicated to Birdie Munger. If a position of leadership meant simplistic portraits, that's probably why he remained awkwardly in the shadows. His life was never black and white.

At the service's end, the bicycling greats unveiled a gorgeous bronze plaque with both a lengthy epitaph and a surprisingly well-drawn image of Taylor. It was based on a photograph taken of him in Paris as he bore down on Jacquelin, his jump in full flower. He was in the streamlined scorching position that at one time made doctors fear for the health of a rapt nation. The epitaph read:

World's champion bicycle racer who
came up the hard way without hatred in his heart,
an honest, courageous, and God-fearing,

clean-living, gentlemanly athlete.
A credit to his race who always gave out his best.
Gone but not forgotten.

In a palpable way it wasn't just his epitaph but all theirs.

They were part of a continuum that continues to this day and will certainly never end. The fascination with speed has not abated, nor has the race to challenge the boundaries that fix us to the pedestrian earth. An extreme example can be found each year at Speed Week on the Bonneville Salt Flats in Utah, where cyclists tuck into the slipstream behind the world's fastest-moving vehicles and hope to budge the speed record upward. In 1995 a Dutch cyclist was clocked at a world's-best 167 mph.

The urge to go faster and the tools to make it so are a modern pursuit as well and no less an obsession than they were a century ago. Records will continue to fall, though not nearly the way they once did. There is an inevitability now that there once wasn't. Moreover, the records only inch forward—no more do they lurch ahead in great big gulps. Major Taylor's best time for 200 meters, a now recognized international distance, was 11 seconds, only a half second off the current world record. His time for the kilometer (57 seconds) is only a shade slower than the French and Aussie speedsters who annually take turns owning the mark. As far as the bicycle goes, the nineteenth-century cycling stars—and Taylor most of all—wrung almost everything out of it they could.

Epilogue

THE STORY OF MAJOR TAYLOR isn't widely known in America; ironically, it has historically seeded itself in a more fruitful way in Paris and Sydney, where the appreciation for the bicycle and the men who first rode it is undiminished. In the latter capital an old-timer continues to display, in his Derby Street shop window, a picture of Taylor riding to his heroic victories in 1904.

At first glance it seems Taylor's accomplishments occurred too long ago, in a time that is neither understood nor valued. But the story hasn't vanished; it continues to circulate, passed between hopeful people like some ancient instructional text discovered in a long-buried time capsule. Only of late has the story found a home with young African American racers and old bicycle aficionados; with an Indianapolis mortgage broker and a Worcester copy editor; and with a string of Taylor relatives spanning the country from Hawaii to Boston. As the story moves through all these hands, it has gained strength, energy, and relevancy. A few years ago it arrived back where it started—in Indiana.

I found out by accident. I plugged the name Major Taylor into a search engine and discovered several clubs and teams named in his honor. The one, however, that caught my attention was Team Major Taylor, a club formed at the University of Indiana. Its expressed purpose was to diversify a nationally revered bicycle race most associated with white fraternity kids. It was the race featured in

the movie *Breaking Away*: the Little 500. I did some research. The
African American population at Indiana University was something
on the order of 3 percent. The African American fraternity houses
on campus numbered zero. Finally, the number of African Americans who were national-caliber racing cyclists wasn't much more
than a handful, and yet the best and brightest had been lured to
Bloomington by a charismatic alumnus and the hope embodied in
Taylor's 1928 autobiography, *The Fastest Bicycle Rider in the World*.
Team Major Taylor's mission was to both integrate and win the race
that seemed reserved for others.

I called up Courtney Bishop, the team's founder, and found
myself drawn deeper into his team's story. On my first visit Bishop
invited me into his suburban home and gave me a two-hour presentation complete with video highlights, posters, news clippings, and a
story that was appallingly familiar. He had the marketing chutzpah
of Billy Brady and the demanding training methodology of Birdie
Munger. "He is obsessed," a friend told me.

Each April, Bishop explained, the Little 500 drew crimson-
clothed alumni back to Bloomington and filled the grandstands at
Bill Armstrong Stadium with 25,000 rabid fans. The bicycle race's
traditions date back to 1951, when the son of pioneer Indy 500 race
car driver Howard Wilcox constructed an event to honor his father's
memory (he died in a crash the year after he won the 1919 race).
Howdy Wilcox Jr. used the Indy 500 as his blueprint but replaced
autos with single-speed Schwinn bicycles and Speedway pavement
with the campus' smoke-colored cinder running track.

The "retro" relay-style event took off. For a half century it has
stood as one of America's iconic amateur sporting events, celebrated
by publications from *Outside* to *Sports Illustrated*. The weekend
showcased the wholesome, hardworking heritage of Indiana and
the virtuous, almost lost world of amateur athletics, the magazines
explained.

* * *

WHEN COURTNEY BISHOP ATTENDED his first Little 500 as an undergrad in the late 1980s, his first reaction was "Wow. I mean, 22,000 people cheering and sitting shoulder to shoulder—I thought it was the greatest event I'd ever seen." Bishop was himself an athlete, a mile runner on a perennial championship track team. However, another reaction lingered far longer. "I looked around and didn't see a single black person, I mean not one." Bishop asked around and discovered that most of the minority students attended a university-sponsored picnic on the other end of campus. That was disturbing enough to Bishop, but the aura of the race was such that the Little 500 was the last place you'd go if you were a person of color. "Black students told me, 'Why the hell would we go to the Little 500 to watch a bunch of white fraternities ride around the track?' The more I thought about it, the more wrong it all seemed."

Bishop graduated, joined the workforce, and returned for post-graduate work in 1991. He hadn't forgotten about the Little 500—in fact, his return had a lot to do with it. He scoured the campus to find potential black participants and received the university's permission to ride in the Little 500 himself. As a grad student, technically he wasn't eligible, but the university applauded his mission, allowing him a special exemption because he was a symbol of diversity and because (according to Bishop) he represented absolutely no threat to win the race. His team, IMO (In Memory Of) Major Taylor, finished dead last. "My dream was to have hundreds out there supporting what we were doing. If we had ten folks there, it was a miracle, and I'm counting janitors, people hauling stuff—you know, everybody."

Out of the "worst experience in my entire life," Bishop hatched a plan of redemption—to find, pay for, and enlist a team of skilled African American teenagers who would attend Indiana University and compete, truly compete, for the Little 500 championship. If diversity was an issue at IU—and many thought it was—the Little 500 was the Berlin Wall. All he needed was four black kids, four latter-day Major Taylors, who raced bikes. There was a problem. "From 1992 to 1998 you could've circled the globe and not found four black kids who raced bikes. You know what I mean . . . anywhere. People were like, 'You're looking for what? Black teenagers that race bikes? Like, good luck.' We called every velodrome, clubs, teams—I called and called and called. And got nothing, nothing, and more nothing."

I first met Team Major Taylor (TMT) in January 2005, four months prior to that year's race. Bishop had found its members in South Central Los Angeles, Trinidad, and Detroit. A few were seniors, now on their fourth and last try at the Little 500. They lugged rollers, bikes, and donated CycleOps wind trainers across the slushy parking lot and into the basement room of a dorm where they could set up in front of a theater-sized TV screen. An African American co-ed who happened upon the incongruous sight simply stood and stared. "Can we help you out?" one of the team members finally asked.

Several members had been on the inaugural 2002 team. They told me they had read Taylor's autobiography at Bishop's request but hadn't really understood it until they were weeks away from their first Little 500. A rival team questioned whether one of the TMT riders was truly amateur, as the rules stipulate. The atmosphere quickly turned ugly as charges and countercharges flew. On practice day, the eve of the race, the other thirty-two teams laid down their bikes, refusing to practice with them—a public display of both rider unity and, it appeared, racial hostility. All of the protesting riders were white. The school's president pleaded with Bishop to voluntarily remove his team from the race in order to preserve the peace. Bishop and the team insisted they were going to compete and if the president was concerned about unrest he should hire more security. They received a police escort to the stadium. When they walked in and were introduced, many of the 20,000 fans whistled their disapproval. Their black T-shirts were particularly infuriating, in part because few knew what to make of them. They read simply: "Who is Major Taylor?"

Team Major Taylor finished ninth in 2002, second in 2003, and fourth in 2004. When I watched them work out that snowy day in January I was impressed by many things about them, not the least of which was their maturity. They had little in the way of obvious commonality. Bishop had found them in scattered cities with widely varying home situations and school reputations. Each of them said he felt something vital was at stake—*that* was what pulled them together. Their steadfastness showed. In the stifling heat of a dormitory basement they did countless intervals in huge gears. When I left, Simeon Commissiong, Kenny Burgess, Steven Ballinger, and Ali Camah were set up wall to wall, like a blocking wedge, sweat pouring down, faces etched in pain, as if the 200-lap, 50-mile race were coming down to the finish line.

ON RACE DAY 2005 it was 70 degrees, perfect, without a headwind. The cinders on the quarter-mile track were firm and fast. Precisely at 2:00 P.M. the first of three paragliders dropped out of a cloudless blue sky and stuck a landing in the grassy infield of Bill Armstrong Stadium, the Little 500's checkered flag in hand. Twenty minutes later—after the national anthem, a stadium sing-along of "Indiana, Our Indiana," and a shower of fireworks—the race announcer rumbled five magic words: "Gentlemen, mount your Schwinn bicycles."

The perfect day was expected to yield the perfect race, particularly for the sprinters of Team Major Taylor. Instead, what will be remembered was the perfect wreck. It occurred on the first lap, only moments after the pacing Indy car pulled off the track and the starter's green flag waved. Racers who had paraded around the track in perfect three-by-three order seconds earlier were still bunched together and nearing maximum speed when a rider lost control and clipped wheels with another. The pack—abnormally clustered because the Indy car driver couldn't shift up into second gear—detonated like a land mine had been tripped. Eight rows back, Simeon Commissiong dodged the initial wave of bikes and bodies but couldn't escape the next. When he arose his peerless tricolor jersey was grubbed with cinder and his bike buried beneath a heap of mangled Schwinn look-alikes. Twenty-five of the thirty-three starters were taken down, making it the worst crash in at least forty years.

Eight laps later it was Steve Ballinger's turn, and TMT mechanics were once again racing across the infield to pick up the pieces. All day it happened. They crashed, they got up, they chased. After Ballinger's wreck it would've taken a Herculean effort to finish in the top ten. With three-quarters of the race completed they stood eleventh. Then Ali crashed, leaving the left side of his torso, from shoulder to knee, a bloody, pulpy mess. They hit the deck six times in all, perhaps a record for a contending team. Of all the casualties in the race—and the medics were busy all day with neck immobilizers, backboards, and disinfecting scrub brushes—no other team was punished as much. They should've finished last, if at all, and not sixteenth.

"We could've given up but we didn't," David Leiter told me. He'd been a late addition to the team, which wasn't particularly unusual, except he was white. "We never did." It was noticed. When Ballinger arose from his wreck in the 170th lap an improbable wave of applause came from the heart of the fraternity cheering section, the same section that had jeered the team four years earlier. A gimpy Commissiong grabbed the bike from him to take up the chase, though he'd dislocated his shoulder in the first crash and later aggravated a hamstring injury trying to make up for it. Also noticed was when Leiter made his debut for TMT in lap 41. Somebody in the large and mostly African American TMT cheering section held a sign that read: "Go Dave Go, You Are So Hot." Officially TMT was no longer an all-African-American team but an all-everything team composed of a white walk-on Jew, a doctor's son from St. Louis, a poor black Muslim from L.A., and a young family man from Trinidad.

As the Dodds House squad claimed their first-place trophy the Team Major Taylor riders linked arms in a huddle on the opposite side of the track and listened to a man who in no way sounded like he was done chasing people for money, nor okay with a moral victory. "This is not going to be our final legacy, do you hear me?" shouted Bishop, his damp eyes boring into theirs and his face contorted with emotion. "We are not done. We are not done. We are not done!"

An hour later, IU vice president Charlie Nelms, the school's second-highest-ranking African American official, sermonized the fans and supporters of Team Major Taylor. They'd gathered in the courtyard of a nearby academic building. "Do me a favor at next year's race," he began, his preacher's beat turning every head. "Open up your mouths, put your hands together. Why is it we still feel like guests at this university? We are not guests, do you hear me?"

He went on, settling his eyes on the riders, who'd sprawled themselves on a brick landing. "Didn't I see blood on your body, Ali?" "Yes," said Camah. "And Simeon, didn't I see you limping across the infield?" "Yes," said Commissiong. "Well, hear me a moment. You didn't claim the prize, but you know—we all know—you've already won. It isn't the prize that really matters, is it? It's the stuff inside. Team Major Taylor showed today they have the stuff inside. We have the stuff inside."

A YEAR EARLIER I'D MET Lynne Tolman selling raffle tickets at the foot of George Street in Worcester. Hundreds milled about on a warm July day, most craning their necks to try to see the top of the same breathtaking hill that Taylor trained on. He was the first ever to

conquer the sheer 500-foot ascent without stopping. When a motorcycle attempted the feat it failed.

The annual Major Taylor Hill Climb, the raffle, and just about
everything else to do with Major Taylor and his association with
Worcester is Tolman's idea. She's a copy editor from the *Worcester
Telegram* who has devoted the last ten years of her life to reviving
interest in Taylor both locally and nationally. She has published
articles, organized fund-raising events, and spearheaded a drive to
commission a statue of Taylor to be placed downtown in front of the
public library. I suspect she encouraged the small frame maker in
western Massachusetts who took the original specs and truss design
from an old Taylor bike to make a modern version. The glass case display at a local Applebee's restaurant, with trophies and photographs
and the script headline "Worcester Whirlwind," is her doing, too.

The date of the race I attended was significant. Sunday, July 25
was also the final day of the 2004 Tour de France, the one where she
correctly presumed Lance Armstrong would notch his historic sixth-
straight victory. But before there was Armstrong—especially in
France—there was Taylor, which was the point she was making.

The cyclists who intended to sprint up the George Street incline
were the most diverse crowd of cyclists I had ever seen at a bicycle
race. There were cyclists looking for something to do, a national
masters champion named Paul Curley, recreational weekend warriors, families, EMT bike patrols, and several jeans-wearing bicycle
messengers who rode trim single-speed bikes. They were the modern-
day scorchers—rebellious, funky, and expert bike handlers. Each did
a long track stand—a technique in which the rider balances the
bike in a stationary position without his feet touching the ground—
before the race starter commenced his countdown. It was a maneu-
ver Taylor made famous when he raced Jacquelin in Paris. In the
background, a disc jockey repeatedly played a bluesy tribute song,
"He Never Raced on Sunday."

The climb was almost alleyway narrow, a strip sandwiched by large brick manufacturing buildings. It was a short and not-so-sweet paean to Worcester's glorious industrial past. You could imagine the shoppy smell of combustion and almost hear the noise of a clanging bell signaling the end of a work shift. Back then the ascent would've been extra bruising on account of the cobbles. These were all things Tolman hoped everyone noticed.

A racing bike messenger flung his bike from side to side with a violence that was astounding. He wore a Brandoesque white tee and a spike-studded belt, and he had the shaggy blond hair of a California surfer. He finished in 24.13 seconds, the best time of the day. Later, Tolman arranged a match sprint between him and some of the other top finishers. It was a touch of old school: a trio of top racers, zooming up the hill in a brutish contest of superiority. Spectators clanged bells and screamed things like "Punch it, punch it!"

The last few meters were endless for some of us. "You died up there," my eight-year-old son observed, though he was watching all the way from the bottom. "How could you tell?" I wondered. He just could, he said. The finishing sprint, Taylor's specialty, was the toughest thing in the world to do, Tolman consoled me. After race day, she had a hundred-plus new believers.

Afterward Brian Chapman, the victor, introduced himself to a little old man named Joe Cote. Cote had an ancient brown frame slung over his shoulder and was showing everyone who would be showed what he had. He believed the century-old bike was one of Major Taylor's, and for the next hour the old Worcesterite regaled Chapman and a few other young bike messengers with the legend of the Whirlwind. He claimed to remember Taylor coming to his door to sell his autobiography. When I left, an hour or so after the race ended, they were still there, the old man and the kids sitting around a vacant parking lot listening to stories of a guy who'd lived on Hobson Avenue. When I told Lynne Tolman she lit up like a light.

Two years later, Tolman announced that the Massachusetts state legislature had approved, after her decade-long battle lobbying for the funds, to set aside the money for a Major Taylor statue, the first monument in Worcester to recognize an African American. The artist's model was Simeon Commissiong, TMT's ace sprinter. The city also agreed to rename an adjacent artery Major Taylor Boulevard. Marshall Taylor's greatest fear—that he would slip away into anonymity—was a thing of the past.

TEAM MAJOR TAYLOR CYCLING CLUBS have proliferated around the country—in Oregon, New York, and most notably Los Angeles. Team Major Motion rose from the ashes of South Central L.A., where rioting in the aftermath of the Rodney King verdict illuminated the neighborhood's wretched despair. In the mid-1990s a thirteen-year-old troublemaker named Rahsaan Bahati was placed on a cycling team as punishment. Two days each week he had to attend a program where he was taught how to race a bike. "I did it because I thought it was motorcycles when they said it was bike racing," Bahati told me. "When I found out it was bicycles I tried to quit, but my parents wouldn't let me." In inner-city neighborhoods bicycle racing commanded the respect of no one.

Bahati would bury his tight shorts deep in a gym bag. One day when a teacher asked him to reveal the contents of the bag, he refused because he feared the ridicule he would receive. The standoff got him expelled from school. In the interim somebody gave Bahati Taylor's autobiography, and something clicked. He was among the first to join an all-black junior team called Team Major Motion, and by eighteen he had won two junior national championships and a major pro event and had earned a contract from the professional team Saturn. Overwhelmed by his sprinting ability, the March 2003 issue of *Bicycling* predicted he could be the next Major Taylor. He was the first African American to enter pro cycling in over a decade.

"I went all over Europe, where there are no blacks racing bicycles, and I remember once in Belgium a little girl coming up to me and asking if she could touch my skin. I said, 'Sure—it's not going to feel any different, you know.' " When several promising young black cyclists were asked whom they respected, they mentioned Taylor, then Bahati. And yet he endured several roller-coaster years in which he was profiled in *People* but then found himself unemployed when none of the major cycling teams thought he was worth taking a chance on. The rap was that he didn't train hard enough.

He said he found himself rereading the Major Taylor autobiography with the patience of a scholar, as though there were clues he needed to find. At twenty-three, he was the same age Taylor was when he went abroad for the first time and wrote,

> Well, I am sinful, right enough
> As sinful as can be,
> But I was fit for wearing wings
> When I was twenty three

In 2005, Bahati reemerged, finishing second in a national road race, approximately ten spots higher than the reigning Tour de France champion, Lance Armstrong. The same prominent team manager who told me he'd questioned Bahati's commitment said he noticed a major change. He hired him in 2006.

AFTER YEARS OF LIVING abroad with her military husband and their three children, Karen Brown Donovan, forty-three, had just moved to Washington, D.C., in the spring of 2005. There were stacks of boxes everywhere in their new Georgetown home—another symbolic wall separating her from those who wished to step beyond the well-known parameters of her great-grandfather's story.

Karen is the keeper of the story, the legal guardian of the papers and artifacts that remain. She had found out a lot about her family, but I had come to convince her that there might be more, that the story of Major Taylor, the cycling champion, was merely a portion of a greater story—a story of a man and a woman at the turn of the century who fell in love and fought for each other with an ardor that can barely be conceived. There were those incredible letters he wrote Daisy—how he ached for the kiss she would send him off with before each of his races, how he lamented the treatment he received and the punitive fines he had to pay for things he didn't do. "When a man is married and has a good wife as I have, and a nice little baby girl, he will take a good deal, and stand for many things that he would not were he not married," he reflected. "I stand for many things now that I never thought I could put up with."

Karen Donovan had read those letters and admired their sentiment; she doesn't know what divided the couple, only that Daisy spent the remainder of her life—she died in 1965—living with her social worker daughter in Pittsburgh. She never traveled after her husband died, and her privacy was paramount; it's unclear to Karen where she was buried. I would later find out that Sydney arranged for her cremated remains to be spread at a nearby garden sanctuary. "I do know this," Karen told me when I met her in D.C. "No mother was more loved. Sydney looked after her."

SYDNEY TAYLOR BROWN was the couple's only child, born in Australia in the days after Taylor's showdown with McFarland. She was 101 years old in the winter of 2005 and lived in a nursing home in the Squirrel Hill neighborhood of Pittsburgh.

Her father lavished attention on her as a youngster. When he traveled he daily wrote her postcards and letters. "Now kiss little Sydney over and over again for me," he wrote his wife during a trip abroad in 1909. When she became a young woman he bragged unabashedly to an old friend, "Sydney is a fine athletic girl, and attends the Sargent School of Physical Culture, Boston. This is considered the best school of the kind in this country. She won two firsts and a second at the last athletic meet there." She was raised in a household with servants and famous visitors; she remembered W. E. B. Du Bois, Booker T. Washington, and the boxer Jack Johnson. The latter supposedly began racing bicycles before he took up boxing, inspired by the sensational Taylor. "Johnson entered a five mile race at Galveston, fell rounding a curve, and injured his leg," the biographer Geoffrey Ward wrote, explaining his turn to the fight game.

When I met Sydney she was fading. Her voice was a whisper and her words spare, as if there were only so many left. She had had her own rebellious years and plenty of her own difficulties, but she seemed happy, thoughtful of others, patient with a visiting writer who read letters her father had sent to her when she was a bonnet-wearing five-year-old and he was a superstar athlete. When I asked her, "Does it seem ages ago or does it seem like yesterday?" she smiled.

On Sydney's bedside table was a picture of her son, retired brigadier general Dallas Brown. He was one of the first black generals in the military. On a regular basis people wished to see her. She was weak, and her family—her granddaughters Jan and Karen—did an admirable job of safeguarding her. They didn't always know what to make of the obsession with their family. One man was halfway to disinterring Taylor for a second time in order to bring his bones back to Indianapolis when the family nixed the project. White people, blacks, moviemakers, authors, songwriters, cyclists—everyone wanted to touch what was theirs. Whoopi Goldberg, Malcolm-Jamal Warner, Spike Lee . . . It was a burden. There was the expectation that Taylor's descendants—though they are lawyers and writers and generals—must be something greater, something for all negritude, as the author Richard Wright put it. "I always wondered if I should've gone down south during the civil rights protests," Dallas Brown told me. "I'm still not sure if I should've, but a friend told me there are those who open the door and there are those who walk through. My grand-father opened the door, and I guess I walked through."

And then there was Sydney. She was dying—the last direct link to the last heroic man whom everyone wished to touch but couldn't. She once said that the things "Mr. Munger told him about being good and clean and righteous carried over into his later life." He was a very controlled man, she remembered, who didn't keep whiskey around and wouldn't suffer card playing. "He was either smart enough or stupid enough to stick with it," she continued. "I think that if he hadn't adhered to them so closely he would have enjoyed his life more and my mother would have enjoyed her life more."

When she died on May 13, 2005, her eulogists characterized her as a strong, independent woman who ably served her family, friends, and herself. Her ambition was considerable. She had gone to London and Normandy during the war to help the segregated black troops; later she helped author a book about the black experience in Pitts-burgh. Her personal choices weren't easy. When her husband said he would divorce her if she went to Chicago to pursue a master's degree, Sydney defied him and enrolled anyway. She was "the daughter of a world champion cyclist," the obituary read, "who went on to make a name for herself." The similarity she shared with her famous father was the knowledge that it wasn't easy.

The day I saw Sydney she showed me the picture of her father she kept in her dresser drawer. She did so only at the insistence of her church friend, Mrs. Cook. She didn't much like the photo, though it was initially hard to understand why. He was in the prime of his being, muscular and proud, astride a bike he could ride faster than anyone. When I asked her what she didn't like about the photograph, she said softly, barely, that it didn't look like him. No? She stiffened. No, she told me. "His skin was much darker."

Bibliographic Notes

With Major Taylor and Louis de Franklin Munger the most obvious requirement in exploring their extraordinary bond is Taylor's 448-page 1928 autobiography *The Fastest Bicycle Rider in the World: The Story of a Colored Boy's Indomitable Courage and Success Against Great Odds* (Wormley Publishing, Worcester). Of all the people Taylor could've dedicated the book to, he chose Munger.

The window to understanding Munger began with the discovery of a December 28, 1924, feature story in the *Springfield Republican,* titled "Bicycle Champ of Other Days Living in City," which profiles Munger and describes the broad arc of his doings. The article didn't answer everything, but it did suggest the enormity of what he did and wished to do and why he may have been drawn to Taylor. It has also helped substantiate that their friendship extended beyond racing right up through their final years. Munger was present for Taylor's first professional race at Madison Square Garden in 1896 as well as his last, an old-timers' event held at the Newark Velodrome in New Jersey in 1917. Munger described how he'd driven all night to be there, possessed, he said, by the need to shove off his friend a last time. Taylor won the race.

The story of the bicycle in America has been expertly chronicled, most recently in David Herlihy's wonderfully informative and elegantly illustrated book, *Bicycle* (Yale University Press, 2004). The

French-born Pierre Lallement, the bicycle's initial U.S. patent holder, could have no better champion than Herlihy, who sniffed out a historical bias (the credit for the bicycle has typically gone to the Michaux brothers) and convincingly documented the mechanic's prominent role. There are other works that inform this chapter such as Robert A. Smith's entertaining *A Social History of the Bicycle* (American Heritage Press, 1972) and Stephen A. Goddard's *Colonel Albert Pope and His American Dream Machines* (McFarland & Co., 2000), a biography of cycling's immensely influential tycoon.

The Boston-area newspapers—at the time there were a handful of major dailies—had some of the earliest concentrated cycling coverage in part because Pope's business was based in the region. Unlike researchers even twenty years ago who had to exclusively rely on non-indexed microfilm, I benefitted from several free online databases such as the Library of Congress's "Chronicling America" and Readex's America's Historical Newspapers, in addition to select newspapers such as the *Boston Globe,* the *Brooklyn Daily Eagle,* and the *New York Times,* each of which is now searchable. The multiple newspaper sites provided access to such newspapers as the *San Jose Mercury News* and New York City's the *Sun.*

Munger's record attempt in which he "suffered a violent collision" with a horse carriage appeared in *Outing* in January 1886. He never wrote about his family, but census records provided a helpful glimpse. The 1860 prewar federal census shows his parents, Theodore, twenty-six, and Mary, only nineteen, having been married less than a year and farming a section of her family's stake in Cedar Falls, Iowa. In the 1880 census, Theodore and Mary live in Detroit with their four children, including Louis, who's listed as working in one of the city's blind-making factories. His great-grandfather Simon Gurley was raised by Indians and later defected to the British side in the Revolutionary War. As a wanted man with a bounty upon his head he, too, ended up in Ontario to live out his life in the rural farm-lands. A certain rebellious spirit is a documented part of the family bloodline.

CHAPTER 2   FLIGHT

The Taylor family story was virtually untold until Andrew Ritchie's 1988 book *Major Taylor: The Extraordinary Career of a Champion Bicycle Racer* (Bicycle Books, San Francisco). It is a marvelous piece of scholarship, adding layers to the family saga and true depth to a story almost nobody knew. (Another superb resource is the Major Taylor Association, which maintains a great website with regular updates at www.majortaylorassociation.org.)

Mr. Ritchie spent countless hours interviewing Taylor's surviving daughter, Sydney Taylor Brown, and was the first to probe the rich personal papers that the family then possessed (those same papers—photographs, ledger books, and letters from 1897–1904—are now held at the Indiana State Museum in Indianapolis and have also been recorded on microfilm by the University of Pittsburgh). Richie's book addressed a lot of what Taylor's autobiography didn't, but he also left room for additional research and exploration. In addition, Sydney Taylor Brown, whom I met shortly after her one hundredth birthday, seemed to have her own share of biases, and perhaps even misunderstandings, about her father and her family history. My goal, having the benefit of the foundational research already done by Mr. Ritchie, was to dig a little deeper and question everyone and every-thing—not out of mistrust, but simply because family stories are so frequently tangled and unwittingly corrupted with the passage of time.

Gilbert Taylor, Major's father, was one gaping hole and Dan Southard, the white boy who befriended him, another. In Gilbert's case the frustrations were many: his Civil War service, proudly alluded to in Taylor's book, proved impossible to document despite repeated searches at the National Archives. Gilbert Taylor's death was another mystery since the accepted date by Taylor's biographer Ritchie was 1909. It was only upon comprehensively reading Indianapolis's the *Freeman,* "the leading colored newspaper in the nation," did I locate some mention, albeit vague, of Gilbert Taylor. A family sketch of the Taylors, which a local columnist published July 30, 1904, mentioned that he had recently been killed by the railroad cars. He would've been approximately sixty-five years old. Several newspapers such as the *Worcester Spy,* the *Worcester Telegram,* or the *Indianapolis Recorder* should've published a death notice, but none did.

The other part of Taylor's upbringing that seemed suspiciously incomplete was the tale of his temporary adoption by a well-to-do Indianapolis white family, the Southards. The original source of this story was Taylor's own autobiography, in which he describes his friendship with Dan, a young boy his same age. Innumerable regurgitated accounts of this relationship have never produced full names for the Southard parents, an occupation, or any detailed personal history that might give an indication of why and how this situation occurred. Daniel Southard III, a grandson living in Connecticut and an amateur genealogist, offered a marvelous entrée into the family's background and helped take the story out of the frustrating category of semimyth and into a factual, and even more fascinating, grounding. The family's personal history was both supported and enhanced with other reference works about the railroad period in Indianapolis, including turn-of-the-century histories, such as *History of Indianapolis and Marion County, Indiana* (1884), fine modern reference efforts like the *Encyclopedia of Indiana* (1994), and William J. Doherty's doctoral dissertation *Indianapolis in the 1870s* (Indiana University, 1981).

CHAPTER 3   FIRE

Floyd McFarland was the unusual man in that the normally forgiving Taylor singled him out in his autobiography for some of his harshest commentary. McFarland's untimely and luridly brutal death prevented him from penning his own thoughts on his career in cycling, a work which would have undoubtedly been rich. The McFarland family, however, is recorded in the San Jose city directories of the period, and in early-twentieth-century obituaries; they also had a routine presence in the news sections and gossip columns of the *San Jose Mercury,* a paper that dates back to 1851. San Jose researcher Bonnie Montgomery put together a fine dossier of information on the McFarland family, no small feat with a family of seven whose journey spanned Civil War Virginia to northern California (and a few states in between). *Hardesty's History of Wirt County; West Virginia History,* volume 1, and early-20th-century reference works on the region provided insight to the conditions around the war. Also helpful in explaining their California experience, and the segregated history of African Americans in Santa Clara County, was the History San Jose Research Library and the California Room at San Jose Public Library. The seminal work on the latter topic is the *History of Black Americans in Santa Clara Valley* (Garden City Women's Club, 1978). The vibrant era of cycling in the other "Speed City" is well portrayed and documented in Barbara H. Houghton's *Cycling: In and Around San Jose: 1890–1900* (1978). Photographs in Ralph Rambo's collection show a joyriding group of San Jose Road Club wheelmen stacked in front of a tavern; another depicts a quartet of Adonis-like racers at the Alameda track with a grandstand backdrop packed to capacity (some of the spectators are actually dangling their feet off the loge rooftop).

A number of sources informed the material on Taylor's adolescent development, including his own autobiography, personal scrapbooks of Taylor's, and period newspaper accounts. The racial tension in Indianapolis at the time, which prevented Taylor from racing on the area tracks and made life troublesome for his coach, Birdie Munger, is best described in historian Emma Lou Thornbrough's *The Negro in Indiana Before 1900* (Indiana Historical Bureau, 1985). In the book Thornbrough cites an *Indianapolis World* editorial circa 1900 that sums up the onerous prevailing mood: "Either the Negro of this city must bestir himself, keep his weather eye open or he'll wake up some morning to find himself reduced in the matter of civil privileges to the level of his brethren in many Southern cities, who are subjected to all sorts of humiliation without recourse or relief."

CHAPTER 4   SIX DAYS

The year 1896, the date of the Madison Square Garden Six-Day in which Taylor turned pro, is generally recognized as the year when the sport peaked in America. The market indicators were at all-time highs: bikes made, bikes sold, riding academies, and members in the League of American Wheelmen (LAW). According to Smith's *Social History of the Bicycle,* Americans spent an estimated $200 million on bicycle repairs and accessories alone, and another $300 million on bicycles. He reported 500 separate plants of varying sizes manufacturing accessories for bicycles; he also pointed out that the assembly line setup of those plants would be the precursor to an even bigger and more demanding craze, the automobile. Peter Nye's U.S.-bicycle-racing history *Hearts of Lions* (Norton, 1988), a well-written book with comprehensive detail on several of Taylor's rivals, makes the distinction that some 2 million bikes were made in 1897 as compared to fewer than 4,000 cars. Articles from *Harper's Weekly, Century, Scribner's,* and all other major magazines and newspapers from the era offered further evidence of the sport's unfathomable popularity. "In and about New York, for example," observed a *Century* writer, "there are at present something like half a million bicycle riders. On pleasant holidays, they swarm like flies upon all the parkways."

The Garden's focal point in the craze—as both a stage for huge annual bicycle trade shows and a venue for track racing—should surprise nobody. While the original Garden had an open-air design and would've been highly impractical for a December showcase event, the new Garden, completed in 1890 (just as the cycling fad was gaining steam) had racing in mind from the outset. The 1896 Six-Day drew the saturation-style coverage of a modern-day Super Bowl; it also drew luminaries and fledgling racing promoters like Billy Brady. Brady's writing about the Six-Day in his autobiographical *Showman* paints a vivid portrait of a time and place never to be seen again. Though the sport was already transitioning from amateur to professional racing, Brady accelerated the process, moving it in the direction of something he knew well—prizefighting.

The Six-Day race accounts were long, detailed, and drama filled. In addition to the New York newspapers, the cycling press also weighed in. There were dozens of cycling specific journals, including *Bearings, Bicycling World, Cycle Age, Referee,* the *American Wheelman,* and the *Wheel.* The *American Wheelman* ran one of the first photographs ever published of Taylor and noted that he rode the six-day "like a general rather than a major." The most complete collection of vintage cycling magazines is the Transportation Collection at the Smithsonian's National Museum of American History in Washington, D.C.

CHAPTER 5   NEW YEAR

Though three-time Tour de France winner Greg LeMond is undoubtedly the most famous California-born bicycle racer, the state produced an astounding number of talented and celebrated racers almost a century earlier. In addition to Floyd McFarland, there were his fellow San Joseans, Hardy Downing, Otto Ziegler, and Orlando Stevens, all of whom won their share of races. The moment when East met West and the racers began to integrate into a true national circuit was excitedly documented in the national magazines, especially *Bearings,* beginning in November 1895. As pleasantly shocked as the easterners were about California's natural beauty and soft, sunny climate, they were equally so about the advanced state of racing on the left coast. In Pasadena alone (a city of 9,000) there were fifteen bicycle shops, according to a 2004 exhibit at the Pasadena Museum of History. The 1900 edition of the Rose Parade featured some 350 bicycles adorned in flowers.

The racing circuit was young and evolving but was already dealing with the complex issues that are familiarly modern: how to keep the almost Hellenic purity of athletic contests while maximizing entertainment appeal. The circuit riders were popularly characterized as "money chasers," meaning their motivation was occupational, not something far loftier. In the 1990s, Hall of Fame NBA basketball player Charles Barkley shocked viewers when he said he was not a youth role model; such a statement was not something that would've had to been said, much less debated, one hundred years ago. A superb article about the evolution of athletic competition in America was published in the July 1895 issue of *Scribner's.* The author, Duncan Edwards, explained that prestige-clamoring athletic clubs were the corrupting culprits, because they made sure they had a "sufficient number of speedy legs to run and jump and a sufficient number of muscular backs to throw weight for their clubs, irrespective of any social requirement of the owners of those backs or legs." The whole game had been cheapened, Edwards wrote.

Perhaps the most honest and well-balanced portrayal of pro

cycling—and a cautionary tale for all modern sport—is Daniel Coyle's deeply researched book *Lance Armstrong's War* (Harper-Collins, 2005). As Coyle put the finishing touches on his manuscript, the Tyler Hamilton scandal ripped apart the sport, followed a few years later by another tainted American champion, Floyd Landis, judged to have cheated. Those cases, and others in 2007, seemed to frame Taylor's resistance to far more benign corrupting influences—such as Sunday competition—as even more remarkable.

CHAPTER 6   TOGETHER

The populous social movements that rose during the Gilded Age were tremendously influential, especially for young men and women. The YMCA brought legitimacy to physical competition, calling its mission "muscular Christianity"; the organization's origins are told in Clifford Putney's *Muscular Christianity: Manhood and Sports in Protestant America* (Harvard University Press, 2001) and C. Howard Hopkins's *History of the YMCA in North America* (Association Press, 1951), as well as in the archival files at Springfield College, the movement's base of operations beginning in the late-19th century. Taylor never specifically commented on his association with the Christian Endeavorers, but according to his date books, he was in certain cities, like Boston in 1895, when those conventions took place. Much of the information about the Endeavor movement came from newspaper clippings throughout the 1890s in the *Boston Globe,* the *New York Times,* and periodicals that are archived on the Cornell University database "Making of America" (www.cdl.library .cornell.edu/moa/). A more general and personal resource for information on evangelical thought was my friend Philippe Berthoud, a French native living in the United States who founded a successful youth soccer mission.

CHAPTER 7   TWO SECONDS

All athletes live within a world that only they fully understand. Their psychological triggers—what makes them perform to the utmost of their ability—is almost always a mystery. What is far easier to identify with, or at least admire, is the physicality of what athletes do. Propelled by early photography and cinema, the sporting fandom began to take keen notice in the 1890s. The era of physical culture rose up hand in hand with the emergence of city living—those a generation or two away from the farm seemed to wish for the feeling (if not the obligation) of physical living. Interest abounded in strong men *and* women, and their performances drew crowds at vaudeville shows, as well as journalists hoping to tell their stories. Taylor's physique, photographed in scanty briefs like a pinup, was one of many that were portrayed to the hungering general public. Little Otto Ziegler, a contemporary who had a series of famous battles with Floyd McFarland, is seen in a similar Charles Atlas–like pose in a picture at the History San Jose Library.

The record-making runs (such as Taylor's well-documented time trials in the fall of 1898) gave birth to sports science, an industry that now touches everything from Olympic training centers to youth club soccer. Some of the early pioneers such as the nutritionist Wilbur O. Atwater, who rightly wondered about what men put into their mouths to make them go so fast for so long, were the inquisitive forebearers to modern giants such as the hyperactive Dr. Bob Arnot. The information about Atwater comes from *Agricultural Research* magazine ("W. O. Atwater—Father of American Nutrition Science," June 1993) and the Wesleyan University Library. The Wilbur Olin Atwater Papers are held at Cornell University's Division of Rare and Manuscript Collections. The robust world of cycling-specific training theories was covered extensively in the 1890s, including by Taylor himself. In an article entitled "Major Taylor on Bicycle Training," he told novices that too much work on the track is all wrong and that "it is not so much the riding one does in training as it is in the attention you get afterward." Ever more scientists and cyclists have wrestled with the correct doses of exercise and recovery. A pair of excellent references are *Serious Cycling* (Human Kinetics Publishers, 1995) and *High-Tech Cycling* (Human Kinetics Publishers, 1996), both by Edmund R. Burke, a scientist who worked with multiple U.S. national teams.

CHAPTER 8   CIVIL WAR

The League of American Wheelmen (LAW) was founded in 1880 as a social and riding organization and as a sanctioning body for amateur competitions. The club's social makeup and amateur mission—the bylaws are fantastically explicit in what constituted an amateur— was bound to collide with the sport's emerging middle-class and professional turn. Its exclusionary side was never clearer than in Article III of its 1897 constitutional charter, which stipulates membership eligibility for "any amateur white wheelmen of good character." Philip Mason's *The League of American Wheelmen and the Good Road Movement, 1880–1905* (University of Michigan, 1957) examines LAW's difficult role, adding detail to more general accounts in Herlihy's *Bicycle* and Smith's *A Social History*. During its heyday LAW also published a weekly bulletin and a monthly magazine. Moreover its political intrigues were exactingly covered in the city dailies as well as the cycling journals.

Taylor's abrupt relocation to Worcester was always troubling if only because he seemed to be a bit young (seventeen years old) to be abandoning his family and following a new employer halfway across the country. A surprising discovery, thanks to articles in the *Brooklyn Eagle,* was that Taylor's eldest brother William was there with him, helping him along. The popular understanding was that Taylor's brothers had jealously distanced themselves from Marshall on account of his advantageous relationship with the white Southards. Obviously, William Taylor's presence with his younger brother in 1895 and 1896 suggests otherwise. Historical detail on Worcester abounds, from large works such as D. Hamilton Hurd's *History of Worcester County, Massachusetts* (J. W. Lewis & Co., 1889) and Franklin Rice's *Dictionary of Worcester and Its Vicinity* (Worcester, 1893) to living monuments such as the still-standing John Street Baptist Church, the place where the adult Taylor was baptized, and George Street Hill, the dizzyingly steep incline tucked between buildings in the downtown. Janette Thomas Greenwood's scholarly article "Southern Black Migration and Community Building in the Era of the Civil War: Worcester County as a Case Study" was an immense aid and offered additional detail on the history of John Street Baptist Church.

Finally, Taylor's interest in African American thinkers and pioneers is well documented in his personal scrapbooks. Tattered clippings of local and world events are tucked between race-win accounts from New York, Chicago, and elsewhere. His interest in an all-black team of pacers, unheard of at the time, seemed to sequence perfectly with the fuller man he was becoming. Much of the information comes from the era's black newspapers, which were thriving in the period. A modern context for understanding what Taylor was dealing with is *The Unlevel Playing Field: A Documentary History of the African American Experience in Sport* (University of Illinois Press, 2003), authored by David Wiggins and Patrick Miller.

CHAPTER 9   NO LIMITS

In 1896 the bicycle boom was a juggernaut, no end in sight, but by 1897 there were already signs that the end was near. Retail stores kept longer hours in order to get rid of their order overruns, Smith reported in *A Social History*. By 1899 the industry was flat and the racing gates were in decline. For a short time the momentum around Charles "Mile a Minute" Murphy's feat arrested the fall. It also forced the sport into more dangerous territory—motorcycle-paced speed runs. Some of the information on the physics of extreme bicycle riding is the result of countless interviews I've done for cycling-magazine stories. Over the years I've visited the Olympic Training Center in Colorado and profiled coaches and trainers working with the premier American teams, Motorola and Lance Armstrong's U.S. Postal. The aforementioned *Serious Cycling* also helped my technical understanding.

Though Murphy drew the headlines, Taylor had forced everyone to look toward machine-generated pace when he set his records the previous year. Human pace wasn't enough any longer. To glean how Taylor felt about his world records at Garfield Park in 1899, one only needs to consult his scrapbook, which contains two pages worth of handwritten split times. His achievements in Chicago were arguably a much bigger deal than his world championship in Montreal a few months earlier. That result had a preordained ring to it due to the absence of Taylor's most challenging rivals (such as McFarland). Still, the 1899 world championships were a red-letter day for Canada. In the fall of 2004 I attended "Le Velo à Montreal," a beautiful exhibit that re-created the time period with posters, period bicycles, and original race medals at the Musée du Château Ramezay in the Old City.

CHAPTER 10   SOMETHING AT THE END

Paris's Exposition Universelle de 1900 was meant to outdo all the other world's fairs that had come before it. There is no doubt on the sports front the French organizers achieved their objective. An indicator of the sporting focus, aside from the long and diverse list of events, was the repeated attempts to draw the American Taylor to France. A French emissary hand-delivered the offer from French promoters Robert Coquelle and Victor Breyer, including the enormous monetary guarantee. There were differing accounts of precisely how much he could've stood to make, ranging from a *Freeman*-reported $15,000 (December 30, 1899) to the *World*'s $10,000, but Taylor himself said it was more like $8,000. A fantastic account of the Paris World's Fair, which helped with my description of it, is Richard D. Mandell's *Paris 1900: The Great World's Fair* (University of Toronto Press, 1967). Images may be viewed online at the National Gallery of Art's virtual exhibit at www.nga.gov/resources/expo1900.

Taylor's troubles in Worcester, including the controversy about his home purchase on Hobson Avenue, were comprehensively documented in the Worcester and Boston newspapers. In February the *Worcester Spy* (which published one of the first Taylor profiles on October 20, 1895), the *Boston Post,* and the *Worcester Telegram* ran exhaustive articles about the contretemps. The national *World*'s headline simply read, "His White Neighbors Object: Major Taylor Buys a House in Worcester's Exclusive District."

The Madison Square Garden Six-Day that closed the millennium was almost an extension of the racing program at Paris, with several European teams brought over for the occasion. Billy Brady's exact involvement in running the show is unclear but he was definitely involved. Brady's disgust at the fixed outcome comes from his commentary in his autobiography. A new general reference on the Six-Day phenomenon is Peter Nye's latest book *The Six-Day Bicycle Races: America's Jazz-Age Sport* (Cycle Publishing, 2006), which describes everything from the building of the tracks to the individual race personalities (including Floyd McFarland).

CHAPTER II　　LA BELLE EPOQUE

Daisy Morris, Taylor's great love, reignited Taylor's career and gave him a new bedrock supporter. Previous researchers haven't had much success digging up background material on her. (Even finding out where she was buried has been problematic. It turns out her cremated remains were held by one funeral home for a time then transferred to Pittsburgh's Homewood Cemetery, where her ashes were spread in the Garden of Rest.)

My journey in understanding what was plainly an incredible love story would eventually take me to a state records depot in Hartford; a rendezvous with her one-hundred-year-old daughter, Sydney, in Pittsburgh; and a visit to Hudson, New York, the upriver town where she was born in 1876. The seedy history of Hudson is marvelously told in Bruce Edward Hall's *Diamond Street: The Story of the Little Town with the Big Red Light District* (Black Dome Press, 1994); it makes for an entertaining counterpoint to the sleepy turn-of-the-century text *Columbia County at the End of the Century*. In Hudson, and later Hartford, state and federal census tracts fleshed out Daisy Morris's family history. In the Worcester town directories, she was listed as a lodger and later as a "domestic," working for a well-known attorney named Elmer C. Potter. None of the census or town history information synced with what was popularly understood about Daisy Victoria Morris's background.

The showdown between Edmond Jacquelin and Taylor, and Taylor's arrival in Europe, is one of the great sports stories of the early twentieth century. The springtime coverage in 1901 was immense, especially abroad where his arrival was treated like a state visit. Two oversized French sports magazines, *La Vie Illustrée* and *La Vie au Grand Air*, published sumptuous layouts with a variety of photogravure print process photographs. Among the many things Taylor brought back with him from Europe were the hundreds of French-language newspaper clippings with bold type headlines such as "La Journee du Negre" and "Noir et blanc." Christiane Jedryka-Taylor, a translator and French-born teacher at the Waring School in Beverly, Massachusetts, was able to decipher some things in those densely written articles that even Taylor might not have known. James Smalls's "'Race' as Spectacle in Late-Nineteenth Century French Art and Popular Culture" (French Historical Studies, 2003) also served as an important reference for the mood of the times and why Taylor was received as he was in Paris. Finally, the handsome Library of Congress publication *A Small Nation of People: W. E. B. Du Bois & African American Portraits of Progress* (Library of Congress, 2003) is a superb summary of the Du Bois–inspired exhibit at the Paris Exposition with a large sampling of original photographs.

CHAPTER 12   TWONESS

The African American literature of Taylor's era, including the many black newspapers such as the *Recorder* and the *Freeman* (both in Indianapolis) was smart, evocative, and dynamic. W. E. B Du Bois' work is well known, but there were many other contributors, such as the poet Paul Laurence Dunbar. For the first time there was an inner view of what the black American experience had wrought, an assessment of how it felt to be equal but not, how it was to be something different than the majority. The artistic freedom enjoyed in Paris at the time Taylor visited was unprecedented: a surprisingly helpful visual reference was the Academy Award–winning film *Moulin Rouge,* which has 1900 Paris as its setting. Taylor's grand reception in Paris, coupled with his continued difficulties in the United States, and perhaps the literature of the period, all combined to form an individual who was understandably less tolerant of the racial status quo. Kevin Baker, the acclaimed historical novelist who recently finished a fictional trilogy on the American immigrant experience, found reference to posters of Taylor in the black neighborhoods of the Tenderloin while researching *Strivers Row* (HarperCollins, 2007); obviously Taylor's influence and celebrity abroad had registered with the black American middle class. Moreover, a black newspaper promoted an upcoming competition by telling its readership to come watch "Taylor beat the white riders." Finally, a post-Europe editorial in the black newspaper *Washington Bee* (August 24, 1901) explained that "Taylor is the central figure; Taylor was the man people wanted to see. Taylor was the great Negro that the refined, the educated, and the Caucasian wanted to see. This is the solution of the Negro question. When the Negro is able to do what the white man can do he will be upon an equal footing with him. All that the Negro needs is a chance."

All of this had something to do with why the story told in the *Colored American Magazine* (September 1902) was creatively altered. Taylor had an agenda other than himself now, and he was going to protect the person "he had fallen in love with at first sight." The black community had reason to put the couple on a pedestal, to anoint them not just a couple but as a royal pair. Even prior to the story in the expansive *Colored American* article, there was a blurb in *La Vie au Grand Air* a year earlier with a photo of a bonnet-wearing Daisy and the caption "La future Madame Taylor" (May 4, 1901). The miniseries movie made about Taylor, which airs regularly on the Starz cable channel and was made in Australia, is called *Tracks of Glory* (1992). It is the only cinematic depiction of Taylor, and its attempt to satisfy viewers with a politically correct family story of Daisy is only one of many historical flaws.

CHAPTER 13   STEAL AWAY

The extremely unstable state of pro cycling in America is portrayed in many of the big-city-newspaper accounts, which gleefully recorded the weekly carnage. As promoters found it harder to fill the stands, they demanded cyclists attempt dangerous, crowd-pleasing speed-trial pursuits. Taylor was one of the lucky ones in that he'd put away enough money not to have to submit to the killing game (an accomplishment proudly mentioned in the *Washington Bee*).

The notion of retirement wasn't as big a deal as it is now in professional sports. Cyclists retired with little warning or fanfare. They understood that sport was an interim phase at best and that it would not extend beyond the time they could regularly win, place, or show. They moved on to jobs that they had left behind; it was as if they were waiting for them until they got through with their little adventure. Undoubtedly Taylor had already begun thinking about what was next—he would attempt to parlay his hands-on technical background by going to Worcester Polytechnic Institute and later, when that didn't work out, he'd start a tire fabrication business. They were smart, logical career moves with one exception: once he retired he was just another black man, facing a society still unapologetically tightfisted with opportunity. He loved what he did and what it gave him, and feared that reintegrating into everyday society was not going to be easy. Unfortunately (though not surprisingly) his autobiography, written in the throes of his post-racing career turmoil, never addressed his "civilian" life problems.

CHAPTER 14   AUSTRALIA

What transpired in France, including his honeymoon after a small Connecticut wedding ceremony on March 21, 1902, was never fully treated in Taylor's own writings. The evidence is a trail of postcards in his Indiana State Museum collection, letters on subsequent visits to Paris without Daisy, and some descriptions by the French journalists and promoters who befriended the couple—Victor Breyer and Robert Coquelle. A frustration is that none of Daisy's letters, which Taylor refers to, have ever been found. Their trip around the world beginning in the winter of 1902 was a remarkable adventure. Daisy received only fleeting notice but clearly from the stops in their travels the adventure was as much about Taylor's desire to show Daisy the world as it was about wins and losses. Taylor was still at the top of his game: the competition in Australia was weak and he'd already beaten the biggest names in Europe.

The Australian leg of the adventure, it being his first stopover, is incredibly well documented (much as his first trip to Europe was). H. "Curly" Grivell's *Australian Cycling in the Golden Days* (South Australia, 1952), magazine and newspaper accounts, and modern papers such as Ian Warden's "Fastest Rider in the World" for the National Australia Library News (February 2007), dig up period stories but also racist illustrations that Taylor didn't keep in his otherwise teeming scrapbook. One shows a clownish-looking Taylor with a large bicycle wheel hovering over his head like a halo. Another modern review of Taylor's Aussie tour is Bernard Whimpress's "Major Tayor at Adelaide Oval" (National Library of Australia, 2005). There have also been other accounts such as Dr. Jim Fitzpatrick's "Major Taylor Down Under on Tracks of Glory" (Australian Society for Sports History Bulletin, 1991), which served as the basis for the aforementioned *Tracks of Glory* film. Philip Derriman's *The Grand Old Ground* (Cassell Australia, 1981) is a history of the Sydney Cricket Ground. Because of that famous pitch's unique ability to accommodate massive crowds, it was adopted for cycling use during Taylor's tour.

Hugh McIntosh, who brought off the Taylor visit, has been entertainingly treated in various books. Among the most complete biographies are Geoffrey C. Ward's *Unforgivable Blackness* (Knopf, 2004) and Ken Burns's 2005 documentary of the same name. A good and highly useful reference is John Hetherington's rare *Australians: Nine Profiles* (Melbourne, 1960).

CHAPTER 15 FEBRUARY FIRES

If there was any doubt Billy Brady was the Forrest Gump of his time, his written account of being in Chicago's burning Iroquois Theater clinches it (*Showman,* EP Dutton, 1937). Brady wrote an additional book, *The Fighting Man* (Indianapolis, 1916), which was serialized in the *Chicago Sunday Tribune.* Dozens of his scrapbooks are held in the Billy Rose Theatre Division of the New York Public Library for the Performing Arts at Lincoln Center. It seems worth noting that Brady proudly declared he bet on Joe Louis to knock out Max Schmeling in another era-defining sporting contest.

Many of the aforementioned resources also cover Taylor's 1904 campaign, the one with McFarland and Iver Lawson. The latter's disgrace in Australia would be temporary—his lengthy three-year suspension was lifted so he could compete in the world championships in London, which he promptly won. A scrapbook of Lawson's is held at the U.S. Cycling Hall of Fame in New Jersey.

As Taylor battled it out in Australia, his father was killed back home. The circumstances are mysterious, as already mentioned, but what had not been understood before was the fact of his father being in Worcester just before Taylor and Daisy got on the train to return to Australia. It's plausible that Gilbert Taylor, at sixty-five, was making his retirement in Worcester and got on the train with his son only because he and Daisy would be gone for a time. Of course, when Taylor returned his father was dead. When Taylor wrote in his autobiography that he was emotionally exhausted and nearly suffered a nervous breakdown on his return from Australia, it's also plausible, though he doesn't mention it, that a contributing cause was the guilt over his father's death. A final factor was his reception in San Francisco. According to the *San Francisco Call* (June 28, 1904), Taylor left prematurely because restaurants would not seat him and hotels refused to accommodate him: "Taylor's money of no account," the headlines read. "Negro bicycle champion finds San Francisco draws the color line . . . Cuts short his stay . . . Local hotels and restaurants decline patronage of man Australia lionized."

Finally, there are the details surrounding the buildup races leading to the McFarland/Taylor showdown: all Taylor biographers have been the beneficiary of immense coverage in the newspapers, firsthand accounts, letter writings, and all the "noise" that transpires in the wake of a momentous sporting occasion. Most of the clippings are contained in Taylor's scrapbooks at the Indiana State Museum. Some of the prominent Aussie papers at the time were the *Sydney Morning Herald,* the *Referee,* the *Australian Cyclist,* the *Adelaide Observer, Table Talk,* and the *Sydney Bulletin.* It's interesting to note that today Australia is one of the sprint-cycling international powers, a legacy that dates directly back to the turn of the century.

CHAPTER 16   THE LAST BEST RACE

In the pantheon of underdog sporting sagas this duel in Australia has never received its due. Taylor's own description of his injured prerace condition is vivid; it is a passage in his otherwise tedious race accounts that shines above all others for the simple reason that it mattered beyond all others. Additional newspaper accounts add richness and extraordinary detail for what was a two-minute-long race.

That the world was changing in ways neither Taylor nor others could then comprehend is without doubt. More than anything historians would see a world that was becoming more intimate—that the things happening in Australia were felt in Africa which were felt in Harlem which were felt in the Arctic. The communication tools were improving, and photography was imprinting its own reality. What happened in Australia was part of a continuum of interconnected happenings, of influences felt not merely among neighbors but among countries separated by oceans and vast cultures. Taylor's underdog victory was arguably the first shot heard round the world.

CHAPTER 17 HOME

Cycling is nothing if not, well, cyclical. Last year McIntosh's Taylor-era creation, the Sydney 1,000, was resurrected at Dune Gray Olympic Velodrome in Australia. The 1,000 in the title is an archaic reference to "guineas," then the common currency. A guinea was worth 21 shillings at the time. Today's equivalent purse would be approximately $92,000.

According to Andrew Ritchie's biography, Taylor's post-Australia debt, incurred when he broke a European contract to race the next year, forced him out of retirement two years later. More onerous, the settlement demanded Taylor race on Sundays. The person who successfully sued for breach of contract, Victor Breyer, was the same person who made him a household name on the occasion of his first visit in 1901. In excerpts from his letters to Daisy, Taylor sounds troubled but resigned. Daisy died, according to her Pennsylvania death certificate, on April 24, 1965. It was the same month and almost the same day Floyd McFarland was buried a half century earlier.

Speed records continue to be hunted and praised. On Sunday, May 13, 2007, the British track star Chris Hoy went to the outdoor velodrome in La Paz, Bolivia (the highest-altitude velodrome in the world at 3,500 meters), and broke the 500-meter record, shaving another second off the record to 24.758 seconds.

EPILOGUE

The modern relevance of the Taylor story is reflected in those who champion his remembrance. The people discussed in this chapter—Courtney Bishop, Rahsaan Bahati, Lynne Tolman, Taylor's remaining descendants, and his late daughter, Sydney—are a few of the many. This spring (2008) in Worcester, a statue in Taylor's memory will be unveiled near the public library, not far from the George Street Hill he trained on and the Hobson Avenue home that still stands.

Acknowledgments

In researching and writing this book I benefited from many people who went out of their way to help me. At Kensico Cemetery in Westchester County, New York, a volunteer who only works Fridays offered to drive around the grounds to inspect tombstones to help solve a mystery involving Birdie Munger. At his seaside home south of Boston the writer and researcher David Herlihy welcomed me and generously offered a road map to the bicycling history terrain. Several descendants of Major Taylor met me at various times in various places: Jan Brown during her lunch hour in Boston, Karen Brown Donovan and her mother, Joyce, in Washington, D.C., and Sydney during a memorable visit to the Squirrel Hill neighborhood of Pittsburgh. Frances D. Cook, Sydney's caretaker, was good enough to arrange that meeting, help break the ice with Sydney, and give me a minitour of the city.

There were others who I didn't meet personally but wish I had. Chief among them was Dan Southard III, the grandson of Taylor's boyhood friend; he was a joy to communicate with—enthusiastic, helpful, and gracious with his time.

The professional librarians at museums, libraries, and historical societies whom I pestered, I owe much to. Kisha Tandy, an assistant curator of the Major Taylor Collection at the Indiana State Museum, suffered my innumerable requests and did so kindly and competently. The Smithsonian Institution's Roger White in the Division of the History of Technology made my D.C. visit go smoothly and added immeasurably to it with a photocopy of an advert for Taylor's 1928 book. The National Archives' Rebecca Livingston was immensely patient in assisting my Civil War research on Gilbert Taylor. Thanks also to Pen Bogert at the Filson Historical Society in Louisville, Wilma Gibbs Moore at the Indiana Historical Society, and Lisa Meadows in the genealogy division at the Indiana State Library in Indianapolis. Also a more generic nod of gratitude to the reference help I received at libraries and town hall offices in Hudson, Ansonia, Springfield, Worcester, Indianapolis, New York, Boston, San Jose, and Beverly.

There were other professionals who helped with the book, including the San Jose researcher Bonnie Montgomery and a Boston college student, Brian van der Boegert. My friend Gina Poirier, a superb graphic designer, put into digital shape some of the vintage photos used in this book. In addition to David Herlihy, I got both encouragement and direct help from the writer-historian Peter Nye and the other Worcester whirlwind Lynne Tolman, who is the lifeblood of the incredibly successful Major Taylor Association in Worcester.

On a personal level thanks to the people who read the book and gave me feedback at some point in its development, including Dan Coyle, Curt Pesmen, and especially my brothers, Tom Balf and Mike Balf. I also want to thank the entire Creamer family, great friends who invited me to Maine in the summer of 2006 to enjoy their companionship and to use the change of scenery to, maybe, tackle a revision of the book. My family—Patty, Celia, and Henry—have all been roped into some research-related wild goose chase during the last several years. I have a picture of Henry in a vintage-bicycle-crammed basement of the Waltham Museum; Celia got detoured to a cycling exhibit in Montreal; and Patty endured the aforementioned summer vacation in Maine in which I excitedly arose each morning to write, rather than, say, paddle up the gorgeous neighboring estuary. To Patty I owe everything, apologies and thanks.

Finally, thanks to Esmond Harmsworth, who read many versions of this book, beginning with a modest proposal. Thanks to all those at Crown, including Lindsay Orman, who helped get this project out the door; and, finally, thanks to my editor, Kristin Kiser, who in spite of all the things, personal and professional, that occupy her time, she managed to make me feel that this was a project she was going to see through and not let up on. She gave me her word at the outset that we would work together and she kept her end of the bargain—and then some. I am deeply appreciative—and absolutely lucky to have such an editor in my corner.

Index

African Americans. *See also*
   segregation/discrimination
   activist, Ida B. Wells-Barnett,
      129–130
   anonymity of, 24–25
   black skin remover, 44–45
   colorism, 164
   Du Bois' Paris Exposition
      exhibition, 170–172
   Du Bois-Washington split, 121–122,
      203–204
   in France, 172–173
   in Indianapolis, 28–29, 39–40
   Plessy v. Ferguson, 49
   in San Jose, 37, 247–248
   in the Spanish-American War, 129
   Taylor and the black community,
      121–122, 151, 186–187,
      202–203, 253, 284–285
   Team Major Taylor (University of
      Indiana), 255–261
   in the Union army, 24–25, 225
   in Worcester, 124–125
agon, 128, 129
air-resistance, 134–135
Albion Cycling Club, 125
American Bicycle Company, 145
American Mutoscope Company, 71
American Racing Cyclist's Union
      (ARCU), 118–120
Anson, Cap, 132
Ansonia Evening Sentinel, 192

Arend, Willy, 168
Armstrong, Lance, 183–184, 188, 249
Aronson, Oscar, 158
athletes and athletics
   African Americans and, 5, 48–49,
      129–130, 132, 176, 247–248,
      253
   desire to prove someone wrong, 41
   inspecting and measuring, 94–96,
      173, 175, 176
   level of desire and success, 33
   nutrition, 94–96
   popularity of, 11, 131–133, 227
   sprinters, 109–110, 112, 247–248
   training and performance, 92–96,
      278–279
Atwater, Wilbur O., 57, 94–96
Australia
   decline of bicycle racing, 244–245
   promoter, Hugh McIntosh, 207–208
   Sydney (1903), 206–214, *210, 213*
   Taylor-McFarland showdown
      (Adelaide), 5, 235, 236–242
   Taylor-McFarland showdown
      (Melbourne), 226–232
   "White Australia" policy, 205
Australian Superbike, 247
automobiles, 143, 181

Bahati, Rahsaan, 264–265
Bald, Eddie "Cannon," 51, 54, 66, 74,
      76, 89, 91, 249

295

ABOUT THE AUTHOR

Todd Balf, a former senior editor for *Outside* magazine, writes for *Bicycling,* the Sunday *New York Times* quarterly *Play,* and other publications. He lives in Beverly, Massachusetts, with his wife and two children, and does his writing in a backyard barn he shares with every bike he has ever owned.

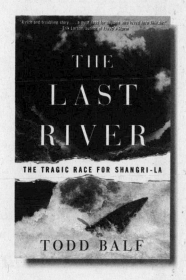